Calendar

Vanessa Berry

Vanessa Berry is a writer and artist who lives on Gadigal land. She is known for her work on memory, place, and objects and is the author of the books *Gentle and Fierce, Mirror Sydney, Ninety9* and *Strawberry Hills Forever*. A renowned zine maker, she has produced the zine *I am a Camera* since 2000. She is a Lecturer in Creative Writing at the University of Sydney.

Vanessa Berry

Calendar

UPSWELL

First published in Australia in 2025
by Upswell Publishing
Perth, Western Australia
upswellpublishing.com

Upswell operates in the city of Perth, on ancient country of the Whadjuk
people of the Noongar nation who remain the spiritual and cultural
custodians of this beautiful land. We acknowledge their continuing
connection to country and express gratitude to elders past and present for
their strength and creativity...Always was, always will be, Aboriginal land.

ISBN: 978-1-7637331-1-4

 A catalogue record for this
book is available from the
National Library of Australia

Illustrations by Vanessa Berry
Cover design by Chil3, Fremantle
Typeset in Foundry Origin by Lasertype
Printed by Lightning Source

Upswell Publishing is assisted by the State of Western Australia
through its funding program for arts and culture.

Are objects halted time?

Clarice Lispector, *Agua Viva*

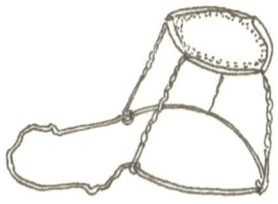

1. Champagne Wire

The wire muzzle from the top of the champagne bottle perches on the kitchen table as if it might scuttle away. Too meticulously constructed to immediately discard, it had been something to tangle my fingers in as we talked our way towards midnight. The hours, the minutes, then the seconds ran down, and the pop and fizzle of illegal street fireworks greeted the new year.

This year my resolution was to write a calendar, inspired by the short-lived French Republican calendar from the late eighteenth century. This calendar reordered the months and weeks and renamed the days, dedicating each to an object related to rural and farming life. Day of the strawberry, the rake, the pine nut or the ladder, an object for every day of the year. To determine the objects for my calendar I wouldn't plan it out in advance. I would wait, every day, for an object to reveal itself to me.

The first is the champagne wire, poised in the centre of the kitchen table. In the quiet new year's morning I pick it up, turning it over to inspect it. One edge is loose where it had been untwisted to be removed from the bottle. This was where the old year escaped, and the new one slipped through.

2. Heart-shaped Pencil

On the radio a psychologist cautions 'commit to nothing'. Her advice cuts through my search for a pencil amid the mess of my desk. 'After all the years of the pandemic, and with all the pressures of daily life, go easy on yourself,' she continues, as if to warn me about my plan for the year ahead.

As usual I find the heart-shaped pencil first, a red, heart-shaped cylinder, embossed with 'Heart Shaped Pencil' in ornamental script. It had come from a stationery shop in Kichijoji, Tokyo, hidden away above street level atop a real estate agency. The store sold items of high novelty specificity, as inessential as they were delightful. From a display of potato-chip-shaped paperclips and miniature keychain cameras that served as flashlights, I chose the heart-shaped pencil. That I intended it as a souvenir and didn't plan to use it has ensured it is reliably there whenever I most need a pencil.

Why fight it, when all the rest hide. I take up the heart-shaped pencil and write the date at the top of the page and underline it, going slowly with the unfamiliar numerals of the new year. The scratch of the pencil lead against the paper is the whisper of something before it has to be anything at all.

3. Seashell

Turning out my pockets at the end of the day, sand scatters as I draw out a balled-up tissue, a black elastic hairband and a flat piece of shell with curled edges. One side of the shell is corrugated and dull, the other pearlescent and gleaming.

Following the shore and the line made up of seaweed and flotsam, I was in search of a shell for my pocket. The waves continued their perpetual motion, strong and quick, one then immediately another. The weather from the ex-tropical cyclone was moving down the coast. This one had been called Seth, as if it were a polite teenage boy. Beyond the breaking waves, further out, were the bobbing figures of surfers, occasionally one emerging tall to ride the wave in.

The shell would hold this day for as long as I could recognise it against the other shells I had picked up in a similar way, on other days. My own tideline of shells and sea glass extends along my bookcases and windowsills, from walks beside the ocean, a diary without dates.

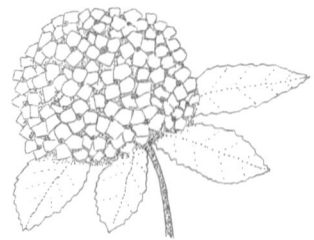

4. Hydrangeas

Flowers are another calendar to follow and now the hydrangeas are out, pink pompom clusters along the weathered grey fence. The heat and the stillness of the slow first days of the year bring me déjà vu. An overlay of this time every year, hydrangeas all the way back to a wooden house with striped brown awnings like painted eyelids.

Behind it was a garden with fruit trees and vegetables, and azaleas, geraniums, and hydrangeas by the back wall. Depending on what the hydrangea bushes were fed you could change the colour of the flowers, baking soda to turn them pink, coffee grounds to turn them blue. This was a coffee grounds house, the hydrangeas the same strong blue as the sky.

Beside the hydrangeas I liked to sit on the gritty concrete steps that led down to the garden, practising the mental trick that enabled me to stop time. From the step I could press pause on it all: my grandfather removing the stinkbugs from the orange trees, the sprinkler ticking on the lawn, the bees hovering above the hydrangea flowers.

5. Green Raincoat

The green raincoat hangs behind the door. There, in the corner of my eye, it is the green of a praying mantis or a string bean, hooked on the handle by its hood, waiting for rain.

The grey sky outside leads me to pick up the raincoat and shrug it on. I become a bright green blade, setting out into the weather. The summer shower has little force to it, but it intensifies enough to make me pull up the hood and tug down the sleeves as I cut through the housing estate. Dark-tinted windows, garden beds planted with feathery grass, and my careful steps on the slippery path that leads down towards the tram line. A malfunction has suspended the tram service for at least a year, but I look both ways before I cross all the same.

6. Christmas Bauble

Some places have kept their Christmas decorations up into the new year, though they have an increasingly stale, forgotten look. They go so quickly from being cheerful to having the stubborn persistence of something still demanding attention, the last guest at the party, unwilling to accept it is time to go home.

Driving along Arthur Street, before the Harbour Bridge on-ramp, I'm not thinking about fading Christmastime or anything much apart from the automatic actions of following the road. The lanes of the on-ramp are high above the motorway. A narrow paved strip, half a metre wide at most, separates the lane from the railing.

Midway along, a tree grows from a crack in the concrete, a casuarina, tall enough in shape and dimensions to resemble a Christmas tree. The glitter and shine of its decorations catches the light and my eye. Someone has risked their safety to cross the lanes of traffic and tie ribbons and baubles to the tree's branches, giving me the gift of noticing this young tree growing on the precipice, putting down roots in this tenuous place.

7. Junk Mail

At least once a week a small booklet printed on thin paper appears in the letterbox. Hundreds of these have been stealthily delivered to me but I barely even look at the offers. My eyes skim over jumbles of letters and numbers and images of scorched, oozing pizzas without troubling to consider any of it.

When the plant name I've been trying to remember finally comes into my head, I reach for something to write it down on. The first scrap of paper to hand is one of these booklets. The back page has a useful blank margin around the edges of an advertisement for the 'One Day Price Slice'. I write 'Yesterday Today and Tomorrow', the name of the tree that has white, mauve and purple flowers all on the same bush.

Examining the booklet more closely I turn it over to find a pink neon font, 80s Miami style, introducing the 'Deliciously Cheesy Duet of the Cheese Toastie Crust'. A landscape of meat and cheese is offered by way of illustration, a crater with stalagmites of grilled cheese at the edges. I stare into it as if it is a puzzle that I might be able to solve.

8. Airline Blanket

Stitched into the label on the corner of the brown plaid blanket is one line in Korean, two in English, 'Please leave on the seat after use'. The blanket wasn't intended to be spread out over a lawn damp from overnight rain, ants patrolling its corners. Its expected fate was to travel from flight to flight, passenger to passenger, covering fitful attempts at sleep.

A message lights up my phone, a photo from New York, taken from a high window, looking down towards the street. It is more snow than anything else, caught thickly in the tree branches. Below, a trail of footsteps extends along the white pavement. Sixteen hours behind and a full day's journey away. Imagining this distance I watch a plane ascending, crossing the sky above the ragged tops of the tall fig trees which obscure the horizon. Earthbound on the airline blanket, I follow the plane until it disappears into the blue.

9. Pomander

Between the clothes in the drawer my hand closes around something. A plastic pomander, moulded into the shape of two slim gloved hands pressed palm to palm. I take it out and shake it to rattle the wax chips inside, releasing its dusty lavender scent.

The pomander has followed me for much of my life, hidden among clothing, persisting by stealth. When it arrived, as a childhood gift from an aunt with Avon connections, I marvelled at its finely etched details as if it were something precious. I would reach under the clothes in the drawer to extract it, the powdery scent issuing out through a pattern of holes that mimicked lace.

The pomander was one of a series that included a dainty boot, a frilled parasol, and a sunhat. Packaging was everything for these creams and lotions which all had the same cloying, talcum-powder smell. Avon products were housed within vessels of any shape: pineapples, turtles, keys, cars, cuckoo clocks, and a series of dolls with skirts that held measures of perfume. They were an early lesson that things could be other than what they seemed.

10. Blue-striped Thermos

On the rocks above the Mahon pool I am in my usual place, back resting up against the side of a sandstone hollow wide and smooth enough to sit in and be sheltered from the wind. People walk up from the pool on the path that follows the edge of the rocks, ascending with slow steps, leaving trails of seawater and wet footprints behind them.

Pressing in the button in the middle of the thermos cap, I enjoy the sturdy click that releases the seal. As I do this I notice the scratches on my hand, thin red lines from the fine sharp points of the cat's claws. Then I see the thermos, too, is scuffed and scratched. In the blind-spot vision of familiar things I haven't noticed its dents, or that the dark blue stripes of paint are scuffed, or that the plastic lip at the top, with embossed instructions for opening and closing it, is chipped. Although I use it every day it is a surprise to suddenly realise it is in such a worn state. The tea inside is as hot as ever. As I pour it into the cup, curls of steam are pulled up by the wind, stealing the heat that the thermos has so reliably kept.

11. Peach Stone

What to do with it, this tough pitted stone, with its pattern of furrows?
I examine it for long enough that it doesn't feel right to discard it.
Instead I leave it to dry on the windowsill, beside the shells and sea
glass, between an incense stick that smells of toffee and a miniature
plastic pretzel.

The peach had been an ordinary supermarket one, chosen from a careful arrangement on the indented tray that had protected the peaches
in transit. Cutting it up into slivers, I made a deal with myself: with
every sentence I wrote I would eat a slice as a reward.

Well, I broke the deal pretty much immediately, eating the entire peach
before writing anything. I sat with the empty plate, the blank screen,
and the stone, which was a kind of conscience, hard and enduring.

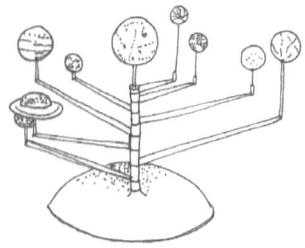

12. Orrery

Tens of thousands of pieces of space junk are orbiting the earth, a space archaeologist says. I turn up the volume to listen properly. The junk is made up of satellites and pieces of rockets and spacecraft, and the more of it there is the more chances there are of it colliding and making even more junk by breaking apart.

This talk of space junk sends me looking for the orrery. There are many beautiful, finely made orreries in the collections of science museums and libraries, but this one is small and basic, for a child to learn the order of the planets. Eight rubber balls are each mounted on a metal pin at the end of a grey plastic arm which can be moved in turn to circle the sun. The sun is at the centre, a ping-pong ball painted red and dotted with yellow spots like a strawberry.

The planets have an uneven, scuffed texture, Earth a swirl of blue and green, only just recognisable from its distinct colours. I push it so it moves around the red ball sun, turning in a slow sad plastic orbit.

13. Sticky Note

A scientist attempting to make a strong adhesive instead produces a weak one. The glue is just strong enough to stick and then be peeled away without a trace, exactly the opposite of what he intended. At the same time, a colleague is struggling to keep bookmarks in his hymn book and this new weak adhesive is just the thing to fix the problem.

The day starts quietly enough. I'm working at my desk, looking through *Exercises in Style* for the pages that need scanning for the course reader, peeling off sticky notes to mark them like the devout scientist must have done with his hymns. From the living room I hear S answer his phone. His voice takes on such an unusual tone I go to the doorway to better hear what he's saying. The caller is on speaker, and I recognise the doctor's voice as he urges 'go now, go today'.

The spiral of a bad dream takes over. My sticky notes fill with the details of radiology clinics, each a square yellow island bearing a bland medical name and a phone number. They scatter loose across my desk, corners curling, not adhering to anything. It is difficult to find a biopsy appointment at short notice, but we call and call, and eventually find a place. When it is booked I collect up all the notes and scrunch them tight in my fist, hoping that this might end up peeling away, leaving no trace on us.

14. Ride-on Car

The shock works through, moving in waves. We won't know for a week. We cry in the kitchen then try and do our usual things for a while. Mid-afternoon I take my work out to the front step but soon close the laptop and just sit there, watching the street, where there's always something going on, or going by.

On the footpath opposite a man has his attention sunk into his phone as he walks with slow, loose steps. Ahead of him is a child in a ride-on car, the kind more often seen in roadside trash piles than actually in use. The toy car is shiny and black, a miniature Range Rover, and the child is positioned in the centre of it, proportionally giant. She turns to stare at me as if I am the one doing something unusual. The car must be on some kind of autopilot, for it keeps on straight as she continues watching me.

We lock eyes and for a split-second we switch places. I'm sitting tight inside the ride-on car, trusting that no harm will come to me as it leads me forward on the smooth road ahead. Then the car turns the corner, and with a jolt I'm back on the step.

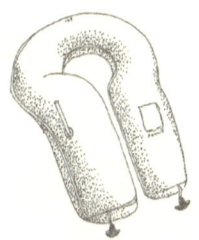

15. Life Vest

The moment I hold onto from the dream of the plane crash is when I bob up again like a cork, in the dark blue ocean, the wreckage behind me. I am both in my body and outside of it, feeling and observing at the same time. It is cold in my lungs, this insistence of life.

16. Broom

All day the corellas are in the trees, eating the skin of the hard green hackberries. I watch how they snip off short lengths of leafy branches and hold them in their upraised claws as they nibble at the fruit. Once they have done so to their satisfaction they drop the leaves to the footpath below, and clamber along the branch looking for another. As people walk past I hear the berries popping underneath their steps like they are walking over bubble wrap.

At the end of the day the corellas move off towards the river, Goolay'yari, and I take up the broom from its position by the front door. It's almost my height, a wooden broom with horsehair bristles and peeling varnish on the handle. I move out to the pavement with it like it is my sturdy, whiskery dance partner. We sweep up the fallen berries and bundles of leaves, gliding over the pavement together.

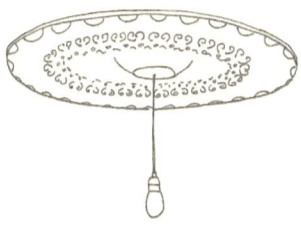

17. Ceiling Rose

In my twenties I lived in a house that was old enough to have ornamental plaster features in the rooms. The two plaster faces on the
moulding of the central archway were our hallway goddesses, even
with their noses and hair chipped, and around every light fitting was
an ornamental plaster wreath, a ceiling rose. Lying in bed I would
stare up at it as an aid to daydreaming, the details of the scrolls, flowers, and vines a maze to follow or get lost in. Now, living in a newer
house, I stare at a ceiling where the light fitting comes down out of a
small plastic dome. The only roses are the ones I bring home to put in
a vase and I have almost forgotten that a rose can be anything else but
a flower.

Sitting at the station platform, sighing over the late train, leaning
against the brick wall of the eternally locked waiting room, I look
up to the underside of the awning. Two long fluorescent battens are
switched on, ineffective in the daylight. Between them, muted under
a coat of arsenic-green paint, is a ceiling rose exactly the same as the
one I had spent so much time staring at, the same scrolls and flowers,
the same tangled vines to follow.

18. Magic Lantern Slide

At the beginning of *Swann's Way* the narrator is troubled by his magic lantern. Intended as a comfort, the lantern's projections over the walls of his bedroom fail to enchant him as they depict a medieval legend of a falsely accused heroine. He watches the story fill the room, unhindered by the folds of the curtains or the doorknob. The disruption is overly stimulating, he explains, leading as it does to melancholy thoughts and feelings.

Balanced in the corner of the window frame is my own magic lantern slide, a black and white photograph showing a cluster of bare oak trees with whiskery branches, labelled 'Oaks in Cadzow Forest' from the 'Tree Studies' series. It was one of hundreds of magic lantern slides for sale at the flea market in the dimly lit and draughty former cinema across from Newtown station. 'Uncertain Smile' reverberated in the cavernous space as I held up trees, flowers, and landscapes against the lightbox.

During the day the light shines in through the slide, revealing the scene of the winter forest. Behind it, outside, branches of a real oak tree glow pale green in the summer light. The world inside the slide is a cold one by comparison.

19. 'Good Morning' Pickle

A day has many other days inside it, bottled up like the 'Good Morning' pickle in its jar, one lonely cucumber suspended in brine, a souvenir from the Estonian Cafe.

It had briefly been my favourite cafe and when I visited it I would order a slice of lemon cake and chat to the barista. We talked about the snowfields in Estonia, prompted by the tourist poster of cross-country skiers on the back wall. We talked about writing when she asked what I did, then about our cities, Sydney and Tallinn. I confessed that I didn't understand the pickles in the baby-food jars, which were for sale along with other groceries. Why was there only one? Why were they called 'Good Morning'?

She grinned and said, 'you go out the night before, then...' She picked up a jar and mimed drinking down the brine, waiting for me to piece it together. A hangover cure? She nodded. 'You eat the pickle,' she said, 'and drink the juice.'

A few weeks later I arrived at the cafe to find it had closed down, its windows papered over with multiple copies of the poster of the cross-country skiers. Soon all trace of it having been there was gone. All I had to remind me was the pickle in the jar.

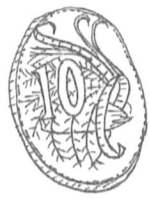

20. 10c Coin

The day before S goes back to the doctor we visit our tree. We cross the reserve that makes up the hollow of land around the creek, between houses on one side and an industrial estate on the other. The tree's tall branches spread wide, so it fills the sky when we are on the grassy creek bank underneath it. From here the creek flows onwards, enlarging to the river, the bay, the ocean.

We spread out our blanket and lie back to look up into the branches. The wind flows over, rustling the leaves. Everything is calm but persistently alive and changing: the breeze, trickling water, ants in the grass.

A girl dressed in a Superman costume appears, looks down at us and asks, 'what are you doing?'

'Counting the leaves,' S says, 'thirty-thousand and one, thirty-thousand and two...' She turns and darts away, responding to a voice that calls her name. We sit up, drink our tea, don't talk about tomorrow.

Before we leave we walk clockwise around the tree's wide trunk. The bark has deep furrows like basalt columns, and we look over it for a place to put the coin: 10 cents, thin and silver, the lyrebird. On one part of the trunk there's a shiny, spotted fly, iridescent blue with lighter blue spots on its body and bulging black eyes like it is wearing sunglasses, resting near a furrow deeper than the others, marking the spot. 'When this is over,' S says, 'we'll come back to retrieve our coin.'

21. Pebble

In the waiting room I hold S's hand and in my other hand I hold a pebble. I squeeze it so its pointed edges dig into my fingers, so the discomfort of this becomes the difficult thing we have to face. The pebble is a piece of granite, sharp like a tooth, black with glitters of quartz, picked up from under our tree as I gathered up the blanket the evening before. Compelled to reach for it, I knew to trust my instincts. In my hand now it absorbs the moment, makes this one small part bearable. A patient leaves the doctor's office and then a short, interminable time passes before we go in together, to hear the news that we had feared.

22. 'Rossignol' Drinking Glass

One of a set of four, each with a different bird with a French name: *rossignol, mésange, rouge gorge, rouge queue.* A small glass, good for a gulp of water to take a tablet, or for a nip of brandy, poured up to the point where it just touches the bird's claws.

The shock has given over to fear. Unpegging a shirt from the washing line a wave of it came to take my breath and I sat on the lawn to cry, head in my hands. The scene of the doctor closing the door, his white gown billowing as he said, 'Now, you do have a problem'. Cancer, yes, but 'a good kind', the doctor continued, reading out the diagnosis, its terms angular and complicated. A bump against my knees brings me back to the present, the cat, Soxy, telling me *I'm here I'm here.* So the rest of the day goes, a cycle of upset and comfort.

Later S has the *rouge gorge* and me the *rossignol.* The conversations of people walking past filter in, just muffled enough to be indistinguishable as I take tiny sharp sips. Then someone comes by singing a line of melody in a sweet high voice. I look out the window to see her, a woman wearing a brown sequinned dress. The Rossignol, with the night unfolding before her.

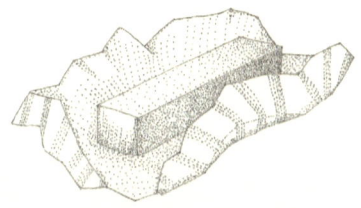

23. Caramel Wafer Wrapper

The message on the edge of the shiny red and gold wrapper gives me pause every time: 'more than 6,000,000 of these biscuits made and sold every week'. Hundreds of people must be reading this statistic at this very second, which means at least some must be sitting at a kitchen table like I am, feeling numb from something difficult they are going through. The taste of the wafer is sweet comfort to me as I flatten out the wrapper, smoothing out its creases. The wrappers are too shiny and smart to discard. I use them as bookmarks, and when I sort my books they flutter out, like golden tickets.

24. Flipbook

Oh, to be the *première danseuse* who is the star of the black and white flipbook, turning cartwheels as her one and only task. On the cover of the book she is in a constant state of readiness, one hand on her hip, the other lifted up above her head, ready to plunge towards the floor and take her weight. Her legs kick up, following the arc, until she stands again, her frothy petticoats settling around her. Definite and deliberate, she trusts her body and the ground beneath her.

I flip the pages and she cartwheels again, her feet almost brushing my thumb at the edge of the page as she kicks up. The sequence ends just before she stands completely upright. Her skirt is rumpled, her hands upraised, so she is forever within the motion of turning the world upside down.

25. 'Gotcha' T-shirt

In the early 1980s the Gotcha was advertised as a versatile garment that enabled the wearer to perform a wide range of activities. Playing tennis, reading in the park, feeding parrots, writing 'I Love You' on a mirror in lipstick, doing aerobics or minor home renovations. A snugly fitting t-shirt, available in a rainbow of colours, made all this possible.

Whoever originally purchased my Gotcha left it in the packet unworn; the right occasion to wear it must never have arrived. Twenty years later it began to enact its destiny with me. The shirt is bright yellow, the colour of egg yolk or daffodils. I wear it for a better mood, an attempt at sunshine.

26. Found Photograph

We find the photograph as we sort through books, trying to bring order to the piles stacked up against the shelves. 'What about this one?' I say, picking up a biography of The Beatles. Before S can answer, a photo falls out, landing on the carpet face down. Written in blue biro on the back is 'Fancy Dress Social 1980'.

A photo taken before setting out for a party, a record of the outfit and the night's fresh hopes. A woman stands against the exterior wall of a house, dressed in black with platform boots, costumed as Peter from KISS. Her face is disguised by thick white makeup with black cat nose and whiskers, in between which her red-lipsticked mouth grins.

She's standing just left of centre in her suburban stage set, with a fibro wall behind and painted concrete underfoot, and potted plants to either side casting shadows against the wall. By her wrist there is a brown blotch, which at first I think is a speck of dirt on the photograph's surface. I try to flick it away before I realise it is in the image itself, a brown moth resting against the wall, wings outstretched, lured by the same light that made the photograph.

27. Lucky Squirrel

From a basket of miscellaneous jewellery on the op shop counter, among the cheap earrings, I picked out a brooch in the shape of a squirrel. Made of dark green plastic it had a delicate expression, its paw raised up to its mouth as if nibbling on a nut. As I examined it I felt a presence at my side. 'That's a good find,' a woman said icily. When I stepped away from the brooch basket she quickly fell to searching it.

She was correct, because days went right when I wore the squirrel. I had serendipitous encounters, I found what I was looking for, everything went better than expected. The squirrel was clearly a luck charm and I started to ration it, only wearing it for job interviews or difficult medical appointments, on the kinds of days when life might change.

Pinning it to my scarf I knew the squirrel was superstition, magical thinking, something to put between myself and the world. But the power of such a thing, although small, can give a necessary bravery. Sitting beside S in the surgeon's consulting room, I drew on my courage. The surgeon was pointing out the irregular edges of the tumour in the grey undulations of the ultrasound image, explaining how the surgery to remove it would proceed. 'See you there,' he said to S, as if they were arranging to meet for a morning jog.

The most commonly used noun in English is 'time'.

every year the Earth and the Moon move 3.8cm further apart.

Clocks in advertisements are usually set to 10 past 10.

28. Odd Spots

In difficult times, mundane things come into weird focus. A coffee pot that needs emptying. The heel worn out of a sock. A packet of sanitary pads with unusual facts printed on the paper backing. The kinds of scraps of information people call 'factoids', a word that sits on my tongue like it doesn't belong there. Facts about fish and hippos, that the official name for a hashtag is an octothorpe, that ketchup was once sold as a medicine, and that sea otters hold each other's paws when they sleep so they don't drift apart.

When the Odd Spots first appeared I found them incongruous and a little annoying, like someone who tries to cheer me up when I'm dedicated to a bad mood. Then I came round to them, what was the harm? When hummingbirds are the only birds that fly backwards, and your thumb is the same size as your nose, and cheetahs can't roar, and the sea otters appear again, floating paw in paw in this sea of discretionary information.

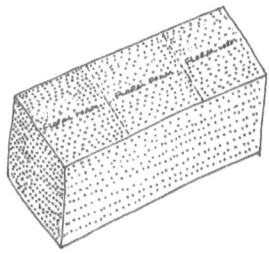

29. Green Floral Foam

In one of the kitchen cupboards, beside the box of milk-money envelopes, blocks of green, gritty foam were stored along with the leftover
ribbon roses from when my grandmother had worked as a florist. She
had great reverence for this absorbent substance that would keep
flowers alive simply by sinking their stems into the block and then
pouring in water. The foam came in slabs as solid as cake. When no
one was watching me I would press my fingers into it to feel the cells
of the foam collapse, as if it contained a life-giving substance from
which I, like water for a cut flower, could draw sustenance.

30. Padlock

At the centre of the bridge that crosses the river, locked onto the railing, is a padlock with two names engraved in it. The padlock is heart-shaped and iridescent gold, the date etched into it from two months earlier.

Underneath the bridge submerged branches trail plastic bags. The mangroves struggle to breathe through the bottles and dog-chewed tennis balls around their roots, and at low tide a sulphurous odour rises from the muddy banks. Even so, like Rae and Ellie, I know this to be a special place, where the river persists despite its despoilment, its tides flowing with the pull of the moon.

The river was clean compared to how it used to be, another walker told me, while we were looking up at tawny frogmouth owls nesting in the high branches of a casuarina tree on the northern bank. 'When I was a kid,' she said, 'we would get from one side to the other by jumping between the tops of the cars that had been dumped in it.' We turn to the river, imagining it this way.

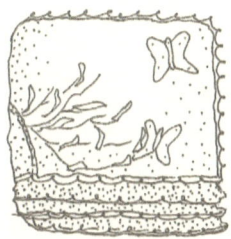

31. Face Washer

A rainbow, butterflies, and flowers make up a washcloth scene edged in purple crochet. I crumple it under cold water in the sink, wring it out, and put it on the back of my neck, a cool touch on this humid day.

It came from a tiny suburban arts and crafts store, with a window display of doilies and knitted baby toys and a handwritten sign, 'All Hand Made'. Walter had been keen to take me to the store, which is staffed by retiree volunteers, lifelong knitters who have the power to rapidly generate baby clothes and woollen hats with a few clicks of their needles.

Everything for sale was either for the very young or the very old, apart from the face washer. When I bought it the volunteer at the counter, admiring its purple border, said 'I have my bedroom in that colour'. In a flash I saw the room with its meticulous colour-coordination, a ruffled valance on the bed, figurines with doilies underneath them on the dressing table, everything in tones of lavender, mauve, violet. 'Lovely,' I had said, not knowing how to respond to this sudden intimacy.

32. School Desk

The school desk must have absorbed every possible attentive state, from concentration to distraction, confusion to boredom. Around the sides of it, beneath the beige laminate surface, is where students carved their initials and messages into the soft wooden edges, HU 4 UV, or KORN. On the underside are shiny stiff wads of chewing gum, adhered to the top of the desk's aluminium legs.

The gum and the carved-in initials give the desk a restlessness. We move it around in the house. Sometimes it is in the living room, where papers and receipts mound up into a messy, sliding pile on top of it. Sometimes it is set up in the middle of my study for me to teach on Zoom. Waiting for the class to start I watch the trees outside and the neighbour's cat high-wiring across the top of the fence. I clench my teeth and fight the urge to pick up a biro, press its nib into the soft wood at the side of the desk, and carve in a message of my own.

33. Rose Quartz

In the middle of the road is a scattering of something pale and crystalline, unusual in colour and texture. We go closer to inspect it. A big broken lump of rose quartz, shattered from falling to the road and further from cars driving over it. It is a shock to see this pale pink stone, representative of tenderness, smashed like this.

Since S's diagnosis we have been more alert to the appearances of signs and assurances. We gather up the largest pieces and bring them to the front steps, even though it is probably a bad thing to handle rose quartz that has been pulverised by car tyres. There is no guidance for this specific situation online, but any newly acquired crystal should be cleansed of residual energies, one website informs me. The full moon, salt, or rainwater will assist.

Later, as I carry the pieces of quartz out to the garden, I like to think the misty rain is working on me too. It catches in my hair and on my arms, forming a cool layer, a soft armour.

34. Perkins Paste

For a time you could still occasionally find pots of Perkins Paste for sale second-hand. It might seem ridiculous that anyone would want to buy or sell a forty-year-old pot of glue, but sometimes a listing would appear: 'Perkins Paste. Container half-full, paste has dried up. Label intact. $50.'

The paste came in a distinctive crimson-pink pot with a white lid, under which a spatula was attached. The end of the spatula was crimped, like tiny teeth, to aid spreading the glue, a thick, white paste that dried in clumps on the page if not carefully raked smooth. Glue of my childhood, a school requisite. Anyone who remembers it will tell you how it was edible, with a taste vaguely sour, vaguely potato. I was probably the only child not to try it. The label guaranteed its safety in all regards – 'sticks quickly, cannot spill, non-toxic' – but I was too afraid to taste it, not believing that I would remain similarly unharmed.

The paste ceased production in the 1980s, so there is no chance of tasting it now, although I have one of the pink pots. Sometimes I take off the cracked white lid and push the tiny teeth of the spatula into the pad of my thumb, thinking how I might be different now, if I had been bolder then.

35. Cat Bell

The cat is all white, apart from a black patch under her chin, as if her head has been underlined for emphasis. As she walks along the top of the wall beside me, the bells tinkle on her collar. They are round silver bells, a whole row of them, like sleigh bells, and their sound moves in time with her light footsteps.

In the morning I had woken up to the church bells ringing from the top of the hill, a low, serious clanging. Whenever I hear them I travel with the sound, over the treetops and the railway line, until it dissipates. Bells are like voices, calling me to the moment, reminding me that today, like every day, will hold something distinctly of its own.

The cat keeps up as I walk along the pavement beside the wall. On top of the bricks she moves in step with me as if we are in a cartoon, and she is my thought bubble following me along.

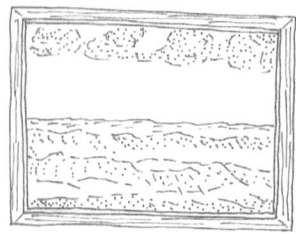

36. 'Song of the Surf' Framed Print

A framed picture is leaning up against a fence in the alleyway, discarded by a row of bins. The brown paper backing is torn and the hanging wire snapped, but I have a sense about it, a suspicion that the image will be something for me. Turning it over, I find a painted seascape of a shimmering grey ocean.

The green-grey sea surges under a yellowish sky, where a stripe of clouds indicates the receding storm. The waves are high, only the very tops of them curling, sunlight making a shining path across them. It is a scene to clear the mind, the waves and sky open to carrying whatever the viewer needs them to.

The label on the back gives its origins as 'Pictures of Distinction', a company in California which produced framed prints of landscapes, seascapes, and portraits. Immediate atmosphere for a room, a scene to escape into, a vista to stare at as you sulk, pushing peas around your plate, or to lift your eyes to in frustration, hoping to disappear into it.

37. Hand-drawn Poster

Sticky-taped to the wall at the end of the row of shops is a poster on blue paper, edges curled by rain. Its awkward childish lettering attracts me and I lean down to read its message:

Save The Tree
Call council and be a part of the
Fight!
to save the tree

Beside it is a drawing, in the same carefully wrought style as the text, of a tree with red flowers...oh no, not that tree! The flowering gum at the train station entrance, which every summer bursts into red fireworks, and rainbow lorikeets come to feed on the flowers, weighing down its branches.

Around the corner, the tree is cordoned off. Two of its branches have already been removed, sawn down to stumps, to make space for a demountable building that contains the toilet facilities for the construction worksite. Further fences and bollards extend out behind it, wire and plastic, no unauthorised access.

38. Bicycle Bell

From the window I watch a man wheeling the bicycle away from where I'd left it with the pile of discards on the verge. His white sneakers match his white hair, vivid in the fading light of the evening. As he pushes it he tests the brakes, which squeal from lack of use.

It had been hard to put the bike out, but it was rusty and unridden. Before I surrendered it to the street, I took the ladybug bell off the handlebars as a memento. A few years before, at a repair shop, after the bike mechanic had recorded my name and number on a piece of cardboard cut from a cereal box, I heard him giving instructions to his junior. 'Move the bell around,' he said, 'so you don't break it when you turn the bike over.'

Such care for a plastic ladybug. He had no way to know that the bike had once belonged to my friend, Helen, who had given it to me the week before she died. His care that day made me realise that her spirit would stay with the ladybug bell and that, one day, I would be able to let the bike go.

39. Hot Air Balloon

Soon after the first untethered hot air balloon flight, in which two men had ascended with the balloon and flown over Paris, a balloon mania swept through the city. Many people had seen the balloon in the air. A crowd came out to the streets, and others climbed to their roofs to watch it flying over, blue and gold and ornately decorated with suns, zodiac signs and the face of the king. Floating aloft the aeronauts had a sense of calm and stillness, as if it were the earth below moving rather than their balloon.

For those who longed to fly with them there were miniature balloons, made of paper, that could be sent up into the sky by means of a small fire in a pan underneath. By day and night these colourful paper balloons could be seen overhead, held up by the heat of the flames, although it was not long before these small balloons started to cause fires and were banned, decreed to be too dangerous.

Our own paper hot air balloon hangs suspended from a hook in the hallway ceiling. Made from strips of card in rainbow colours, with a paper basket hanging underneath, it reminds us of the night we made it. Friday the 13th, up late, strips of coloured paper around us, the tinny sound of the Altered Images cassette in the background. We floated above it all. Our new love came with the feeling that we knew each other in the past, present and future all at once.

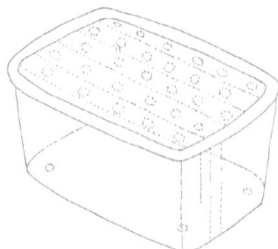

40. Tupperware Container

Once S is through the calls from the hospital we use the last hour of light to walk to Cup and Saucer Creek. We sit by the wetland, watching the swamphens bustle around their nests and the colours change in the sky. A man walks into this scene with a purposeful stride, out from the row of houses that back onto the reserve. He has something he needs to do, something to do with the Tupperware container he is carrying.

Inside the container is a grey-brown frog. The man takes the lid off and with a confident, practised move keeps a firm hold on the container as he propels its contents towards the pond. We watch the frog flying through the air, high over the fence and the reeds, then landing in the water with a glop. 'They like going in my pool,' he says to us with a shrug, as if this is any old regular evening.

41. Digital Wristwatch

Only patients are permitted in the hospital, no visitors. From the entrance I watch S going further in and down the corridor, until he is out of sight. As I turn to leave I look up to see that the round, tiled sign on the hospital roof is a figure of a nurse carrying a teapot on a tray. This is something, as is the lorikeet feather I find on the foreshore path, and the heavy bunya cones in the grass behind the school named Rivendell.

At home it is hard to know what to do with the knowledge that his surgery is happening at that very moment. I read the beginning of Christa Wolf's *Accident*, which unfolds over a day on which the narrator's brother is undergoing a major operation, which is also the day after the Chernobyl nuclear accident. There is no equivalent environmental catastrophe for me, apart from the slower, continuing one, held within the day's intense heat. To her brother in the operating theatre the narrator transmits a message as a beam of energy, that everything will be all right.

I breathe in *all*, exhale *right*, and move my hand to S's watch. When I came back home from the hospital I had put it on, clipping the metal band so it clasped my wrist. A digital Casio, the numbers on its grey screen running fast by nine minutes, chasing the future. Against my skin it feels warm and alive.

SLUMBER NET
for day wear, for night wear

42. Slumber Net

At the hospital pharmacy, beside a row of teddy bears and above a display of combs and scented hand creams, is a cardboard cut-out of a woman's face in profile. Over her head is what looks to be a loose kind of cap, until I see that it is made up of many layers of thin black hair nets. 'Slumber Net, for day wear, for night wear' is written on a pink panel underneath the model's shoulders. She has a serene, optimistic expression, refreshed after her slumber.

On the phone that morning we had exchanged sleepless night stories, S in the ward with the sounds of machines and the restlessness of other patients, me at home with too much energy fizzing along my nerves. Both of us had watched the 4am thunderstorm flash in the sky. I stare at the Slumber Nets in a tired trance, as if they are an antidote for sleeplessness.

43. Souvenir Dish

One of the items I have persistently come across in my years of op-shopping are melamine dishes that commemorate tourist land-marks. No one much wants to buy other people's souvenirs. The dishes are not particularly useful or desirable, too small and oddly shaped, someone else's discarded memory. This is exactly what turned me on to collecting them.

Most are for postcard places, the Trevi Fountain or Trafalgar Square, but occasionally there are more unusual destinations. The one I choose for today commemorates the International Road Federation conference in Montreal, 1970. The dish features a highway under construction through an Italian forest, where heavy machinery and trucks are in the process of laying the asphalt. Under a green beach umbrella a worker operates the machine that smooths and compacts the road surface, as other workers prepare the ground ahead. Unlike the usual landmarks, which remain much the same from year to year, it commemorates something temporary, more difficult to recognise.

44. Chess Set

With S back home from hospital we sit up in bed with the chessboard between us, lining up the pieces on either side. The last time I played chess I was a child, imagining identities for all the pieces. The pawns had only one note like Beaker from The Muppets. The knights showed off in sidesteps, the Queen was consistently serene and powerful, and the King was the stiff bewildered presence around which the game circled.

We pause our halting game to see if there is still a chess column on the puzzles page of the newspaper. There is, and it announces that the world's oldest Grandmaster, Yuri Averbakh, turned 100 this week. It was only after contracting Covid last year that he was no longer to be found in his usual corner of the Moscow Chess Club. However, he reported that he was doing well, 'taking into account how far I am from my youth'. The article included a sequence of moves from one of his favourite games, written in the emphatic, obscure argument that is chess notation, where !! stands for a brilliant move, ?? for a blunder, and !? for the unexpected move that opens up interesting possibilities.

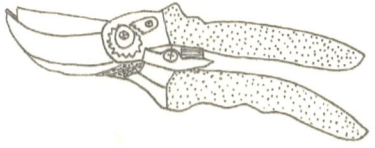

45. Secateurs

Growing up in a family of gardeners, I respected the power of the secateurs. Heavy and sharp, they were an invincible tool for adults to take up purposefully as they went out into the garden. There they would proceed to make decisive snips with the bird-beak blades. Sec, sec, sec, and a pile of cut branches would grow.

Now the secateurs are a weight in my pocket as I walk to the park, a former bowling green where people let their dogs off leash and stand in groups to chat on the neat square lawn. At the side is the old ter-raced bowlers' garden, with a row of rose bushes marking out its edge.

Not far from the roses a group sits with their dogs, black poodles of various heights, like an arrangement of different takeaway cup sizes. Most of the group ignore me, apart from one woman who watches me with an intense focus, wise to my intentions. I eye off the rose I want and pause beside it, hoping to appear as if I have been stopped by a sudden realisation.

She keeps staring, knowing I am up to no good. Both of us hold firm in our positions. When another poodle owner appears at the other side of the park and this momentary distraction causes her to turn, I strike. The secateurs bite, the pink rose is in my hand.

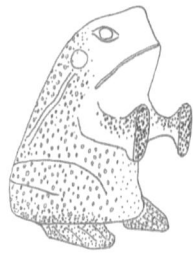

46. Toad Doorstop

The bronze toad sits up on its back legs and holds the door open with its upraised front feet. It performs a gesture more like a mime artist trapped behind an invisible window than a toad. As if in protest at this unnatural position the toad has a grouchy, resigned look, understandable from the eternal task of holding back a door or waiting to.

Without the toad in place the door will swing shut, following the pull of the breeze as it flows through the house, moving the heavy hot afternoon air out and away. The day comes to life again in the early evening, as people set out walking and cars start up, and buses roar past in either direction. Outside I hear the cat in the garden, light footsteps rustling as the noisy miner birds squawk down at her from the oak tree. The layers of pale green leaves stir, animated by the wind. Outside everything is on the move. Only me at the desk and the toad at the door stay stubbornly in our fixed positions.

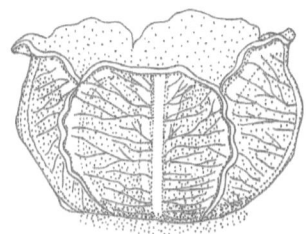

47. Jardinière

Some of the jardinières are painted with flowers, others are shiny smooth and lustrous, or have a blue-green or yellow glaze. Some are ceramic, others brass. One is moulded to look as if it is made from cabbage leaves. Some are wide, with handles or claw-feet; others are more like vases, upright and accommodating.

The jardinières hold ferns, succulents, cacti, and orchids, the kind of plants that grow well in the filtered indoor light. Each suggests the different room it had once been a part of, while also making up this particular living-room arrangement, a gathered intensity of different eras and objects coming together in the present.

When I visit my friends here I sit in the same armchair, at home among their books and plants, their big-eye dolls and art deco vases, happy to be inside their world of things carefully chosen. I take my place in the tableau, as much a part of it as the ferns and the orchids.

48. Four-leaf Clover

This one from beside the playground where the magpies like to line up on the fence. This one found on a difficult day, walking back to the car, a small note of hope. This one from the vacant lot with the friend who showed me the best way to find them. This one from the patch in the park with the sculpture of the dispirited astronaut, a patch which flourished until it was mown flat. This one from the day I didn't want to go home without finding one, and a woman asked me if I'd lost something when she saw me looking intently at the ground at the edge of the bowling-green park. 'No,' I said, 'I'm finding something.'

49. Elderflower

Derek Jarman's garden diary records his time living in windswept Dungeness. Here, at the very south edge of England, the land is forbiddingly barren. His cottage looked over a flat beach of shingle, towards the nuclear power station that dominated the horizon. It should by all expectations have been a bleak place, but Jarman loved its stark, wild beauty and the challenge of making a garden there. Through his diary, I step inside his days. On one a friend comes to visit, they drive around the nearby towns together and they gather elderflower, which they later fry in batter and sprinkle with sugar for supper.

When I worked as a museum guide there was an elderflower bush beside the small stone building that contained the ticket office. In summer it flowered in bursts of tiny white stars. One day, a tour group from a retirement village arrived in a minibus and I stood waiting to greet them beside the elderflower, its white flowerheads nodding in the wind.

A woman came up to the elderflower and reached towards it. '*Holunderblüten*,' she said, quietly. She turned to me to explain. 'I haven't thought of it since I was a child. My mother would dip them in batter, fry them, and sprinkle them with sugar, and we'd eat them. *Holunderblüten*,' she said again, turning back to the flowers.

50. Gripe Water

The bottle of Gripe Water, there on the shelf of Fiji Market, carried the same claims to restoring infant health that I remember from when I was the infant who needed restoring. On the label is an illustration of a baby with a snake in each hand, tightly grasping their necks to vanquish them. 'Celebrated Gripe Water', the label reads. 'Important to Mothers. Assists teething. Promotes digestion. Establishes the constitution.'

The strong baby on the bottle was in contrast to my own sickliness every time I gulped down a slick sweet tablespoon of it. My grandmother believed it had the power to cure all minor ills, although it was a patent medicine more popular in the 1880s than the 1980s. A mildly alcoholic mix of sugar, bicarbonate of soda and dill oil, it was a medicine and a time-travel elixir. A spoonful of it made me feel antique, like I was a figure in a sepia photograph.

51. Salt and Pepper Shakers

In the antique store the air felt thick and soporific, as if the room contained an entire summer's worth of heat. The hundreds of salt and pepper shakers, arranged on shelves that ran the length of every wall, only added to the claustrophobic atmosphere. As I swooned in the heat the man who ran the shop came up beside me to tell me how he and his wife had collected them all. They'd had only six sets when they were married, he told me, but their collection grew to be over five thousand, the largest in the country.

It was a double vision of every colour, shape and size, rows of ducks, pigs, and cats, and weirder things like sticks of celery and poker machines. A cluster of foot-shaped salt and pepper shakers were printed with the slogan, 'I walked my feet off in...' and different hand-painted placenames.

It was impossible to choose but I decided on a pair of plastic anthro-pomorphic oranges with big eyes like the animated orange that sang the aria from *Carmen* on *Sesame Street*. They were sold as souvenirs of Florida, the shop owner told me, wrapping them in tissue paper, as they are also souvenirs of his collection and that hot afternoon.

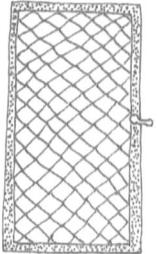

52. Screen Door

At the end of the day I sit on the front step, leaning against the screen door, moving my attention between the blush of sunset in the western sky and the sheen of rain on the road. It is storm season, every day threatening to break into rain by the evening. Tonight only the edge of it catches, the thunder a cautionary purr, the rain gentle.

The doorstep is not quite inside, not quite outside, a good place for a time that is not quite day, not quite night. Today's news cycles through my thoughts. Ukraine on the brink of war. An earthquake in Aotearoa, medium intensity, with only minor damage. A rail strike here, no trains on the entire city network. International travel has resumed today, and people are arriving at the airport to the gift of a jar of Vegemite and a city that is trainless and gridlocked, the afternoon heat rising, counting down to the storm.

53. Train Ticket

In my copy of *The House on Mango Street* is a bookmark, an old train ticket the size and thickness of a business card. Printed with the date and destination, they were dispensed from a cumbersome machine that had a button for every station listed in alphabetical order. I missed so many trains from the last-minute pressure of having 300 buttons to choose from.

April 20th, 2009, 9:09am, Petersham to Chester Hill. That day in my journal:

Mon. 20.4.2009 Outside the bank, a man and a little girl gather up a scattering of $1 coins. A broken white plastic bag is in his hand, I can see the whole sequence of events, I go to help them but then think better of it, something too personal about it.

At the Salvos, $10 for two jumpers and a pair of white flared polyester exercise pants (Slazenger, but too stylish for sportswear). Then on the station waiting, two teenage girls pace up and down the platform whispering conspiratorially. They shriek at the freight train as it goes by, at the same high pitch as its scraping wheels.

54. Computer Mouse

The surgeon moves the scroll wheel on the mouse with a clockwork rasp as he reads down through the report. Every movement in the room is heightened while we wait for his verdict. S sits tensely beside me as I clench my hands, watching the rectangle of the screen reflected in the surgeon's glasses. I look back down to his hand covering the mouse, the same hand that had done S's surgery. It must be a precise and steady hand, though there is nothing about it that's distinctive in the way he uses the mouse. He mutters a few acronyms, scrolls further down, nods, holding us in suspense. Then he ungrips the mouse and slides both hands over the desk towards us. He turns them, curling his fingers to give us two thumbs up. 'Good news,' he says.

55. Tessa Armchair

The Tessa armchairs in the lounge room had smooth leather cushions and polished wooden armrests and swivelled on a heavy wooden base. A forbidden thrill was to spin around on them, an excitement heightened by my parents' warnings that the chairs would not stand up to such treatment. Obedient, I rarely tried it. I would sit in my father's chair and let it envelop me as I examined the objects on the copper-topped coffee table beside it: a pipe, an ashtray, a box of Redhead matches, a pile of boating magazines.

When my parents separated the house was packed up and most of the furniture disappeared into storage. The chairs re-emerged when I was a teenager, when I no longer wanted to spin around on them. Instead I liked the idea of disappearing, slipping into the gap between the seat and the armrest, which harboured the remote control or things fallen out from pockets. I would sit and let the chair envelop me, slide my hand down by the side of the cushion, hoping for coins, hoping that the rest of me would follow.

My mother still has the Tessas and we each sit in one, talking about S's appointment. It went okay, I tell her, but the surgeon said we would have to wait for more results. I turn the chair ever so slightly on its base, slipping my hand down into the space beside me.

56. Road Sign

The motorway cuts through the fog, a runway through a cloud. On an incline my car struggles to overtake a semitrailer piled with hundreds of orange plastic crates. Scraps of white fluff are flying off the sides and I realise they are feathers. Through the sides of the crates I glimpse the huddled shapes of chickens.

The music stops and a news bulletin starts up. A voice fills the car with the headline that Russian troops have taken control of Chernobyl. There is nothing to do with this information but let it settle in the pit of my stomach and keep driving.

I start up the section of the hill that has the varying speed limit when it rains. The signs that indicate this have a symbol of a cloud emitting a storm of thick short dashes: 90 when raining here, 100 otherwise. There's no rain, but a feather is stuck to the side of the windscreen, and the description of the invasion continues, and I don't quite know the right speed for these conditions.

57. Washing Machines

On the highway that runs through Mayfield is a notorious corner lot. In it hundreds of broken washing machines and other bulky appliances are lined up across the cracked concrete, trees and pampas grass growing between them. Exposed to the sun and the rain, the washing machines prove their indestructibility by being barely even rusted, although most look to be in some way broken.

A second-hand appliances store had been here, a warehouse with a painted sign of a hand with '2nd' on the palm on the front wall. When it burnt to the ground the plume of smoke could be seen from across the city. The wreckage was cleared away, leaving the corner temporarily vacant. Then the washing machine collection started, becoming a library of spare parts for the appliances store which renewed its operations across the street.

I walk down the rows, stepping over the rubble of broken safety glass on the concrete, past the machines with shiny silver drums revealed by missing lids, their hoses unhooked and snaking over the concrete, moving deeper into the whitegoods graveyard.

58. Dixibell Margarine Container

In 1969, a new design for the Dixibell margarine tub featured in its newspaper advertisements. A slender, red-nailed hand reached out towards the plastic box, which was said to be a revolution in spread packaging. The revolution was in its reuse. Once you had finished the container of Dixibell, which, being polyunsaturated, could be consumed in great quantities without adverse health effects, the box could be used for 'food pieces, olives, nuts etc.'

The boxes came in a rainbow of colours, but this one is a sunny artificial yellow, befitting the spread that, as most people know or wish they didn't, would be grey without the addition of food colouring to improve it. Margarine names try for the same effect, either glowing – Sundew, Meadow Lea, Daffodil, Flora, Golden Pastures – or extraordinary: Miracle, Praise.

Some of these margarines are still manufactured and sold in plastic tubs printed with artificial sunrises, but not Dixibell. Even though the redesigned, curved, 1980s-era containers could be glued together to form a passable model of a space shuttle, it wasn't enough for the brand to endure.

59. Wooden Apple

A wooden arrow pierces a wooden apple, making an 'impossible object', a kind of puzzle which appears to defy what is physically possible. The arrow passes through the centre of the apple, through a hole only just wider than the arrow's stem. The arrow's tip and the fletching at the end of it are both too wide to fit through the hole, but there are no seams or joins on either the arrow or the apple to indicate how it might have been assembled. How did the arrow fit through the apple?

On the base of the apple is an old phone number, written in biro, beneath a name smudged to the point of being unreadable. Why not try it? I don't expect it to connect but it immediately starts ringing and, as is my usual habit, I count the rings. Five then ten then fifteen then twenty, then the ringing stops and the line goes dead, and I can't tell if I have been disconnected. Then, out of the blank hiss, comes a rushing and a whistling. The sound of an arrow, flying fast.

60. Bread Tag

At the supermarket I reach up to pull down a loaf of bread from the top shelf of the rack. Pulling the tail of the plastic bag I expect the loaf to follow, but the bag opens and the slices start falling out of it. I reach up to stop them and recoil at the softness of the bread against my hands.

Only a few seconds have gone by but people are already staring in the way that they do in the supermarket when order is disrupted, when a bottle of pasta sauce is dropped in an aisle, or a bag of rice spills. Maybe the person responsible is wilfully destructive. Maybe this is how everything starts to break apart.

There's a problem with the bread tags, the storeowner reassures me, releasing my hold from the slice of bread I am clutching. 'It's okay,' she says, although I am immobilised with embarrassment, as if I was the one with the problem, rather than the bread tags, which are now made out of cardboard, not plastic, and hold with a softer grip.

61. Ticker Tape

For one party, we built an Eiffel Tower in the back garden. Made out of sticks and tape, draped in fairy lights, it stood almost two storeys high. Underneath it we demonstrated the Proust Prognosticator to our guests. This was a box decorated with a photocopied portrait of the young Marcel Proust, the parting in his hair just off centre, a white orchid in his buttonhole. From his mouth a thin strip of paper protruded.

The party game went thus: ask Proust a question, then pull on the strip of paper until you reach the end of the sentence, a quote from *In Search of Lost Time*. Our friends had at first been shy with Proust, as if he really was an oracle, and his answers were serious determinations, but it was funny to pull and pull on his ticker tape. It unspooled from the hidden mechanism, a sticky-tape dispenser loaded with long sentences.

The morning after the party I picked up these strips of paper from the garden, where they were twisted up with blades of grass, bottle caps and scraps of baguette, and put them up around the house where they have remained ever since. On the shelves of the bookcase: 'But sometimes illumination comes to our rescue at the very moment when all seems lost; we have knocked at every door and they open on nothing until, at last, we stumble unconsciously against the only one through which we can enter the kingdom we have sought in vain a hundred years – and it opens.'

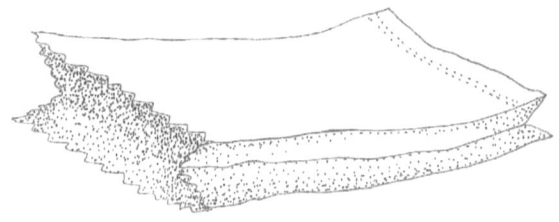

62. Paper Bag

Headlight-shine on the wet road, smell of barbecue chicken and cig-arette smoke. Broken glass on the pavement, traffic banked up at the lights, the night's torn edges. The heightened energy either sweeps you up or casts you aside. Standing back against the glass of the convenience store, I look towards the curve of the road for the bus to rescue me, as the crowd streams by.

At other times I have been one of them, surging past, shoulder to shoulder with my friends. It was my hand with green fingernails crumpling a paper bag around the bottles inside, sweeping past the people waiting for the bus, barely noticing them. I remember how it was, to want soft edges, to cling to the night or for the night to cling to me, to take my shape.

63. 'Winning Post' Chocolate Box

The cardboard box, green with the insignia of a gold horse approaching the finishing line printed on the lid, once held 'Winning Post' brand chocolates. Inside the box is a slip of paper that describes the potential of the chocolates to win friends, hearts and approval. Their soft centres were 'lusciously varied'. 'They're good to eat…and good to eat often!'

I imagine who might have kept it for so long that I would find it for sale half a century later. Perhaps two sisters, given the chocolates by a new neighbour who hadn't yet figured out that they weren't the least bit sweet. The sisters sat together at the kitchen table, deciding what to do with it. 'Is it possible the chocolates are poisoned?' the older one said. 'Remember those stories, back from when we were young? Who says that it doesn't still happen?' No to the chocolates then, but the box was worth keeping. That part of it, at least, was useful, they decided, putting the box away in a cupboard.

64. Gargoyle

Just visible above the temporary fencing, on the side wall of the building revealed by the demolition of a warehouse, is the top of an old, painted sign. It is wide and eye-catching, a yellow background with the word 'Gargoyle' painted across it, cut through with a red line. Below it perches the stylised figure of a red, scaly dragon.

The dragon looks down to where the mud is churned up from the deep tracks of the earthmoving machinery. On this stretch of Parramatta Road the layers peel away with every demolition, revealing more signs from the past. Only a few months before an advertisement for Plume Motor Spirit had been uncovered further down the hill. A century ago this had been the motor garage strip. Now the businesses sell mattresses, wedding dresses, and specialist bicycles.

Beside the construction site is one of the bike stores, and outside it a cyclist stands waiting, disguised under lycra and an aerodynamic helmet. He watches me crouch down to angle my phone through the gap in the fence, trying to capture the gargoyle.

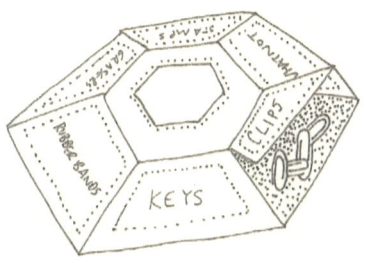

65. Desk Organiser

Made in Japan in the 1970s, the desk organiser is a hexagonal box made of brown plastic, with a decorative gold border printed on the lid of each compartment. A button on the base gives the box the ability to spin, so as to move between the categories labelled on each of the lids: stamps, erasers, rubber bands, keys, clips, and 'whatnot'.

Whatnot is the compartment for everything else that is not stamps, erasers, rubber bands, keys or clips. It is the unclassifiable, miscellaneous, various, odd, and assorted, always the best and most interesting of categories.

Whatnot holds a badge made out of a White Rabbit candy wrapper, a 45 rpm record adapter, 11 small white buttons on a string with a $1 price tag, a silver scarf ring, two SIM card tray ejector pins, a long metal screw, a nail, a black and white pebble made into a pendant, an orchid plant clip, an 'A' shaped fundraising token for Anzac Day 1941, and the tips of two Caran D'Ache wax crayons (kept from childhood).

66. Ghost Sign

At another building site the awning has been ripped away to reveal a painting of an ocean and a wide blue sky. A cruise ship surges forwards, the white smoke from its chimney merging with the thin, ornamental clouds above. Beside it a plane is taking off, its triangular wings and thin curved nose identifying it as the supersonic Concorde.

Once the pinnacle of elite air travel, Concorde jets travelled at twice the speed of sound, as passengers sipped champagne and ate truffle pastries and syllabub. The Concorde mostly flew the transatlantic route, but in 1985 there was a special flight from London to Sydney. To commemorate their arrival the crew were photographed holding a giant cardboard pocket watch, displaying their arrival time of 4pm, evidence of their record-breaking journey, only 17 hours. The passengers then transferred to the QE2 cruise liner, the slow-going ocean equivalent of luxury, which was waiting for them in the harbour.

This event must have so captured the imagination of this suburban travel agency that they commissioned a painting of it as their sign. It was the kind of leisure and luxury they could make real. Now, with the scene revealed again it is a fantasy trip, an illustration of a time gone by.

67. Coathanger

The day's object always makes itself known, often repeatedly if I don't immediately take notice of it the first time. In the morning I hold a handful of wet shirts from the washing machine. Outside the rain is so intense it looks to be in solid lines like in a Japanese woodblock print. A brisk, insistent wind blows in through the window, swirling around me, lifting the cuffs of the shirts. I improvise, putting the shirts on coathangers, opening the cupboard doors on either side of the narrow kitchen and hooking the hangers through their handles. Immediately the shirts begin to dance their way dry.

During my appointment the doctor advises me about back pain and posture, trying out a new analogy. 'Imagine you are a coathanger,' she says. 'Your head is the hook, straight and in the centre, and your shoulders are the triangle beneath it.' I can feel the hook overlaying my head like it is a line drawn in a caricature. The line descends downwards, looping around itself to make my neck and shoulders. It makes me sit straighter, for a moment, until the line unclasps itself. The wire untwists, keen to escape its structure.

68. Great Artists Magazine

The Great Artists arrived at the newsagency weekly, one by one, 96 in total. These magazines, printed on thick glossy paper, were designed to be filed away in speciality binders that collectors could send away for. The leather-look vinyl and gold embossed lettering of the binders aimed to transform the series into an encyclopaedia. The same company produced other series that could be similarly collected. Along with the artists, there was also *The Great Writers* and *The Great Composers. Golden Hands* for craft. *Fate and Fortune* for mysteries. *How It Works* for mechanics. *Story of Life* for biology. *Discovery* for history. *Superwife* for domestic advice.

There is often a stray Seurat or Van Dyck from *The Great Artists* in the op shop bookshelf or sometimes a larger bound collection shelved with the reference books. Or a stack of them appears in the street library with number 95, Matisse, on top. I can't place why I recognise the cover image until I realise I have recently seen the artwork in person. It had been Matisse's last self-portrait, 'The Sorrow of the King', a collage so big it took up an entire wall of the gallery. It is a sweet bright sorrow with yellow leaves like fire. S said from beside me, 'He's sad to be saying goodbye to life, because the world's just so beautiful.'

69. 'Day in the Life' Scarf

The scarf is a grid of squares like a calendar, each containing a symbol for an activity from a certain kind of New York day in the 1950s: a typewriter, two poodles, a stack of banknotes and coins, a microphone, a chef brandishing a plate and a spoon, a train. Wearing the scarf I am something of this character, rushing around the city from task to task, then onto the train home.

At Circular Quay station a man gets on board with a macaw sitting on his shoulder, a splendid bird, blue and gold, with black lines tracing rivulets around the eyes. The man wears all beige, as if to heighten his bird's vivid plumage. He sits by the doors so the bird can perch on the nearby handrail. Through black-lined eyes the macaw observes everyone in the carriage staring back.

I step closer and the man nods as if we've agreed on something. He gestures, by holding out his arm, that I should copy him. The bird hops from the railing to the man's arm, then to mine. The macaw's grey claws grip tight as he leans in towards the calendar scarf around my neck. He nudges the ends of the scarf with his beak, picking them up and tossing them, rearranging the envelope, the typewriter, and the poodles into a different order of events.

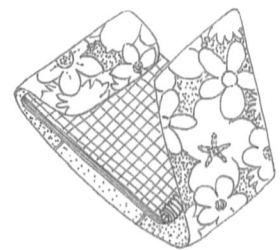

70. Koromogae Cover Notebook

I'm always in search of another notebook, one that might bring out some kind of latent idea or talent. Maybe it could be this one, which comes in a clear vinyl case that seals with velcro. The cardboard insert is a floral palette of yellow and brown, printed with the words 'Koromogae Cover'.

In Japanese *koromogae* is the word for the biannual change of wardrobe with the seasons, switching between summer and winter clothing. A twice-yearly ritual of airing out, washing, and packing away. Used on the notebook, the name suggests that you might change its cardboard cover to match your outfit, in a version of life where everything falls into line with the season.

71. Balancing Wooden Parrot

With the psychic imprint of the macaw's grip on my arm I look over
at the wooden parrot that balances on the edge of the bookcase. Its
beady eye, the yellow feathers painted down its back, and its curved
red beak make for a cartoon appearance. An educational toy, illustrat-
ing the principle of counterbalance, it is a flat curved strip of wood
that balances on one narrow notched claw at the front, weighted by a
ball at the base. When I perch it on the desk beside me it sways back
and forth in smaller movements until it reaches a point of rest. I notice
then that it is painted, for some mysterious reason, as a scholar, wearing a waistcoat and a bow tie, a book under its wing, a pencil behind
its ear.

I bought the balancing parrot from a legendary church flea market,
where the most dedicated shoppers line up for at least an hour before-
hand, empty bags over their arms. Everyone is friendly until the
doors open. Then we set to combing through the trestle tables piled
with objects surrendered by the elderly parishioners: anodised lamps,
typewriters, cardboard suitcases, bonnet hairdryers, any mildly
redundant domestic item that you could or couldn't imagine. Scooping
up anything that catches my eye, I progress through the thicket of
people and objects until I can carry no more. The balancing parrot is
the perfect emblem of this challenge.

72. Ballerina Music Box

The box has a shiny black lacquer coating which highlights a scene outlined in red, of rocks, trees, and Mount Fuji in the background. As a child I thought it elegant even though the ballerina inside was plastic like a cake decoration. When I wound the metal key on the side of the box she would turn in circles to the forlorn tinkle of *Swan Lake*, slowing and slowing until she came to a stop.

When I open the box the ballerina is gone, although there's nothing missing from the collection of lockets and former luck charms in the velvet-lined compartment. There is only the plain metal pin where she had been attached, in front of the mirrors that once carried her reflection. I lean down and my face fills the centre panel. A bad-news face, with puffy eyes and thin frown.

The tune I was slowing to came from the surgeon. He had called S to say the panel of specialists had discussed his case and it wasn't as straightforward as they had first believed. He would have to go for more surgery soon, and then radiation after that. The hospital would call tomorrow, to book it all in.

73. Pyrex Mug

It is comforting to be at the Salvation Army warehouse, at the edge of the airport, with the landing planes shrieking overhead mixing with the blasting classic hits radio. The sensory overload makes for good distraction. As 'Hungry Eyes' ramps up into the chorus I catch sight of a glass mug among the kitchenware, a promotional item for *Inch High Private Eye*, a sub-*Scooby Doo* animated series from 1973. Printed on it is an image of a cartoon dog with a tiny man standing on its nose.

Like so many once-plentiful mid-century objects, these mugs are collectable now. I realised this when I visited a shop in Tokyo that specialised only in American vintage glassware. The store sold, at surprisingly high prices, glass mugs of every conceivable design. A four-leaf clover? A cheerful peanut? A typewriter? The moon landing? An apple? A masked bandit? A penny farthing? A bear on ice skates? Elvis? A letterbox? A lemon with the slogan 'I'm a hot lemon lover'? A kitten playing with a ball of wool? A giant dog and a tiny detective, whose miniature size is both his superpower and his weakness?

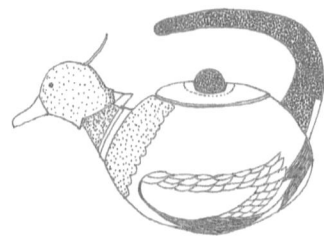

74. Duck Stovetop Kettle

The electric kettle breaks so we go searching for the duck among the piles of occasionally useful things stacked up in the laundry. Here it is, along with cans of spray paint and a block of beeswax: a kettle styled as a mallard duck, with the spout its neck and the whistle the duck's head.

Whenever I think of the duck I remember it first on the stove at a friend's house. I remarked on it every time I went to visit, and when she moved she gave it to me, saying I could use it to water the plants if I didn't use it as a kettle. 'Of course I'll use it,' I said, but then found that water takes a long time to boil in the duck. Steam ejects forcibly from the duck's nostrils and activates the whistle, which blares low and loud like a freight train.

An insistent noise comes to my attention, a background sound growing more urgent, splitting into two tones, unceasing. Maybe it's a siren, or something from the building site across the street, or some kind of evacuation alarm or someone is leaning on their car horn like they do sometimes when they want to prove a point, but why won't they stop? Oh, that's right, it's the duck, I realise, rushing in to find the kitchen full of steam.

75. Claw Feet

The heavy iron printing press in the library basement rests on four lion's feet. They are the size I would expect an actual lion's feet to be, as if this object is the result of an incomplete transformation. In their fight the printing press was almost completely the victor. Only the lion's paws still cling to the ground, unwilling to relinquish their position.

In the quietest hours of the night I imagine the printing press turning back into a lion, which paces the aisles, padding past the students who sleep in the library overnight rather than return to their cramped apartments. The lion makes a circuit of the library, then returns to the basement to disappear back into the machine. As the students wake up, they forget the lions that have appeared in their dreams.

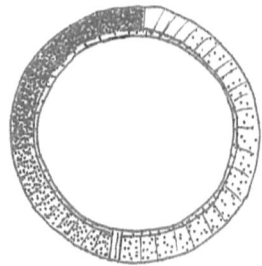

76. Cyanometer

The morning was a 4, pale blue, a little greyish. By midday it had deep-ened to a 17 or an 18, a cloudless canopy, the same colour as Sarina's sky that she sends me in a message, reminding me that the day is fresh and good and full of potential. I send my own clear sky in reply, blue above me as I sit on the lawn across from my work building, behind a row of camellias, just far enough away from the office's forcefield.

The sky is back down to 6 when I present the picture of the cyanom-eter to the class in the evening. On the screen is the ring made up of colour swatches, black to white through blue, numbered 0 to 52. With it, I talk about how writing too can provide a kind of measurement, an assay of emotion and possibility.

When I'm next out underneath the sky it is 36, a dark blue city night. Over in the east the airport glows behind the trees on the horizon. An updated cyanometer would extend through yellow and grey to include the ambience of the night airport and the jaundice of pollution haze, new colours for the same and different sky.

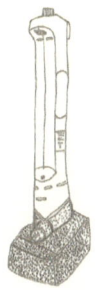

77. Robot

The robot moves slowly down the supermarket aisle, looking some-thing like a high-tech fence post, a white plastic pillar embedded with lights and sensors and cameras. As it glides it emits a barcode-scanner beep. What does it see? Packets of flour, cans of tomato puree. People ducking out of its way, or meddling with its path, or stopping to stare at it, trying to figure it out. It doggedly continues. A note in fine print on the side explains how it scans the floor to detect hazards, and also, if you come close to it, 'a photograph may be taken of you'. Too late. I am already in its memory.

When robot vacuum cleaners were new technology it was reported that one had gone missing from a hotel beside a motorway in England. Theft was suspected, and appeals were sent out that if found, the robot vacuum cleaner should be immediately returned. It was no use to anyone without its docking station. In fact no one had taken it. The robot had successfully breached the automatic doors and escaped. A day later it was found, battery depleted, under a hedge, by the road leading to the motorway onramp.

78. Philmar 'Unique' Jigsaw Puzzle

The tape sealing the edges of the box is brittle and yellow and flakes away when I peel it back. Pictured on the box is a painting of a street parade with the carnival queen, wearing a wide blue dress, holding the floral reins of the two giant model swans at the front of the float. Inside the box this scene is broken up into fragments of sky and pattern. A few pieces have faces of the people in the crowd, looking hopefully out of the jumble.

The last person to meet their eyes was Tom, who had checked the puzzle, as recorded on the underside of the box in wide, uneven lettering: 'Tom, OK, June '79, Checked.' Tom had started with the edges perhaps, or with an easily recognisable central detail. He had pieced together the trees on the hill in the background, moved along the strings of bunting, assembled the watching crowd. I do the same, bringing together the pink and gold throne and reconstructing the queen's face from where it has been split over two pieces. I lock them together and move on to her blue skirt decorated with flowers, hovering like a dragonfly over this artificial world.

79. Writing Set

This week, staying on Gathang country, we drive to the closest town with high hopes for what we might find. Among the collection of books in the church hall op shop I find a folder of notepaper, printed with a bouquet of daisies in autumn colours. An orange bud on the envelopes and sheets of notepaper, plucked from the bunch, a message ready to unfurl.

Back at the house, I inspect it further. One envelope of the eight is missing, along with one sheet of paper. The trace of the letter written on this sheet is on the top page of orange-bud notepaper, where the pressure of the pen from the page above has left an impression. Angling it up to the light, I try to make it out, but it is unreadable. I overwrite it with my own letter:

I'm writing this with the sound of the wind in the trees, and the waves breaking against the shore of the bay below the house. It is so peaceful it is another different life. If I could set the conditions of this life, would I make it so there was nothing difficult to face? I don't know. I am thankful for this quiet time before things become harder again.

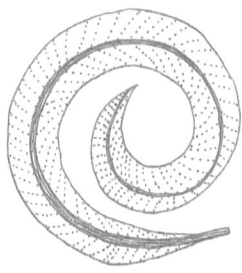

80. Spiral Leaf

On the path through the bushland a freshly fallen leaf stood out, curled into a spiral. An insect had eaten away the inner edge, setting the leaf off balance as it grew, causing it to turn in on itself. It was the shape of a comma, of things to come. I picked it up as the souvenir of the walk, put it on the bedside table so it could lead on to the next day.

In the morning the leaf had curled into a tighter comma, making me notice them in the morning news, in two powerful pauses. 'What I saw, I hope no one will ever see,' a foreign diplomat said, leaving the remains of the city of Mariupol. Devastated buildings, people trapped in the bombed remains of their shelters, unrelenting days of fear and loss.

Then in Sydney, outside Government House, Lismore residents protested alongside a pile of debris from their flood-ruined houses. They threw wet, destroyed objects out from the back of a truck: a cloth doll saturated with mud, strips of carpet, blankets. In Lismore the same piles were stacked up along the streets, everything people had owned sodden and destroyed. The protesters stood behind a muddied wooden door, holding it to display its spray-painted message: 'Morrison, your climate mega flood destroyed our homes.'

81. Pencil Tin

The tin was a long, flat rectangle, with an illustration of a lake scene on it, an example of what might be possible with a combination of Water Green and French Grey and a patient hand. The comprehensive set of all the pencil colours, arranged in two plastic trays that moved through the spectrum of colours, made me feel as if I might do something important with them, bringing together Scarlet Lake with Burnt Umber or Rose Madder Lake with Sap Green.

Unable to resist personalising the tin, I had painted a corner of it white and drawn a face on it, a happy round head with a fall of long black hair. In this way my grinning face interrupted the scene, like a novelty balloon that had drifted into the country landscape.

On the inside lid I had continued, drawing beside the list of the colours the same face with hair in pigtails, a butterfly, a snail, and a cloud filled with asterisks. The presence of my cartoon alter-ego only seemed to diminish the possibility I might use the set for extraordinary things, but my urge to fill the blank spaces had been too strong.

82. Silica Gel Sachet

A sachet contains about a teaspoon of the stuff, granules crunchy like gravel or rock salt. Not that it should be put on a teaspoon, because every packet of silica gel carries the warning DO NOT EAT, so much so that the warning and the name meld together: silica-gel-do-not-eat.

With its capacity to draw in water vapour silica gel folds up space, each granule made up of millions of tiny pores, so a teaspoon of it contains a surface area as big as a football field. It hides a secret immensity in the sachets inserted into shoe boxes or packages of nori or bottles of vitamins, to be ignored or discarded, a sideline object beside something else that is more demanding of attention.

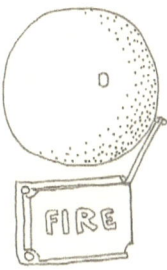

83. Fire Alarm

When the alarm starts up the class is quiet, heads down, writing. It doesn't sound like the usual fire alarm, it is softer, more textured, more alive. We all look towards the ceiling, where the sound is seeping through, difficult to ignore. It is the sound of a ghost teasing us, whistling 'ooooh' at the windows. Soon we realise it is made up of voices, a choir in the hall upstairs singing the rising and falling tones of a fire alarm, up and down, an uncanny call.

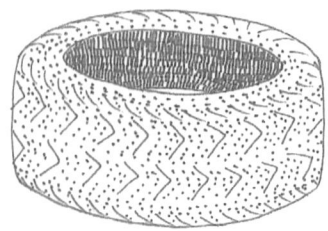

84. Car Tyre

A lentil can be used to deflate a tyre, by putting it under the cap of the valve. Rescrew the cap and air will begin to hiss out, and soon the tyre will be flat. The owner of the SUV will be angry, but as the flyer tucked under the windscreen wiper informs them, 'you will have no difficulty getting around without your gas guzzler'.

A tyre can be used to make a swan. Draw the outline for the head and body on its surface, then cut into it with an angle grinder. Turn it inside out, stretch out its wings. It is more difficult to do than you might expect, but it is worth persisting to make this metamorphosis.

A garden can be planted in a tyre, once it is cut open and its edges trimmed to make a zigzag around the edge, like a patty pan for a cup-cake. You might notice two such planters by the side of the road, put out for rubbish collection, and pick one up to carry it home. 'Do you want some help?' a group of teenagers might ask you, begrudgingly polite, seeing you struggle with it. No, no, you gasp, polite in your own insincere way, arms fit to snap.

85. *Looking in Junk Shops*

Published in the 1960s, the trio of pocket-sized 'junk' guides aimed to educate novice collectors about the mildly useful, highly embellished objects from the nineteenth century that were then readily found in British secondhand stores.

'Each entry is rather like the window of a junk shop,' wrote the author, John Bedford, at the start of *Looking in Junk Shops*, the first in the series. I open the book at horse brasses, amulets that were used to decorate horse's bridles, then an array of pincushions, then a 'barge' teapot, distinguished by having a smaller version of itself on its lid. Victorian-era detritus, their logic for existing almost forgotten.

The first volume covers major styles of pottery and porcelain and the more common decorative items, but by volume three, *Still Looking for Junk*, there are entries for the mote skimmer spoon (a long spoon punched with holes, used to skim off stray tea leaves), potichomanie vases (decorated by collage), and apple scoops made from the shank bones of sheep. Why are these things of such interest, Bedford asks, before providing his answer: 'perhaps the things of today are too near us to have enchantment.'

86. Street Directory

The street directory contains the city as it was half a century ago, presented in maps and lists of swimming baths and movie theatres. On the cover is an evening scene showing the then tallest building, the AWA tower, its metal spire a central beacon.

The maps inside parcel up the land into grids of streets and blocks of colour indicating parks and waterways. To make the maps easier to read at night, the introduction states, 'strong colours have been specially selected'. Thick black outlines give the shape of the land and the streets, cut through by yellow highways.

Interleaved with the maps are scraps of paper with directions handwritten on them: a notice for altered city bus routes, a pamphlet for a smash repairer, and a slip of soft orange paper. The orange page gives me a jolt of recognition, as if I have seen it before, but it's not the note that's familiar, it's the street names. They describe a route to Lucinda Street, where I lived for the first five years of my life. It was a place so significant to my parents that they had come close to naming me after it. Ever since, Lucinda has followed me around, another self, a person I could have been.

87. Polaroid Photograph

Beginning in 1979, the artist Jamie Livingston took a Polaroid photograph every day up to the day of his death in 1997. They are self-portraits and photos of friends, lovers, parties, trees, shadows, rooms, and objects, as random and deliberate as any daily moment can be. Sometimes I look up the current date in his archive, and see what photo comes. Thirty years ago today, a group of friends made shadow puppets. A dog, a frog, a lizard, a bat, and a fifth hand that makes no shape but stretches out, reaching across time.

Taking down a tin of my old photos, I pick out the first Polaroid I come to. Inside the square white frame two women are wearing men's suits and have eyeliner-pencil moustaches drawn on. Pressed close together, shoulder to shoulder, one has a round face and almost-closed eyes, the other high cheekbones, purple hair and an intense stare. Our faces are lit up by the camera's flash, our own spotlight, highlighting our opposites-attract expressions.

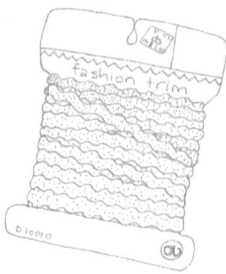

88. Rickrack

Rickrack sounds like the shape, up and down like a soundwave, a braid that exists for no other reason than to decorate the hems of skirts or the cuffs of sleeves. For further uses consult the *Nufashond Rick Rack Book* of 1916. The instructions inside are for making fussy objects like decorative pincushions, doilies and guest towels, heavy on embellishments.

It is for dolls dresses and party costumes and I am drawn to it although I will never use it, liking how frivolous it is, always surprised it still exists in the days when making a lavish pincushion is no longer a good use of one's time. I know I will leave it as it came, wound round the cardboard, forever holding its potential.

89. Van Van Oil

The image on the bottle of Van Van Oil is indistinct, the lines blotchy
and imprecise, a photocopy of a photocopy of a photocopy. The only
recognisable detail is an angel with wide, spreading wings, in the midst
of a chaos that could be trees or houses or devilish creatures.

The bottle of Van Van Oil, for good luck and protection, came from the
Farmacia Million Dollar in Downtown LA. It was my first and only
visit to the city I had already visited a thousand times in films and
daydreams. Outside of the movies it was blue sky and pollution haze
and motorways, the rundown movie palaces on Broadway, the iron-
lace staircases of the Bradbury Building, and hope made material in
the aisles of the Farmacia.

The shelves were stocked with oils to heal a broken heart, tame bullies,
drive away evil, make the devil run. Attract the person you want,
repel the person you don't. Bring the city's angels around to your side.

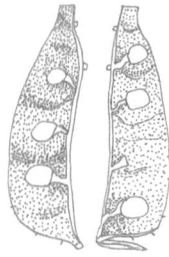

90. Model of a Pea Pod

In the university museum the teaching model of a pea pod stands upright in the display cabinet. Enlarged, with its two almost-symmetrical halves, it has the look of a set of lungs. But this is botany class, not anatomy. A teacher would have used the model to explain how the pod was a fruit and the peas its seeds, naming its parts – the hull, the midrib, the funiculus – as the students took down notes or drifted into other thoughts.

The pod has a realistic, waxy appearance, so solidly green that to look at it is to fall into the colour. Set snugly inside it are three peas on the left and three on the right, with one empty stalk for a detachable pea which could be further disassembled to show its layers – the testa, the radicle, the cotyledon.

The artificial pea pod has a robust, waxy life, a sheen to its skin under the lights. Whenever I visit the museum I go to look at it, to imagine curling up at the end of the empty stalk and the pod closing protectively around me.

91. Tugboat

From the hotel room I look over at the tugboat moored across the river, beside a row of shoreline palm trees being pushed asymmetrical by the wind and rain. The name 'Lydia' is painted on its side, above the tyres lined up along the hull, a protective buffer against the coal ships and chemical tankers that the tug guides in and out of the narrow waters of Newcastle's port. Today Sea Neptune is due, and Doric Pioneer, the CS Olive, and Noble Salute.

In Mulubinba for the writers festival I am thinking about extraction and dislocation, as I drink decaffeinated instant coffee made up from a sachet, and look over towards the opposite headland. This stretch of land was artificially created from ballast, rubble from Europe, Asia, and America that weighed down the ships on their journeys south. The ballast was replaced by an equivalent weight of coal at the Newcastle ports, an exchange of displacement.

I find a map that shows how the ballast was built up around an island to join it to the mainland, creating the wharf. The names are recent and European – Bullock Island, Throsby Creek. I look out the window again, across the water to where a ship named Lydia waits by a rubble wall of displaced stones, a map of the world crumbled into pieces.

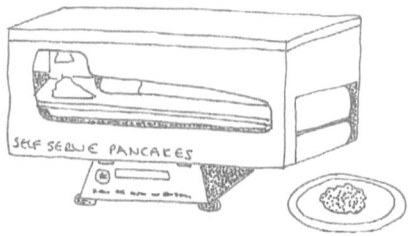

92. Automatic Pancake Machine

In the hotel dining room I lean down to watch a puddle of batter moving along the conveyer belt inside the automatic pancake machine. It flattens out between two hotplates as a screen displays 'Making 01 of 02', as if it is printing a document. Beside the machine are bowls of multicoloured sprinkles and mini-marshmallows, to further feed my inner child.

As the display screen changes to 'Making 02 of 02' the first pancake emerges from the end of the machine, edges frilly like a doily. The pancake tumbles onto the plate below and I try to think through the sequence of events that have led up to the existence of the automatic pancake machine and me standing watching it. If only I could under-stand each event like the component of a machine, able to be taken apart and put back together, readily described and understood. Every object is this way, with tendrils that extend across time, into histories that pull close, never separate from the here and now.

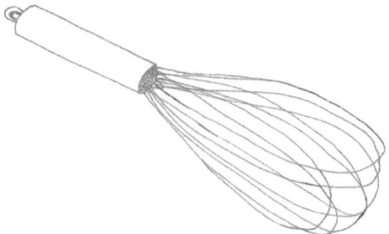

93. Balloon Whisk

A whisk waits on the bench as Julia Child separates eggs, describing the action as she tips the yolk between the two halves of the broken shell. Her low singsong voice has high inflections, as if trying to escape itself. No escape for the egg yolks in the bowl, which she whisks vigorously, describing how this helps the yolks take the heat with 'more equanimity'. The yolks grow pale and slick, compliant for the next stage of the process.

Child's kitchen was as homely and rustic as mine is narrow and cluttered. It is Sunday night and I am working on whisking a sauce. Whisking brings equanimity, I imagine telling my viewers, don't be fooled by the vigorous action, it is hard work for a calm result.

Tonight's recipe is for dealing with the unexpected. I don't want to think about S going to hospital soon, so this is the sauce I make when I want to distract myself as much as possible, when I want to keep my hands busy, when I know the days will pass no matter how I feel about them doing so.

94. Roycroft Library Book

The books that originally came from the Roycroft subscription library are hard-bound in black cloth with a yellow label affixed to the cover. Above the hand-lettered 'Roycroft' is an illustration of two fish with big eyes and long noses, the library's emblem.

The Roycroft was a subscription library and bookstore located on Rowe Street, the laneway of artisan shops, studios, and cafes that was the cosmopolitan centre of mid-century Sydney. The library was below street level, under the sign of the two fish locked together into a circle. It was known for its literary collection, for stocking banned books like *Brave New World* and *Down and Out in Paris and London*, and for offering, as its advertisements promised, 'personal, courteous attention'.

Sometimes a long-forgotten novel is requested from the university library storage, where the Roycroft fish undetectably hide. In the foyer, on the shelf of books recently retrieved from the stacks, I notice one. Black cover, yellow label, Elizabeth Bowen, *The House in Paris*. When I open it the pages are soft and worn, speckled with foxing. I flip through to find a line that fits my mood: 'After that, the days here began to slip by faster and faster, not touching anything as they passed.'

95. Half a Cup of Coffee

Against the front of a vacant house, covering over the long crack at the centre of the wall, is a real-estate sign. Rather than present a photo of the interior it displays an aerial shot of the block of land and a description: 'The upside of this home mostly lies in its future, but it's a very bright one indeed.'

The house is derelict, with windows boarded up and rusted guttering sagging at the corners. It's clearly deserted so I go in through the gate and down by the side to look around. Cool stale air emanates from inside, a sour scent of mould and broken plaster. At the back of the house steps lead down into a yard overgrown with grass and sword ferns.

Among the green something white catches my eye. By the top step is a joke coffee mug that looks as if it has been sliced down the middle, a shape too long and narrow to comfortably drink from. 'You asked for half a cup of coffee' is printed on the side in thick brown lettering. A last cup of coffee in the garden from who-knows how long ago, a mucky brew of stagnant rainwater inside it.

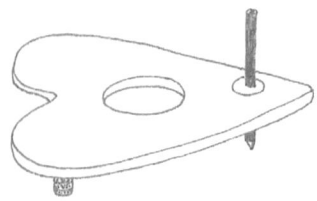

96. Planchette

It is, they say, invested with the power of prophecy; it can answer any question put to it regarding the past, present, or future – in short, it is a sort of inanimate wizard, under the guise of an extremely simple-looking little instrument.

There's a *something* in all this, an intelligence separate and distinct, but the instrument is not one which it is advisable to place in the hands of any morbidly disposed persons, who might be inclined to accept an apt answer as a direct communication from the unseen world.

Her opinion about the planchette was that it worked intelligently only with those who yielded to its influence. Her own planchette had been very fractious at first, she told us, but had soon become amenable to her touch. With those who did not yield the planchette refused to work.

Whether the achievements of the machine are due to spirit influence or unconscious nervous effort the writer is not prepared to say. While some believe, many doubt. They say that to ask a question of Planchette is an interview with nothing.

Spirit! Have you a message for me?

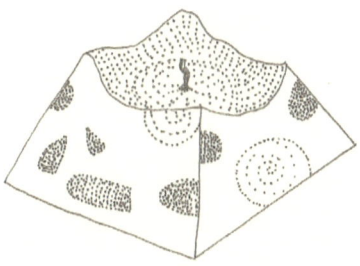

97. Candle

The candle is for my birthday, but mostly for S. I had driven him to hospital in the first grey hour of daylight, as the rain continued its steady rhythm. Arcs of water fanned up from the tyres of the cars and people huddled under bus shelters, cursing the grim sodden morning.

Inside the hospital, after filling in the paperwork, we followed the corridors until we reached a set of double doors that seal away the operating theatres. In the middle of a row of vinyl chairs we sat close together, like the wet myna birds we had seen under the awning at the hospital entrance. Then a nurse came to take S further in and the doors swung shut behind them.

Back at home I lit a fresh candle, a pyramid of white wax with chips and circles of colour inside it. The wick crackled as it caught the flame. The candle was the psychedelic-patterned kind I had coveted as a teenager, when I believed I could become the person I wanted to be simply by owning particular objects. Although candles did not trans-form me as I thought they might, they remain good companions, softly and slowly burning through the hours.

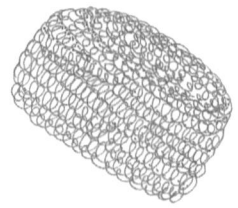

98. Steel Wool

The pad of steel wool is made of tiny shavings of wire, thinner than hairs, meshed together into a stiff pillow. With it I scour the saucepan, though it does little to remove the layer of carbonised sugar syrup that has fused to the metal from boiling dry.

My head reverberated with the sound of the smoke alarm and I felt chastened, an embodiment of the woman from the 1980s insurance advertisement who is distracted from deep-frying a pan of chips when she's called away by the ringing phone. 'Sally,' she says, smiling, settling in for a chat. A moment later the kitchen is on fire and she cries out, 'Oh my goodness the chips!', remembering all too late.

My own caller had not been as friendly. The syrup was about to boil as she whispered in my ear that I should read back over the email I just sent, did I word it softly enough? And what if something goes wrong with S's cancer, what if you get sick next, what's the next bad thing that will happen? Her voice is in the shriek of the freight trains in the middle of the night, it is in the itch of the mosquito bite on my ankle. As I work the steel wool over the burnt pan I imagine I'm pushing her further and further away.

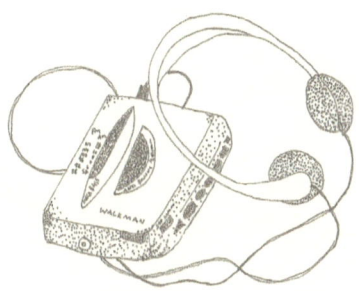

99. Walkman

Under my desk, in a box, hidden by a snarl of leads and cords, the Walkman had been biding its time, waiting for me to rediscover it. I hadn't been looking for it but now I was curious to find out what cassette I had left inside it, the last one I had been listening to who-knows how long ago. A mixtape, with 'more stuff for Vanessa' written on the label in pink pen. I push it back into the Walkman, snap the cover closed.

Slowly, slowly, I inch the front door closed behind me so the latch makes only the faintest click. I leave S asleep, with the bunch of roses in the vase on the kitchen table slowly exhaling their sweet scent through the house.

Heading down the hill towards the river I put on the headphones and press the play button. The tape starts up in the middle of a song. Over a loose beat a voice is singing 'oh dear, what can the matter be' as if it doesn't worry them in the least.

100. Tape Measure

On the metric side of the yellow measuring tape the numbers advance quickly, divided up into the close strokes of the millimetres. Turn it over and the inches are wider, their increments spacious by comparison.

The inch is a human measure, the first knuckle of your thumb or three grains of barley. The centimetre was calculated down from a planetary scale, equal to one-hundredth of one 10-millionth of the distance from the North Pole to the equator. The line was measured to run through Paris, the epicentre of decimalisation. Here the new era of metric measurement coincided with the Republican calendar, which as well as naming days after such things as violets, brooms or guinea fowl, had weeks lasting ten days.

Rolled up tight, this tape measure has centimetre upon centimetre folded inch upon inch, coiled up together in a long strip of yellow plastic. At the end of it, beside where the measurement markings end, COW HEAD BRAND and a cow's head insignia is printed in the space beside the metal clip that seals the tip. This short length, unmarked by divisions, is my favourite part, leading into the unquantified space beyond.

101. Day-of-the-Week Handkerchiefs

When the girl arrives with the basket, I come to the door, mobcap hiding my long ears, hoping she won't notice I don't look very much like her grandmother at all. I think she might have food inside the basket, but all she has brought is a small, shallow box.

The box is printed with a snow scene in red and blue ink. Stars blaze in the sky and a self-satisfied moon smiles down over a hill across which a well-bundled figure carries a basket towards a house. From the steeply pitched roof, a long trail of chimney smoke rises up into the night.

We sit together on the side of the bed and she watches as I open the box. Inside it the white handkerchiefs are folded and arranged so their hand-stitched designs are visible. There is one for each day of the week. Monday's cockerel rings a bell, Tuesday's goat plays a drum, and Wednesday's rabbit rides a hobby horse. Thursday's turtle wears a top hat, Friday's pig policeman has a blue, satin-stitched coat, and Saturday's goose wears a fine red hat. To celebrate the end of the week, Sunday's cow plays a tuba. They are so sweetly and purely good that I forget my hunger.

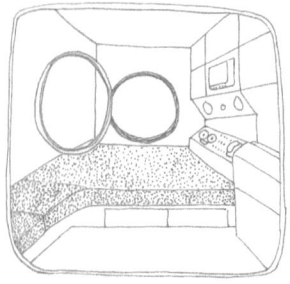

102. Capsule

A minor headline in the day's news announced the demolition of the Nakagin Capsule Tower. This notoriously derelict Tokyo apartment block had been designed by an architect from the Metabolist movement, a group who envisaged buildings which could grow and replenish like plants do. The Jenga-like arrangement was made up of concrete blocks with round windows at their ends like giant washing machines. Despite the architect's intentions, the building had decayed rather than grown with the city around it.

Across the street from the tower, standing in the parking lot underneath an elevated motorway, I had examined the stains on the concrete capsules, how power cords trailed down from the higher levels, and how nets and tarpaulins were draped over its more unstable parts. Despite its broken-down state, the architect's aspirations still hung around it, the vision of the capsule-dwellers neatly occupying their concrete shells.

The apartments were tiny, only ten square metres, their designs based off the efficient interiors of boat cabins. Most, now, were uninhabited. One window, as if it were indeed a washing machine, had a tumble of fabric shoved up against it. Others were grimy and ruinous, but some had curtains or clear glass. I was sure that in one high-up window I glimpsed a face looking down, but by the time I looked closer it had disappeared.

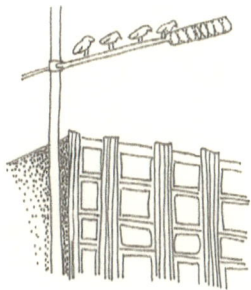

103. Streetlight

The seagulls aren't worried by the rain, lined up on the crossbeams of the streetlights that extend over the road in front of the town hall. It's far too wet for anyone to be lingering on the steps today. The crowd moves like an endless caterpillar rippling along, the slogans on their t-shirts and the patterns on their umbrellas merging into a confusion of symbols.

Beneath the pavement, the beach. The town hall clock chimes for the half hour. As the bells ring the seagulls all take flight. From my position under the supermarket awning I watch them circle above the street, grey shapes against a grey sky, before they resettle on the streetlights in new configurations.

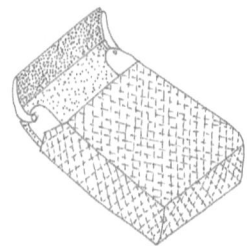

104. Cigarette Case

On our last night together we wrote messages to our future selves. Twenty years, we decided, was long enough to wait for the significant things we would go on to do. Violet tore out two blank pages from the end of her notebook and we began.

She wrote immediately and intensely, head bowed over the page. I went slowly, with long pauses after each sentence. The future was my blind spot. Violet was still intently writing after I wrote my final line: 'with me looking forward, and you looking back.' I could predict at least that much.

I put down the pen and reached for the Glomesh cigarette holder. It was a small, sturdy box with a metal mesh skin and a brass mechanism connected to the lid, which worked to raise up the cigarettes inside. Glomesh was slinky stuff, op shop elegance, a good disguise.

The box was empty and I opened and shut it a few times, feeling the cold metal mesh against my hand. 'Give me that,' Violet said, rolling her letter into a tight cylinder. She put it inside the case, closed the lid and pushed it back over the table towards me. 'In twenty years time,' she said, 'not a moment before.'

105. Romance Novel

The woman behind the counter was reading a book with an impassive face, as if nothing whatsoever could shock or impress her. When I approached, dress draped over my arm, she paused her reading, lying the book open face down, so I could see it was a romance novel titled *Danger from the Past*. Looking down at the dress, which was pink with a voile and satin skirt, she asked, 'Are you going dancing?'

'Yes,' I said, not telling her the full story. I was going to dye the dress black and wear it to a goth club, where dancing meant swaying side to side within a thick pall of dry ice, waving my arms around like tree branches in the wind.

She used to go to the Trocadero dance hall, she told me, in the centre of the city. 'It hasn't been there since the 1960s,' she said, 'you wouldn't remember it.' When she danced there it was wartime and there were shortages of many things. One of them was elastic. She looked at me as if expecting me to understand the significance of this.

She pushed the pink dress towards me, leaning in closer. 'It was difficult to keep our underwear on,' she explained. 'If you felt it coming off, there was nothing to do but kick it away and just keep dancing.'

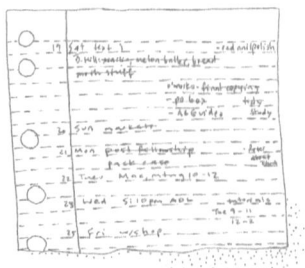

106. To-do List

My lists are written in pencil on the back of an envelope, or an index card, or the reverse of a printed A4 sheet from the scrap-paper pile. It is best if the page has already been used. My superstition is that this moves the tasks closer to being done, and I always like to use a piece of paper to its fullest extent.

The lower left corner is for works in progress, and the upper right for their opposite, for items easily crossed off. Underneath this is the list of messages I haven't yet answered. In the upper left, a thorny patch of deadlines. Below it, life admin, that useful, repellent term to describe chores and appointments.

Occasionally I turn up an old list, with the once-urgent, now-cryptic items on it comfortably set to rest under the lines that cross them out. If only I'd kept them all, I think, when I find a stray list from the past. Every to-do list I've ever made, all those ragged creased pages stamped by teacup rings and scribbles to wake up the pen nib, another way of taking my life's measure.

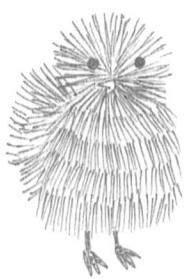

107. Easter Chick

One Easter, when I was working as a guide at a historic house, I was given a packet of 24 synthetic Easter chicks. My task was to place these balls of yellow fluff around the rooms. Two in a copper pot hanging up in the kitchen, peeking over the rim with their black-bead eyes. Others by the carved foot of a chiffonier in one of the bedrooms. Another cluster in the bookshelf in the Children's Room. Throughout the day I challenged kids to search for them, and by the time the house closed there was only a trio that I had hidden too well in the Little Tea Room remaining.

Before driving home I blu-tacked the feet of the three leftover chicks onto the top of the dashboard. Their shapes and expressions were all a little askew, but every time I tried to reshape them into the cute creatures they were intended to be, their eyes and orange-felt beaks slipped further out of alignment. The more I tried to make them what I wanted them to be, the stranger they became.

108. Composition Book

With the sun on my arms and the grass cool underneath my crossed legs, I hold the composition book in my lap. Or the exercise book, to call it by the name I grew up with. Before I knew that they were the same kind of notebook I presumed composition books must have additional features. Exercise is work and practice, and composition is making something, putting pieces together. Over time I came to understand how these activities could be one and the same.

The designs on the covers of composition books suggest their potential. The speckled black and white lines and shapes could be snail trails or mountain ranges. These abstract and irregular arrangements, that might yet resolve into something in particular, were like a static of thoughts, out of which ideas take form.

109. Trading Card for Dr Jayne's, 'The Ghost Story!'

The girl sits in a blood-red armchair, book open in her hands, eyes wide as she looks up from a ghost story. The room around her gives her little comfort, with the mirror hanging crookedly on the wall, and the window framing a view of a full moon behind clouds. The candle is burnt down to a nub in a silver holder, soon to sputter out.

Each card in the series describes a new situation that can be remedied by Dr Jayne's Liniment, Expectorant, Tonic Vermifuge or Sanative Pills. As well as cough mixture and worm pills the company produced a vast range of promotional ephemera including almanacs, trading cards, and fortune-telling games, all preaching the effectiveness of Dr Jayne's remedies.

The cards illustrate scenes such as patting kittens, feeding chickens, or inhaling the scent of morning glory flowers. It isn't until you turn the card over and read the text that you come to understand the lurking contagion inside these scenarios. But do not fear, Dr Jayne's is a trusted family tonic. If, while reading at night, you happen to breathe in a ghost, and come to feel its haunting chill in the pit of your stomach, Dr Jayne's Expectorant will release it, and the spectre will speedily depart.

110. Anodised Apple

The red anodised surface of the apple reflected us as indistinct points of light and shadow, as we sat around the copper-topped coffee table, talking the night away. Enough wine and cigarettes and the hours puddled into a warp of the messy room, jagged music, and the forces of chance that had brought the three of us together.

The apple was ostensibly an ice bucket with a lid, shaped to resemble the fruit. Its instruction booklet, however, described it as a 'year round hostess helper', suitable for soups, stews, scrambled eggs, ice cubes, cocktails, or cold cuts. Illustrations depicted wholesome party scenes with the apple highlighted in red on the family dinner table or at the centre of the picnic rug.

This apple had pride of place in the middle of the table as we listened to the Plug Uglies, talking about everything and nothing, our words settling around the music, disappearing with it. At the end of the side the turntable kept spinning, the needle circling the run-out groove with a hiss and a tick.

In the sudden hush Ryan asked, 'What's inside the apple?' Our blurry reflections loomed in the red aluminium skin as we leaned closer to it. 'I don't remember,' I said, reaching for the lid, 'but whatever it is, it must be a message for us.'

111. Kitchen Tap

In the office kitchenette, waiting for the microwave, I think over escape strategies. The neatest is some kind of extraordinary good fortune, like winning the lottery or receiving a mystery inheritance. Another possibility, requiring more effort, is to patent an indispensable gadget. A time-and-effort-saving invention, compact and clever, like the tap which produces both boiling and ice-cold water from the same spout.

The first time I took notice of the tap was in another university office kitchenette, during a meeting with one of my supervisors. He patted the newly installed tap lightly, like it was a pet, and said, 'invent something like this and you need never work another day in your life'. Every time I use the tap now, this scene returns to me.

As I press the hot water button I put my mind to dreaming up something like it, that fulfils a clear and immediate purpose in the physical world. It is much easier to think of intangible desirable things that are much more difficult to manufacture. Yet again, nothing comes. Everything already seems to exist.

112. Squirrel Pillowcase

In my first waking moment I am eye to eye with the cartoon squirrel printed on the pillowcase. Its eye is as big as mine, mouth the same size too, though it is about to bite into an acorn, and I am wearing a night guard that prevents teeth-clenching during sleep. We are in an epidemic of bruxism, or so dentists report. Anxiety settles in the jaw.

Squirrel teeth, unlike mine, are ever-replenishing. Their teeth continue to grow throughout their lives, only kept in check by gnawing. All rodents are this way, although only certain rodents are featured on pillowcases. Under my cheek all night, the squirrel sits on the branch of an oak tree, holding its acorn, for the delight of the child whose pillow it was intended to decorate, or for the adult who might still find comfort in such things.

113. High Bulk Walk Socks

There's something in the letterbox. A package protrudes from it, too long to fit completely inside.

A packet of walk socks.

The socks, knee-high and thick-ribbed, were packaged with an assurance of summer comfort, and their versatility for business or leisure. To illustrate this is a photograph of a scene in a car, in which a woman in a Jackie O scarf and sunglasses sits in the passenger seat. All we can see of the other passenger who, weirdly, has their legs draped over the driver's seat, is a pair of legs in long grey socks and brown suede shoes. It is a scene of unexpected glamour for socks that, judging by the material evidence, were only worn by elderly relatives in old family photographs.

Standing behind the letterbox, beside the gate, I'm holding the socks as if they are urgent news. I look down along the street for a clue to who might have left them for me. There's just the same pile of discarded mattresses that have been collecting rain for a week and the taciturn neighbour who feeds the pigeons on the corner, not for the love of them, but to deter them from congregating on his own driveway.

114. Ceramic Cats

The cabinet behind the shop window displays a collection of cats. Someone's figurines, newly donated, arranged together for the last time. Inspecting the figures more closely I see that some are also salt and pepper shakers or teapots, and that each of the cats has a mood, whether eager, aloof, sweet or fiendish. Some are positioned mid-pounce, others look restful and self-satisfied, others serious and watchful.

It is the thoughtful, slightly melancholy-looking cats that I am drawn to, like the tiger-striped cat sitting up attentively on a solid ceramic base with a hole for a candle beside it. This is the cat I choose. I take the candle-holder cat out of the cabinet and over to the counter, playing my part in the distribution of the collection.

Over the week, the cats disperse. Someone buys the ginger teapot with the cracked ear, someone else the tabby kittens playing with a ball of wool. Then the long-necked salt and pepper cats are gone, and someone buys the cats with even the most awkwardly painted faces. Then the next week the cabinet has a different display altogether, a new round of recirculating things.

115. Finger Puppet

The finger puppet is made of a wooden bulb, a dog-like head with two long leather ears glued to each side. Affixed to it is a circle of Liberty fabric under which my finger provides shape. It is a tighter fit than it used to be: but of course, last time I did this I was a child.

My mother and I are sifting through our family's collected objects, things that have been around for my whole lifetime. We won't discard anything without assessing its story, then its utility. The finger-puppet dog we will keep, strange creature that it is, with its head painted red like a saveloy, a contrast to the floral fabric that makes up its outfit.

Encountering it again every minor detail of the finger puppet is familiar. The frayed edge of the fabric, the shiny black paint of the dog's round eyes, and how it feels to animate its solid wooden head, to make it nod and tilt as if listening to me as I say, 'hello, long time no see, shall I tell you everything that's happened?'

116. High-school Art Textbook

At the top of the box of books is *From Caves to Canvas*, a high-school art textbook I immediately remember upon seeing it again. By underlining key phrases, I had attempted to impress the details of art history into my memory. My pencil was sharp and at the ready, marking up important details like 'Cezanne painted this mountain sixty times'.

The book had a cover image by Keith Haring, dancing figures, a snake, an angel, and a hula-hooping figure, stout black lines in between them, vibrating with energy. From week to week I followed the sequence of artistic movements, each building on or reacting against what came before. 'In dismissing the past, the eccentric artists of the movement looked to the future.'

The corner is dog-eared at the page with *Le Thé* by Berthe Morisot. Short, thick brushstrokes form the image of a woman sitting pensively at a table, tightly laced into an elaborate dress. Her hands reach out towards the cup of tea, which she has her eye on in the distracted way of someone thinking of something else altogether. The scene kept something of itself obscure and I could come up with a different story for it every time. But all I underlined beside it was 'loose, spontaneous style'.

117. Chalkboard

In the gloomy cobwebbed space underneath our house I find the long chalkboard we used to keep in the hallway, with inscriptions from a long-ago party. What had caused us to write a list as weird as 'sound police', 'offline movement', 'embarrassment loop', 'worm tricks'?

'It's our version of those historical school chalkboards,' I say to S, 'remember that story?' At a high school in Oklahoma, chalkboards were taken down to reveal older boards behind them, with lessons from a century before. Cursive lettering, a wheel of numbers to teach multiplication. A drawing of a girl in a blue dress blowing a soap bubble, and another in a pink dress, standing with a turkey. Beside the pink-dress girl was a grid of days, a yellow circle on every square, counting down to the end of the month.

The chalk had rasped against the slate, dust falling from it as the teacher stood drawing the treble clef with the notes ascending, singing as she went, maybe. At the start of each day she marked off the calendar square with a yellow dot, creating an endless run of sunshine no matter the weather outside.

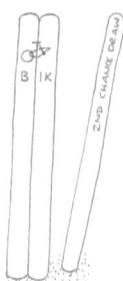

118. Popsicle Sticks

On the rain-wet, grey paving of the central walk an A-frame sign is set up, an orange square with a question printed in the centre. As I draw closer it comes into focus. 'Does Our Society Need God?' Two clear plastic containers are set up on either side of the sign, one for yes, one for no. A pile of popsicle sticks at the base of the sign waits to be cast in one side or the other. Both containers are empty, capturing only the rain. Like everyone else walking past on this grey morning I adjust my course, veering wide to avoid the question.

119. Cameo Brooch

The goddess is carved from a pink cornelian shell, circled by a gold frame. She is engraved in the paler outer layer of the shell, her face in profile with a long nose and full lips, long coils of hair thick against her neck. Cold to the touch, she is a figure of calm wisdom.

The brooch had first belonged to a woman born exactly a century before me, so that I step through the same years at the same age, a hundred years on. In 2028 I will be the same age as she was in the 1928 photograph where she stands under a stone archway on fete day, preparing to tell people what they might have to fear or look forward to.

She had a talent for fortune telling using playing cards and I like to imagine the cards might have suggested me to her. That with them she could see ahead to the woman who would follow her year for year into the future, connected by the calendar and the cameo-brooch goddess.

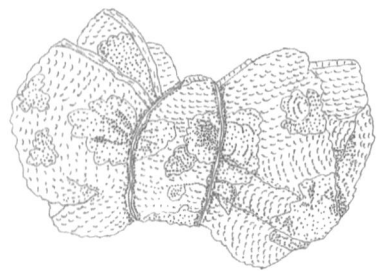

120. Hand Towel

To help with the insomnia which has been rattling my head every night and putting me out of step with the days, S has an idea. He takes the towel from the top of the washing basket, a hand towel with a print of pink roses, and balls it up into a bundled shape which he then secures with a thick rubber band. 'This is an extra brain,' he says. 'It's going to do all the worrying for you, while you sleep.'

He wedges the towel-brain beside the pillow, close enough to my head to make it seem as if it might work, or at least might be worth trying. He switches off the light in the bedroom and leaves me in the quiet. It's the usual situation, too tired, too awake, but then I'm in the room at the back of the terrace house where I used to lie with the big ginger cat beside me and look out through the branches of the jacaranda tree, towards the back of the Esperanto school, and it is a place I haven't been in for so long that I must be in the dream in which all the rooms of my life stack up, opening one to the next, all the way until morning.

121. Dip-N-Set Container

The cardboard box is full of things that had been packed up and sealed away long ago. My mother and I look down into it, in search of something we recognise. A pair of dolls with stiff plastic bodies, their wigs fallen off, clothes faded. 'No one would want these now,' my mother says, arranging their hair back on top of their heads.

More dolls, photographic slide boxes, the pearls from a broken necklace. A jar with asterisk snowflakes and 'Dip-N-Set' printed on the glass, and a twist of curled green and red ribbon inside it.

'What's that?' my mother asks, looking at the container. 'A jar of Dip-N-Set hair-setting gel, with curling ribbon inside,' I say, suspecting I am the only person to have ever uttered this exact sentence. She gestures at the discard pile, made up of a miracle grater, VHS tapes and old road maps, and we return to sorting.

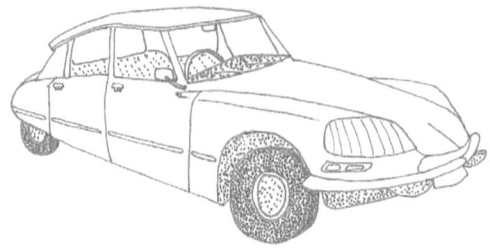

122. Citroën DS

One of the houses I pass on the way to the train station has a collection of vintage cars in the yard. I keep my eye out for the steel-blue Citroën DS that is often parked in the driveway. The DS premiered in the 1950s, a car with a bug-eyed, long-skirted appearance, low to the road, a vision of an alternative motoring future.

Roland Barthes described the DS by comparing it to cake icing, a soap bubble, and an insect. Whatever analogy comes to mind, it is true that it appears to be less a car than a hybrid creature. It operates by a circulatory system of hydraulic fluid, which controls the steering and the brakes, and the headlights move to follow the turns of the wheel, yellow eyes surveying the scene.

One day, I like to envision, the neighbourhood DS might turn its headlights in my direction, lift up from its low resting position, and glide away with me inside. Until it is suddenly gone from the driveway, replaced by a boxy baby-blue Rolls-Royce, a car for somebody else to dream about.

123. Porcelain Doll

Her brown hair matched mine, though unlike me she had blue eyes. Perhaps it is not a good idea to have a doll that's identical, but I wanted there to be a greater resemblance between us. So I called her Lucinda, the name that had come close to being my own.

Lucinda, unchanging under her floral bonnet, kept up the same wondering, open-mouthed apprehension of the scene before her. Her tiny mouth, with two miniature teeth visible inside, exhaled a secret that I had to stay very quiet to hear, but could never quite catch.

I still haven't developed acute enough senses to detect it. I sit her on my desk and wipe her face free of dust with a cloth, then move the cloth to her hands which protrude from the lace cuffs of her dress. They are small and grasping and seem to clutch onto mine when I hold them, although of course it is the other way around.

124. Exact Copy of the Gloves Worn during the French Period of the Directoire, 1796–1799

The gloves were one of a series of historically influenced designs made by Henry a la Pensée, a French fashion label that specialised in luxury accessories. Along with more ostentatious pairs which had puffed sleeves, or layers of tulle for cuffs, the gloves gestured towards the future by way of the past, led by mutton-chop ruffs at the wrists or a pattern of tiny human and animal characters across the palms.

The pattern is divided into a grid of diamonds, inside each a bird, a flower, or a dancing figure, printed in hair-thin lines. The figures are so small and finely rendered that they are impossible to make out from any kind of distance, so only the person wearing them, or someone very close, would be able to decipher them: owl, peacock, a boy with a violin, people in long jackets or jesters' coats performing magic tricks.

The design had been originally worn in the days of the French Republican Calendar, when the months were named for frost, mist, and rain. Ten-hour days, of the goose, lichen, silkworm, rosemary, baskets, oats, or pitchforks, made up the ten-day weeks. Or the day of the gloves, of coming close enough to something to be able to see it properly.

125. Tapestry

Among the awkward amateur oil paintings and faded prints stacked at the back of the shop was a tapestry version of a scene from a Beatrix Potter story. The mother cat sends her kittens into the garden, to be out of the way as she works in the kitchen. She has dressed them carefully in anticipation of guests, the sisters in long dresses, their brother in a blue suit and straw hat. They set out along the path, standing up on their hind legs, dressed up like dolls, on their way to mischief.

The tapestry converts the illustration into a bolder style, along the way changing details in small ways, flattening out the nuances. The mother cat no longer holds a long fork in preparation for making hot buttered toast, the kittens' faces are more purposeful than meek, and rather than look distractedly towards a butterfly in the bushes, Tom Kitten strides ahead, his green-eyed gaze aloft.

The most unusual modification is the change to Tom Kitten's hat. In the original illustration a pale straw hat sits flat on his head, a detail so subtle it is barely noticeable. In the tapestry the hat is the first thing you notice, a bright yellow orb. Around his head it could be a halo, and with one hindpaw lifted he looks about to ascend, to float up to heaven like an angel in a medieval altarpiece.

126. Plasticine Ear

Lying on its side, against the spines of the 7" records that line the back of the shelf, is a dusty, cream-coloured plasticine ear. Although the dust makes me suspect it has been in that position for a long time – between a once-favourite-now-broken coffee mug glued back together with a bird's nest resting on top of it, and a hardback copy of *Middlemarch* – this is the first time I've noticed it.

'What's that ear?' I ask S, pointing over to it in the bookcase. He follows the invisible line out from my fingertip until he sees it. We stare at it together, unable to remember anything about it or why it is there, or to know how long it has been there, listening.

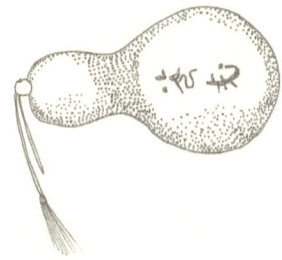

127. Ornamental Gourd

The gourd fits in the palm of my hand, its surface gold-blushed and smooth. It's perfect, I think, until I notice a broken section near the top, glued back into place. A customs official had cut it open with a pocketknife, tipped out the inadmissible seeds, then handed it back to us in two pieces.

It was a souvenir from Yoro, a town just beyond the outskirts of Nagoya. Legend has it that there was once a spring here which ran with a magical saké that had restorative powers. The boy who discovered the spring filled a gourd with the liquid and took it home to his father, who found that his youthful vigour returned after drinking it.

The canopy over the train station platform at Yoro was hung with different sizes and shapes of gourd, some bulbous, others with long curved necks like swans. They swayed in the wind as we tried to figure out the way to the Site of Reversible Destiny. This postmodern theme park, we had read, aimed to alter consciousness through shifting perception of space and landscape. We must have looked exactly like the kind of people who would become lost on the way to such a place. Seeing our confusion, a woman in an apron as yellow as a sunflower came out from the station cafe and gourd shop to point us in the right direction.

128. Tin of Pineapple Juice

The oldest of the secondhand furniture stores on Parramatta Road was housed in a building as aged as the objects inside. The paint on the facade was peeling off in flakes like coconut on a lamington and a painted sign announced a perpetual Two Day Sale.

Along with tired desks and sagging lounges the store sold a range of back-shed items, borderline junk, and among these I found an unopened can of Golden Circle fruit juice from the 1960s. At $20 it was expensive for a fifty-year-old can of pineapple juice, but the idea of the can remaining sealed for all that time captured my imagination. It would be my version of the canned provisions abandoned in early Arctic expeditions that, on rediscovery, were found to be surprisingly edible.

When I bought it the man in the shop said the juice would most probably have turned black from reacting with the metal of the can. At home, speculation upon what was inside was a strong talking point, and my flatmate often pointed it out to her visitors as a concise way to summarise my character. 'This,' she would say, pointing first to the can and then to me, 'tells you everything you need to know about her.'

129. Roman Coin

A few years ago a Roman bust had been bought from a thrift store in Texas, found under a table with a price tag of $35 stuck on one of its marble cheeks. The woman who bought it had suspected it was more than a mass-produced garden ornament and was vindicated when it was identified to be at least 2000 years old.

The bust's last known whereabouts had been the Pompejanum, a museum of Roman artefacts in a replica Pompeiian villa in Bavaria. The building had been damaged in World War II, and it was thought that an American soldier might have souvenired the bust and brought it home, eventually leading to it turning up at a Texas thrift store. But no one knew for sure. Articles focussed on the moment of discovery, the bust under the table, the price tag on the cheek, and the bust travelling home in the passenger seat, secured by the seatbelt, quoting the finder's pragmatic commentary: 'there was no reason not to buy it.'

I read the story out to S and he reminds me of the coin he found while working as a postman. Along his route he had stopped to look through a pile of miscellaneous stuff dumped by the roadside. In the bottom of a drawer, among pencil stubs and business cards, was the coin. It didn't look like much until he held it up to the light and the emperor's head came into view with its ancient, authoritative stare.

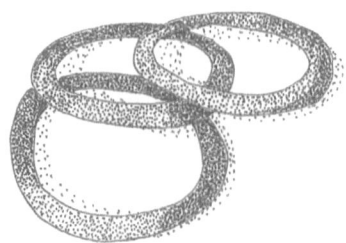

130. Hair Elastic

The law of disappearing things – hair elastics, teaspoons, pencils, socks – is that the more urgently you require them the more their energy is directed to getting caught up, slipping away, vanishing.

Inside the fibres of an elastic hair band the molecules coil like snakes, twisted up together. Pull on them and they straighten out, providing stretch. There is one around my wrist, cutting in. Sorry, mum, I hear your voice telling me that it's cutting off my circulation. Producing high daughterly irritation, because of course she's right.

Worn around my wrist the hair band is a habit that carries my mother's caution and the memory of a high-school mathematics class in which the teacher praised a student who'd just had her long hair cut short. 'All girls do this,' she said, 'when they are ready to become women.' She said it like it was an inalterable rule, that we had no choice to obey.

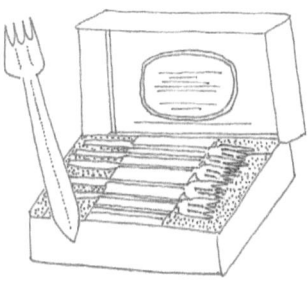

131. Buffet Forks

On the counter of the op shop, where the most valuable items are displayed, was a box of Splayds. Instead of the regular stainless steel these had an unusual gleam. Coated in 24-carat gold, they were the top of the line, the Rolls-Royce of Splayds.

Inside the felt-lined box they were arranged in a configuration I would be tempted to call 'spooning' if it wasn't selling the Splayd short. Designed to combine knife, fork, and spoon in one, Splayds can be deployed whenever a full set of cutlery is cumbersome to manipulate. According to the instructions these situations include 'Eating in bed', 'Buffet dinners' and 'Family mealtimes'. They had been trialled in a Sydney city cafe before being put into mass production in the 1960s.

After that time, judging by the number of mint-condition boxes of Splayds that appear secondhand, they were more often gifted than used. They remained in their boxes, wedding presents that people of my parents' generation found too special or too impractical to actually use. The life in which Scandinavian glassware, crystal punch bowls, and 24-carat gold Splayds were necessary items never quite eventuated.

132. Mouse Ball

When I leave the therapist's office I try not to catch the eye of the next client waiting outside, or rush across the street unheedingly, but I do both, made reckless with the possibility of changing for the better. On the other side of the street I head for the low wall at the edge of the drive-through dry cleaners. I open Notes and tap out a list of the strategies that are going to help me: choice, celebrate small achievements, kind to self, mouse ball.

I have to image-search the mouse ball to understand it: a clear plastic ball with airholes and a hatch in the side. Inside it a pet mouse or a rat can safely run around the house without escaping. As I examine images of this item (for only $9.95, 'peace of mind as your pet exercises') I roll one into my mind's eye.

A grey mouse rolls the ball around the crowded room where my inner critic lives. As it does it pushes aside stacks of papers, most of them long lists of regrettable things I did and said, and things I should have done but didn't, until gradually, in the centre of the room, a clearing appears.

133. Purple Ink

Writing with purple ink I describe the rising moon, the smell of the night, and how it is to sit on the front step and watch people walking past. They in turn watch me, spotlit under the porch light, pen in my hand, ink bottle beside me. The bottle is a faceted shape that allows it to be positioned on its side to reach the last of the ink inside, which smells very faintly of iodine. The words glimmer against the page as they dry and the nib is often thirsty. I dip it in the bottle to replenish it, and write another line.

134. 802 Automatic ColorFone

Every time I open the high cupboard, among the envelopes of x-rays and boxes of old study notes, I see the green rotary-dial landline phone. With its curly cord and thick plastic receiver, it was one of the series of home telephones that came in a range of murky colours with aspirational names: light ivory, mist grey, fern green, topaz yellow, and lacquer red. Now it seems almost as archaic as the Theatrophone, an electrical device that broadcast, through telephone wires, musical performances live from the Paris Opera to subscribers such as Marcel Proust.

We kept this kind of phone in use long after everyone else we knew had upgraded to a push-button model. Knowing there was a quicker way it could feel interminable to wait until the dial returned to starting position after each digit, but I liked how you could do it quietly or emphatically, and how the turns were accompanied by a series of clockwork ticks. This was a safecracking, morse-code sound and with it I imagined that I was tuning in to the switchboard of the universe.

135. Dust Bunny

At floor level there are drifts of air and electrostatic forces that pick up my long hairs like a needle picks up a thread, looping them through fluff and lint until it all holds together into a dust bunny.

Furry and brown-grey, dust bunnies form in the gaps and corners, underneath furniture, an unstoppable accumulation despite the broom, despite the vacuum cleaner. Because the strands of my hair bind them together they seem almost to be a part of me, an extension or an emanation, existing on the cusp of something and nothing.

The longer my hair grows the more readily they appear, and the more intrepidly. They build in the corners and encroach over the carpet, reminding me of how I extend out beyond my boundaries, of how I am entangled.

136. Memory Game

Face down on the table, the cards conceal their identities. Under their grey backs are bunches of carrots, butterflies, watering cans, pears and, strangest of all, pipes with grim grizzled faces carved into them.

My sister and I lay out the cards and start to play, turning over pairs of cards at a time, hoping to make a match. Soon chance is replaced by memory, as I set in my mind the location of the teapot and the whale and the bottle of liquor with a label that makes me imagine it is actually poison. This is the only game I ever feel compelled to win.

I turn a card to reveal the toadstool, then move my hand with a trance-like intensity, willing it to land on its pair. The seal balancing a ball on its nose. I flip them back over and Fiona has her turn, revealing the sun and then the bouquet of flowers, as I concentrate on scoring their positions into my memory.

When I turn over the card that has the pipe with the face on it, I hear its voice in my head. 'The art of memory is like an inner writing,' it says, and then goes quiet, leaving me to find its twin.

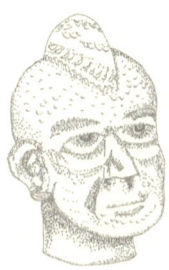

137. Concrete Head

At the front of the house is a garden bed, where the flowering bulbs planted by previous residents bloom on their annual cycle. Snowdrops as winter ends, then bluebells, then later in summer pink crinum lilies, which are big and pretty enough that people reach over the fence to pick them. This low fence is loved by toddlers, who stand on its brick foundation and grasp the top rung of the railing in their little hands, satisfied that finally they have found something of the right size out in the world.

This is all to say, the fence is easy to breach. Someone must have reached across it during the day in order to leave a sculpture of an oversized concrete head in the garden. A concrete head? All I knew about it was that it hadn't been there when I'd left in the morning.

A concrete head. Twice life-size. Big eyes, stern eyebrows, narrow strip of hair on top. A punk turned to stone, in among the crinum leaves.

138. Rabbit Ears Phone Case

Made of black silicone, the case had two long, pert rabbit ears extending out of the top. It came with a ball of fluff attached to a suction cup,
the rabbit's tail which, according to the instructions, could be used to
stand the phone upright. I couldn't try it out because I didn't yet have
a smartphone and wasn't eager to buy one. iPhones had existed for
five years by that time but were expensive, and coveted by some to a
point that made me suspicious.

Quaint resistance. After I gave in, even with the phone kitted out as a
rabbit, I had to adjust to the idea of carrying something in my pocket
that could almost think for itself. In the 1960s the computer in the
Reader's Digest building in Surry Hills, which stored the names and
addresses of the company's mailing list, had been so large that the
entire building was designed around it. Very soon the immense capa-
bilities of the rabbit phone would seem as antiquated as this.

139. Clear Protective Phone Case

Now that phones were larger, novelty cases were a thing of the past, and I housed the new one inside a boring clear plastic case. I decommissioned the bunny-ears phone, consigning it to the drawer to join its predecessors. All of them had once seemed to be impressively slick but now had a crude, bulky appearance, intensified by their years of being hidden away.

The clear case was marketed as if it were an invincible armour, protecting the phone from shocks and, according to the information on the packaging, the phone's user from dangerous bacteria. Evidence for this was an escalating list of 'Disturbing Facts'. We constantly touch our smartphones, it stated. In fact we touch them more than 2600 times a day, and did you know that a toilet seat is ten times cleaner than an average smartphone? My vision clicks back to pandemic mode, where I can see a layer over everything, surfaces and my own skin seething with germs.

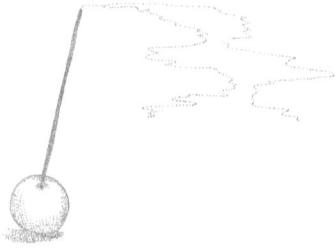

140. Incense Stick

There is a balance of delightful and disquieting things listed in Sei Shōnagon's *Pillow Book*, the inventory she made of moments, situations, and objects from her life a thousand years ago. Through lists and descriptions she records her experiences as an attendant in the Japanese Imperial Court, taking note of things that are truly splendid, repulsive things, things that give you confidence, and things that no one notices. The categories she devised are evocative, as applicable now as then. Some things remain awkward and pointless, or have terrifying names, or are endearingly lovely.

Sparrows with nestlings are one of the things that make your heart beat fast, as does lighting incense before lying down to sleep. When I burn incense, sleeping is about the last thing on my mind, but when I light a stick of it, holding the flame to the tip so it catches alight, I believe in the idea of the curling smoke carrying me away from my immediate world, and into another.

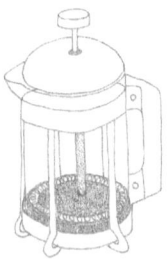

141. Coffee Plunger

At home after S's appointment, I flick the switch on the kettle. The previous visit to this doctor had been when he received his diagnosis, and I had held on tight to the pebble in my hand as the gate swung open into the other kingdom. Afterwards we had driven home mutely, then cried together in the kitchen, afraid of what was to come.

This time we have better news, but when I pour boiling water into the coffee plunger the glass cracks with a short sharp snap. Immediately the water level starts to descend and the coffee escapes out over the bench in all directions, waterfalling off the edge towards the floorboards. All we can do is stand back and watch the cascade. It slows to only a drip and I lift the handle of the plunger to find the base has broken off. The glass disc on the bench is topped by a perfectly neat round of wet coffee grounds.

There is a theory that when objects stop working for us they exert their own kind of power, display their potential beyond their use to humans. Wrapping up the now-bottomless plunger in newspaper, standing in the pool of coffee on the floor, I try to respect its self-expression.

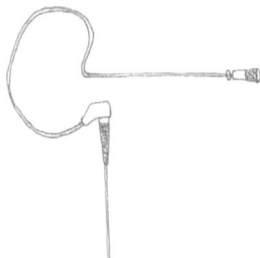

142. Wireless Microphone

For good luck on stage I am wearing an amorphous dress that has a pattern of intersecting shapes like a dazzle ship. It's the right fit for my mood but offers nowhere to clip the battery pack for the wireless microphone. 'I'm sorry,' I say to the assistant, as she tapes the thin wire of the microphone to my cheek.

'It's not your fault,' she says, apologising for touching my hair and my ear, which is too shallow to hold the microphone wire in place. When I ask if they are still called Madonna mics she gives me a quizzical look and replies, 'I've never heard them called that'.

Wireless microphones might have been named after Madonna but Kate Bush was the first performer to use one. During her first tour a sound engineer fashioned one from a coathanger. Without having to hold the microphone she could lie back singing in a red-satin-lined egg, rocking backwards and forwards in it, or be a dancing sprite in electric-blue, singing about being a kite flying under the moon.

When I hear my voice channelled through the microphone taped to my cheek, I imagine my words flying out like bats around a cave. Some disappear into corners of the dark auditorium, others settle with the audience, words to describe the work of writing, and how stepping outside and being under the sky again always makes me feel as if more is possible.

143. Early Twentieth-century Postcard, Woman in a Spiderweb

At the centre of the spiderweb a woman sits thinking, her hand to her chin, her eyes at an evasive angle, escaping anyone who might try to meet her gaze. The silvery fall of the long white sheet she is draped in makes her seem to float on the glossy paper's surface. Perhaps she is Arachne, condemned to live as a spider, or perhaps a less mythological figure waiting for something to ensnare.

Often in cards from this era the message on the back of a postcard has little to do with the image on the front. Thus serious enquiries can come on the back of a card picturing naughty kittens in a basket of wool, or a banal scheduling of a visit can be on the back of an eerie image of a face appearing from a trailing wisp of cigarette smoke.

The spiderweb card carries a message to Dearest Most Bestest from Your Bob. Bob writes: 'Am feeling rather anxious about you, are you better? Bob Glover was in to see me, he says he was very disappointed you did not write as promised.' The card provides only this cast of characters and the briefest of situations: Most Bestest, with the two Bobs in her web.

144. Pompom

It is satisfying to be making something for no particular purpose, just to experience the minor transformations that attend each step of the process. I start the pompom using two cardboard crescents, looping the wool around them, winding and winding, until there's a thick layer all around.

The best part of making a pompom is when it springs together into a sphere. I snip around the edge to release the strands, then thread a length of wool through the middle and tie it in a tight knot. Around the constriction of the knot the pompom suddenly expands into shape, a soft planet with a firm, snug core. Once made there's nothing to do with it but keep it around, to squeeze it for courage, to feel its strong centre inside its soft exterior.

145. Anarchist Poster

I didn't go to work today…

The sleeper is covered by a thick blanket, the folds of it textured with sharp white linocut lines. Her black hair is fanned out over the pillow, framing her face and her closed eyes and slight smile.

I don't think I'll go tomorrow.

She is dreaming on the telegraph pole and on the substation wall and on the facade of the motor garage that closed down years ago. She sleeps as workers assemble at the nearby bus stop in the morning, and are brought back to the same place by the bus at the end of the day. She trusts that with enough repetition of her message, her disruption will eventually succeed.

Let's take control of our lives and live for pleasure not pain.

The street is empty, no traffic, no pedestrians. The traffic lights run through their colours. The city's background hum has fallen into hush, birds are the only sound. There's no one out even to wonder why it is so quiet. Everyone is busy dreaming.

146. Apple Lapel Pin

For the last class of semester I wear the pin, an enamel brooch so small that it is hard to see against my shirt. A tiny red apple, which I had bought attached to a black cardboard square with 'A+ Teacher' written on it, as if on a chalkboard. Every last class brings a shiver of all the classes I've ever farewelled, sending the students out with whatever they will remember of our time together.

In my first year working as a tutor I'd calm my nerves at the op shop after class, getting off the bus midway through the protracted trip home through every compass point of Ryde. The apple must have been intended for a child to give as a gift to their teacher, but I bought it as a gift to self. It was a recognition of personal achievement even if a student had asked me, that very day, 'Is this the first time you've done this?'

147. Corflutes

With the semester over we are driving north, along the east coast motorway. On Biripi country one forested stretch has a sudden rash of corflute signs nailed to trees, the cheese-slice yellow of the ultra-right party, blasting their slogan: *Freedom Freedom Freedom*. The party had spent $100 million on election advertising, their corflutes and billboards emblazoned across country and city alike, all the same alarming yellow. Their greatest impact, apart from visual pollution and an embarrassingly small percentage of votes, was that yellow paint sales vastly increased as people rushed to modify them, calling them out for their bigotry.

The yellow corflutes by the motorway shout their message to the cars which continue on uncaring or unheeding. An additional message spray-painted on a row of bedsheets beside the corflutes doesn't aid their cause. I catch only a few words of it, *virus, pharma, lies*, before the trees continue uninterrupted.

148. Big Banana

There is a queue for photographs at the Big Banana. Three women in long floral dresses wait behind a man in a pilot's uniform, who asks one of the women to take his photo as he moves into position, standing front and centre and flinging his arms out wide. Behind me children shriek around the gift shop, emitting high-pitched pleas for soft-toy bananas which can be affixed to a window by means of a suction cup.

The Big Banana was the first of the 'big things', roadside constructions aiming to lure passing motorists into stopping for a visit. When I was a child, the sight of the banana from the car was a necessary holiday rite but I'd only have a few seconds to examine it, and the fringed leaves of the banana trees on the steep hillside behind it, before the road turned us onwards.

Finally now I know that inside the Big Banana is a walkway, lined by display cases, with exhibits that explain the process of how it was made. First came the choice of the ideal banana from the packing shed, then its division into forty segments, which were precisely drawn and enlarged by means of a surface gauge and graph paper. Another cabinet displays Big Banana commemorative items from the past, teaspoons and trays and postcards, proving that the Banana is a monument to its own existence.

149. Big Joint

The Hemp Embassy in Nimbin is cluttered with prayer flags, sandals, and posters advertising past years of the annual Mardi Grass. The embassy doubles as a department store for hippy accoutrements, with sections for clothing, books, home decorating, and cookware. If I wanted this life I need go no further. A few hundred dollars and I could emerge completely made over.

Hanging from the ceiling is a long sagging fabric slug with LET IT GROW painted down the side, the rips in its covering stitched back together: the Big Joint. In 1999 I remember the joint, or one of its predecessors, was conveyed to Sydney to participate in a number of anti-prohibition actions. It was hoisted atop a ferry and sailed around the harbour, smoke issuing from the end of it, as it did a lap by the Prime Minister's residence at Kirribilli. It drooped over the top of a hot-pink bus in Victoria Park for the Hemp Olympix, which took place a week before the actual Olympics were held in the city. It was a flare of resistance, as the city fell into sporting fervour and a tidier, less eccentric, version of itself.

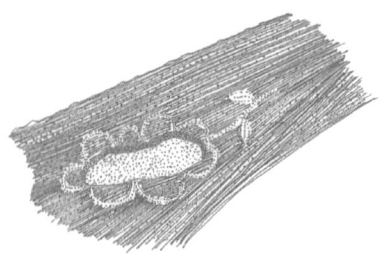

150. Potholes

At the start of the year the rivers on Bundjalung country rose to record levels, submerging buildings, washing away bridges, and collapsing roads down the soft slopes of valleys. Even on the roads that remained intact, rain had weakened the asphalt so much that potholes appeared, deep pits in the road's surface.

The winding, cratered roads crossed creeks strewn with debris: fallen trees, broken garden chairs, twisted metal, and sodden blocks of foam, all of which had been picked up by the floodwaters. Many roads were closed off, made impassable by landslips. We took detour after detour until eventually we found ourselves driving through the centre of Lismore, where the flooding had been the most severe.

The river had risen rapidly, leaving thousands of people in danger, fleeing from the fast-rising water, or stranded on their rooftops, await-ing rescue. When the flood receded there was nowhere undamaged, and what had been people's belongings was now muddy wreckage. We drove through the town centre, where the shops were either boarded up or empty, apart from the toy store, in which models of two life-size zebras and a tiger stood guard in the front window. There were few other cars and even fewer people, but the potholes had been traced around with white spray paint, given petals and stems, made into flowers.

151. Church

A few doors down from one of my childhood homes was a wooden church that had been converted into a house. Its high front wall was, it was rumoured, made from pieces of Hadrian's Wall that had been used as ship's ballast. At night I'd look for lights in its windows, imagining an alternate life in which I lived there.

The wooden church we are staying in is roughly the same size and shape, or close enough to feel as if I am inside that childhood dream. From the desk in the loft I track the day by the sunbeams moving from window to window, their paths tinted red and yellow through the stained glass. Uncoupled from its religious purpose is a contemplative place, good for thinking about the currents that run behind everyday things.

The church had been moved from a nearby town and reconstructed here, on a hill above the junction of two creeks. Before it was moved, after its last service, a photo was taken of the congregation assembled on the lawn outside it. The kids sit in the front, the older generations stand behind. I imagine myself into it at the age I would have been then, cross-legged on the lawn, my shirt tucked in and shoes polished, in front of the grandmothers in pearls and cardigans.

152. Astrological Calendar

A calendar is made of cycles and repetitions, tracking the orbits of the earth and the moon. It is a way to mark time, a method of attention. Dark and light, cool and warm, flowers. It is the right time, or too early or too late. It is a circle, a square, it is something you feel, or know, or forget. It is generations, the inexorable, a life lived or a life to come.

The Astrological Calendar on the poster is presented as a great wheel with a sun in its centre and the moon phases and constellations around the circumference. In the yellow sphere of its sunbeams are columns of densely written text, predictions for the year. 'The conventional calendar is fine for co-ordination purposes,' the text begins, 'the lunar calendar is better for natural and, shall we say, psychological purposes.'

It is mullet season on Bundjalung country and I watch them flipping up from the creek in silver flashes. Perhaps tonight the moon, waxing towards a first crescent, will be visible in the night sky. The Astrological Calendar notes that it is soon the time to plant cabbage and celery, and the moon is in Gemini, making for an inquisitive mood, 'good for chatting, visiting, writing, studying, and driving around'.

153. Gumboots

Pulling on gumboots, I think of an interview with Mary Quant in which she described how her 'Quant Afoot' boots were made. 'A kind of chewing gum goes into a mould,' she said, 'and you get out what you want, like making a jelly.' This thought flashes up then disappears: we are very far away from that world. Wiyabal country, stopped at a roadblock between Repentance Creek and Federal, made of a line of concrete bollards. A truck with the name 'Mud Rat' above the front grille is parked behind it.

We walk in past the barrier and at the bend we see a section of road washed away, as if it has been ripped out, replaced by a mess of broken trees and earth that has flowed down from the top of the hill behind. Deep cracks in the road lead up to the edge where it breaks away. Spray-painted on the road, in big white letters: 'extreme danger.' Even so we have heard that it is possible to clamber over the debris and make it through to the next town. When a man in work gear stops us, we tell him our plan. He shrugs and says, 'some people have tried it', before he turns back to his tools.

We climb down into debris of the swept-away road and begin to make our way across. The gumboots don't really help at all, but it's not difficult to progress, clambering over the fallen trunks and branches like ants over blades of grass, towards the road on the other side.

154. Glitter Stars

A glitter star twinkles in the carpet. It is iridescent pink, the size of a pinhead, concentrating light into a tiny bright point. After I notice the first one more light up, a sparse scattering of them, dropped from a toy or a card, from someone who stayed here before us. Glitter persists. In my early zine-making days people would often send me letters with glitter inside the envelope, ensuring I didn't forget them when it stuck to my hands and was transferred to anything I touched. The punks complained, but the riot grrrls continued to shake glitter into their envelopes, unrepentant.

The glitter stars remind me to go outside and look at the real ones. It is cold and I can see my breaths in puffs of vapour as I walk away from the house. Below the steep bank the creek runs high and fast, a rushing sound like continual rain. When I reach a clearing and look up, the stars shine against the velvet dark of the sky, more than I ever see at home in the city. I begin in the west, choosing a star and saying a name, a friend to bring protection to. In this way I move across the sky, a name for a star, a star for a name, each one a pulse of light, bright and long-travelling.

155. Lace Curtains

Halfway through the drive back home, we stop at the seaside town on Dunghutti country where my family used to spend my childhood holidays. This is a long time ago but little has changed, apart from my sense of scale. A common adjustment, that what the child thought was a vast landscape, the adult walks through as a toytown.

At the Cantonese Inn restaurant the same thin snarling dragons are painted on the windows, breathing fire, their bodies covered in spiky scales, tails curling. On the other side of the window behind them, long curtains conceal the view of the restaurant interior, so the dragons appear to be floating in an expanse of lacy cloud.

We only ever went inside briefly to pick up our takeaway order from the front counter, leaving me to wonder what it might be like on the other side of the curtain. Now I know. Rattan chairs, chandeliers, a painting of Hong Kong Harbour hung on the brick wall. Red carpet, banquet tables with rotating trays in the centre, and the lace obscuring the view of the street, sealing us in on the other side.

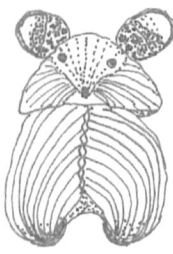

156. Shell Animal

At one point during childhood holidays we would inevitably visit the Shell Shop, which was set up in a basement of a house on the road into town. Clutching a purse with a few dollars inside of it, I would scrutinise the display of animals which had been glued together out of various shells, lined up at my eye level on the other side of the glass.

Today I am an adult looking down into the same display. My whole life in between is bracketed, off to the side because in the Shell Shop no time has passed at all. The same seagrass matting is underfoot, buoys and wooden fish hang in nets to decorate the walls, and the same cabinets display the shells. The only difference is the 'cash only' sign in the window that hints at other, future technologies.

The shell animals are dogs, ducks, or turtles, or frogs smoking cigars or playing trumpets, constructions of whelks and clam shells with beads for eyes and daubs of paint for details. I choose a mouse with two pointy periwinkles for ears, and bring it to the counter. 'What do you think this is?' the same proprietor I remember from decades before asks me. I know I'm wrong as soon as I say it. 'It's meant to be a koala,' she says, 'but children think they're all sorts of things.'

157. Odometer

When I was learning to drive my instructor had a low tolerance for small talk. Worst of all was when my attention was captured by something unusual. Even if I pointed out that the hatchback behind us conveyed five nuns, and they had an air freshener shaped like a white dove hanging off the rear-view mirror, he gave no response, just a gesture to indicate my concentration was better focussed on the road ahead.

In one of our final lessons together he became unexpectedly animated, pointing to the dashboard. I must have been doing something wrong, but what? 'The 2s!' he cried, pointing to my speed of 22 kilometres, then the time, which was 2:22, and then the odometer reading, which ended in 222. 'I look for things like this, it breaks the monotony,' he told me. 'It is a good day when this happens.' I laughed and agreed that it was satisfying, but the moment passed quickly. The numbers changed, the odometer clicking forward another kilometre, breaking the sequence. The instructor pointed back to the road ahead, and settled back into his usual inscrutability.

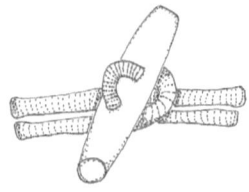

158. Toggles

Ghosts of old technologies lurk in newer ones, preserved in the idioms used to describe their use. Hanging up the phone when there's nothing to hang, making a mixtape when there's no tape involved, message boards without the board, turning something off when there's nothing to turn. A shadow life of materials and gestures. Toggle on, toggle off.

On this cold day, back at home, I wear the quilted jacket with toggles for buttons, long smooth lengths of wood that make me feel like Paddington Bear, sealed up inside his duffel coat. Doing up the jacket before I go out walking I turn the word over, *toggle*, enjoying how it sounds, like the action of threading the button through the loop so it holds fast.

Anti Ageing
Net 80ml 1.68 fl oz

159. Freebie

The promotional cookie is sealed inside a crimped package, its icing printed with an image of a pot of moisturising cream. The biscuit is the same size as the pot itself would be, as if it has emerged from a Willy Wonka world in which all objects are potentially edible.

The biscuit is the very definition of a promotional freebie, something I couldn't dream up desire for, but now it exists and I am reckoning with it. I have never before come across a photorealist moisturiser-shaped biscuit. The freebie angles to seduce me and I put up resistance, uncomfortable at the considerable resources that have gone into it, and its historical trajectory. So much has led to its existence, from the evolution of wheat, to the colonial history of sugar production, to the construction of beauty standards, and the development of printable icing. This is what I hold, in the guise of a biscuit.

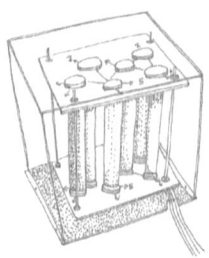

160. Cosmic Ray Detector

At any moment – this second, and the next and the next – fragments of cosmic rays are falling to earth. They break apart into smaller particles and shower down through the atmosphere, undetected and incessant. Before arriving here they might have travelled through space for millions of years.

We sit on a round black carpet and listen to them arrive, channelled through a contraption of six copper cylinders, connected up to a device of circuits and wires that translates them into sound. Each is a long, high-pitched, descending note, the sound of falling, slowing. They sound like electronic wolves, howling in a slow, steady chorus.

The waves move around and through us without us feeling or knowing, and they do so for our entire lives. I close my eyes and listen to the notes descending and fading and remember how my grandfather had taught me about them. He had me try to understand this energy that I couldn't see but was nevertheless all around us, an awakening to forces invisible and ineffable.

161. Hot Water Bottle

The hot water bottle has a rubbery smell that is synonymous with winter. The draughty house resists any attempts to heat it, and the bottle is a warm presence in my lap as I sit at my desk, an obedient, sloshing pet that never tires of its position.

At night in bed I position it near my feet or up by my chest, careful not to make contact with its beak-like top, the touch of which makes me shudder. On top of the beak is an embossed warning, 'do not use boiling water', although I always do, even though it weakens the rubber and eventually causes it to split. More than once the neck of the bottle has cracked and the water leaked out, and I've leapt up in shock from it burning me. I couldn't say I wasn't warned.

The bottle has its own anatomy. The beak flares out to protect the stopper that secures the water inside the rubber body, which is textured with long rows of parallel furrows that maximise the surface area for the warmth to disperse. As I sleep its heat transfers, ebbing away, so by morning it is cold. If you are going past on an early bus you might see me, wearing a long pink dressing gown, tipping up the hot water bottle to water the plants on the porch.

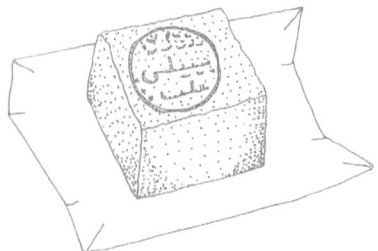

162. Aleppo Soap

The poet Francis Ponge wrote at length about soap, how it is slippery and ever-changing, producing bubbles as readily as writers produce words. Ponge believed his writing was best when objects were in control. 'The object is always more important, more interesting, more capable,' he wrote, '…it has no duty whatsoever toward me, it is I who am obliged to it.' Trust the object, that is, and it will direct how you write with it.

At the back of a shelf, behind a box of scarves, my hand closes around a heart-shaped tin, patterned with roses. Inside it is a layer of tissue paper and underneath that four cakes of soap, brown-green, stamped حلب – Aleppo. They have been stored back there from before the Syrian civil war in the 2010s when, along with so much else in the region, many of the soap factories were destroyed.

Aleppo soap is made of olive oil, lye, and laurel oil, the mixture spread out in a thin layer on a flat surface to set. Then a worker stands on a rake-like contraption with blades underneath, pressing them down with his body weight as he is pulled over the solidified mass to slice it, first one way then the other, across at right angles, dividing it up. The piece I hold in my hand smells sweet and earthy, of sunlight and time, of bay leaf and olives.

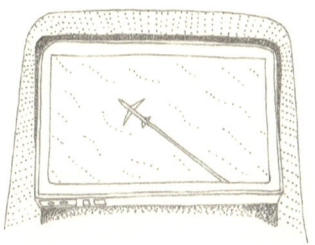

163. Seatback Screen

On the morning flight to Darwin I follow the journey on the screen that is framed inside the back of the seat in front of me. A green thread crosses the continent, the plane an oversized arrow at the end of it. I'm seated over the wing, and beyond the white metal panels I can glimpse the desert country below, the long pale lines of roads, occasionally a plume of dusty smoke billowing up. I turn back to the screen with its cycle of flight information. The pages of maps and lists of ground speed and air temperature comfort me as they quantify the journey, these hours suspended from ordinary time.

As the green line extends north from Broken Hill the image suddenly glitches, replaced with a black screen with a word in plain text in the centre: *Oops*. Through the gap between the seats in front of me I check other screens: a herd of gazelles grazes in a wildlife documentary. The candy colours of a cartoon. Across the aisle a man sleeps as an action movie flashes through a fight scene. I leave *Oops* on the screen and turn back to the window and the sliver of desert visible below.

164. Sprinkler

The sky is wider here in Garramilla, and the dawn and sunset fill the streets with saturating colour. The sunrise glow is fading into blue as I set out in the warm morning, past hotels and A-frame churches and government offices flanked by palm trees. In between there are some of the older houses, built on high foundations, tall spreading frangipani trees in their gardens, a scattering of their white flowers on the pavement.

The mist from a sprinkler is cool on my legs as I walk past the garden at the front of an office building. The nozzles of the sprinkler system hiss, hidden under the grasses and ferns, keeping them green and lush during the dry season. It is Damibila in the Larrakia cycle of seasons, the time of barramundi and bush fruits, clear sky and high clouds. Bird song, the spacious sky, the spray from the sprinkler evaporating quickly from my skin.

165. Sweetheart

At the top of a ramp is an enclosure behind a low glass wall. Inside is the taxidermically preserved crocodile known as 'Sweetheart', scaly and ridged, mouth open, legs in belly-crawl position. An interpretive panel gives his particulars: a male saltwater crocodile, 5.1 metres long, 2.3 metres girth, 780kg.

Strongly territorial, Sweetheart often attacked the boats that came into his billabong, which was also popular for fishing. After dinghies were overturned and Sweetheart took bites at their propellers, a plan was made to catch him and relocate him to a crocodile farm. The capture went wrong and Sweetheart drowned, trapped under a sunken log as his captors struggled to bring him in.

He became a specimen, an exhibit, his skin stretched over a frame, mouth reconstructed with plaster so he was part animal, part sculpture. In the years after his death he was toured to Melbourne and Sydney and, closer to home, was displayed in a Darwin shopping mall before ending up as an exhibit in the museum. As I ponder Sweetheart I hear a whimper and look beside me to see a little girl, wide-eyed and afraid, unsure if the crocodile is real. As her parents usher her away I see she's dropped something. 'Hey, don't forget your unicorn,' I say, pointing to the greyish toy. She looks at me, then at Sweetheart, not trusting either of us.

166. Artificial Lettuce Leaf

Alfred's, locals told me, was the gift shop where I would find the salty plums I was looking for. Also unusual eggcups, chess sets, babushka dolls, fountain pens, and bottle openers. I find Alfred's between an optometrist and the country and western store, unassuming from the street, but inside, everything has a decorative specificity: the babushka dolls are painted with cats, stress balls are shaped like planets, dinner plates have doilies printed onto them.

My eyes range over it all until I fix upon a display of pale green artificial lettuce leaves. Romaine, to be exact, with frilly edges and thick stems, so lifelike they could fool the unwary. I pick one up and it sits lightly in my hand, as a man I assume is Alfred comes up to ask me if I am looking for anything in particular. 'This?' I say, as I hold the unwiltable leaf.

It isn't Alfred, rather his son, Stanley, who tells me it will be the last year of business before he and his wife retire, after running the shop for almost fifty years. It opened after Cyclone Tracy, as the city was being rebuilt. He takes me over to the knife counter for a demonstration of correct knife-sharpening technique, and afterwards points out the guestbook, in which customers have been writing their memories of the store. He hands me a fountain pen with a calligraphic nib, but what can I write underneath Bill and Dot, who've been shopping at Alfred's since Tracy?

167. Lemon-scented Soap

I forget it is Bloomsday until S sends me a photo of the soap we bought from Sweny's in Dublin, the pharmacy where, in *Ulysses*, Leopold Bloom bought that very same object. Sweet lemony wax, coolwrappered soap, produced as a souvenir now. Sweny's continues as an eccentric museum with displays of James Joyce paraphernalia and long-expired pharmaceuticals like boxes of Pure Ethyl Chloride and pots of Wigglesworth's Fullers Earth Cream.

There was a reading of *Ulysses* at the shop the night we arrived, and despite jetlag so severe I felt like I was falling into a dream every time I blinked, we went. Inside Sweny's a woman was making cups of black tea and distributing copies of the novel to the dozen or so people who had gathered to read. 'Nausicaa tonight,' she said cheerfully.

We take turns to read a page each, a Swedish accent, a Russian accent, Argentinian, Irish, and us, all struggling through the chapter which is itself a mixture of voices. Around the circle we cycle through the pages. In one of my readings the soap reappears in the story, a sweet-scented object in Bloom's waistcoat pocket, a punctuation mark in his encyclopaedic day.

168. Tin Star

The star hangs at the entrance to the arcade, which had once been the entrance to a cinema. A metre across, rusty and battered, the star's peeling yellow paint reveals the tin beneath. Before the cyclone it had been at the top of the vertical roof sign, above the name of the theatre spelled out in plain lettering: STAR.

Up close I see that each point of the star is a folded piece of tin, all five soldered in the centre to hold it together. When I have an urge to touch it I remember working at the historic house, and how compelled people were to touch the things I showed them, to increase their connection with the past.

The cinema, like most of the city, had been destroyed in Cyclone Tracy in 1974. In the museum I'd gone into a small dark room in which the sound of the cyclone played, recorded by a man sheltering from the storm, unsure if he would survive the night. Inside the roar of the wind were louder, sharper noises of things colliding, being torn apart. Somewhere amid this the star was wrenched down.

'The acids on our skins are destructive,' I'd say, to explain why the visitors couldn't put their fingers to the wallpaper. But in the entrance to the arcade I second-guess my reticence, and reach out to touch the star's cold metal centre.

BOARDING PASS

ZONE 2
ECONOMY

ZONE 2
ECONOMY
BERRY NANESSA
FLIGHT VA 1356

NAME: BERRY/VANESSA
DEPART: DARWIN
ARRIVE: SYDNEY

1756
2240

FLIGHT VA 1356
DATE 17 JUN 22

DATE 17 JUN

GATE 4 AT: 1735

SEAT: 19A
ETKT
SEQ 00007
FARE
PNR

SEAT 19A
DEST: SYD
SEQ: 0007
1 FARE: I

169. Boarding Pass

The first time I travelled on a plane I was twenty years old, and as the trip approached I grew increasingly nervous. Despite the daily evidence of planes flying safely over the inner-city house where I lived, I believed the journey would end in my plane suddenly dropping from the sky.

'I think you'll enjoy flying,' one of my zine friends wrote in a letter, cutting through my trepidation, 'there are plenty of specifics to observe.' This piqued my interest: I lived for specifics. Before the overnight flight, Sydney to Perth, I sat in the airport bar drinking whisky with my housemates. They were older than me, in their wise mid-twenties, and wrote me notes on beer coasters that guaranteed the plane wouldn't crash, setting out their messages like boarding passes. Only now I realise how kind they were not to tease me. They didn't laugh when I suggested something about me might be cursed and bring the plane down, they just pressed the boarding passes they had made into my hands, and waited for me to live out the proof of their promises.

170. Horse Jump

Back at home, as I drive along Bunnerong Road I notice, in the middle of a grassy lot, a long, low wooden box. It is painted in pastel colours to resemble a row of terrace houses, with a hole at one end as if a meteorite has crashed down through it, although it is the box, positioned askew, that looks as if it might have fallen to earth. Initially I think it is a doll's house and has been dumped there, but then I see the poles and hurdles over the other side of the lawn, and realise it must be for show-jumping training.

On occasion I have seen the horses and riders who practise here, walking along the wide strip of parkland in the middle of Anzac Parade, where the tram tracks used to run. The horses move with a calm gait, slowly and noddingly. The last time I'd seen them here Helen had still been alive. She was only just well enough to leave the house and we had gone for a drive to the ocean. Heading home in the last light of the day, the horses were a delight, a reminder that even in bad, suffering times, there could be magical things.

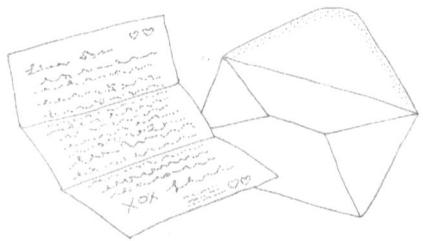

171. Love Letter

Niki de Saint Phalle believed that, of all artistic provocations, there was nothing more shocking than joy. Her Tarot Garden in Tuscany gave form to this idea, a sculpture park constructed as an ode to life and making something joyful and lasting within it.

It had been difficult to get there, wrong turns and high stress on the *autostrada*. Driving the car felt like I'd slipped into a mirror, everything back to front. Then relief, as the mosaic sculptures came into view in the distance, silvery giants springing up from the low fields.

The path through the garden winds around the Major Arcana, between the glittering figures of the Empress, the Magician, and the Hanged Man, who is inside a grotto with the branching heads of snakes issuing out the top of it. Around the grotto are tiles painted with love letters from Saint Phalle to her husband, Jean Tinguely.

They follow the lovers' story, from their early passion to Tinguely's death and then Saint Phalle alone, remembering. Her curling handwriting is framed within the white tiles, which carry drawings of significant objects and symbols: people with tiny heads and bendy torsos, a cat with a wavering body like a strip of seaweed, carnivorous-looking flowers. She is heartbroken, but happy, thinking of their love.

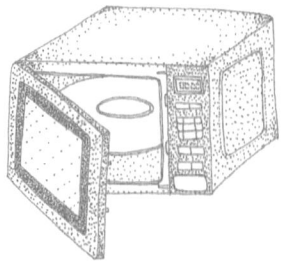

172. Microwave Oven

On the radio quiz, caller after caller is stuck on the question, what was the first food cooked in a microwave oven? 'Well it would either be pizza or a cake,' one caller confidently states. He's wrong, as is the person who suggests noodles, and another who guesses soup. 'You'll kick yourself when you find out,' the host says.

I can't guess either. Everything I can think of is something you wouldn't cook in a microwave oven. Such as the experiment in which you place two grapes on a plate side by side, and microwave them for a minute so they superheat and sparks shoot out at their point of contact. The answer is not grapes. Finally somebody comes on who knows. It's popcorn, of course, cue the song and its popping synthesisers.

The tune fades at my back as I leave the radio and go outside. It is the winter solstice, the longest night of the year, a night for reflection, not trivia. Outside the sky is clear apart from a bank of clouds in the east. Over there a storm must be moving out to sea. As I watch, lightning sparks up in a split-second flash against the dark sky. It flashes once, then again, and again.

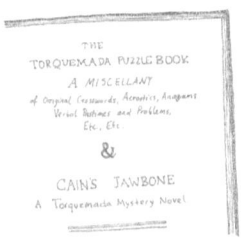

173. Torquemada Puzzle Book

The *Torquemada Puzzle Book* was published in 1934, a small hardcover with a collection of notoriously difficult crosswords and anagrams and other word games, culminating in the 100-page murder mystery 'Cain's Jawbone'. A pink page inserted at the beginning of the story sets out the puzzle and the prize. Send in a list of the correct order of pages, and the names of the murderers and victims, and if you are the first to solve it you win the cash prize. Each page has the lower third kept blank for the copious notes you need to make to solve it. Of the many who have tried, over almost a century, only four people have ever been successful.

Some vital action is happening on each page, an ice-cream dessert is being prepared, or a flight of cabbage butterflies is observed, or the narrator is alone among the marigolds, or notices a certain green ink is the colour of a dragonfly. Each sentence is like a cryptic crossword clue, smugly holding its secret. A rambling, weird confession that washes over you if you're not the puzzling type, or are content never to try to solve it. Sometimes I open it and pick out a line as the day's oracle. Today: 'my life was all short stories, I had come to think.'

174. Dried Onions

The dried onions are still on the bench from the night before, and as I secure the snipped corner of the packet with a clothes peg I notice something unusual on the front. Printed above the product name on the label is 'save your tears'.

'Look,' I say to S, who is drinking coffee at the kitchen table. None of the other spices have an enigmatic additional message I point out, flipping through the packets in the spice box to be certain.

'It's like it was made for you,' S replies, knowing well that I keep a lookout for unusual scraps of text on common things, promotional verbiage that can readily be transposed to some other meaning. Save your tears. Was it tough, was it kind, was it good advice?

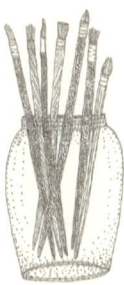

175. Paintbrush Jar

In the late 1990s I saved a newspaper article about Francis Bacon's studio, which was then in the process of being moved from his house in London to a museum in Dublin. The room was being reconstructed exactly, even down to the dust which had been bagged and labelled so it could be sprinkled back in the correct position. The dust was the detail that stuck with me, a tale of reverence that verged on the ridiculous.

Decades later, visiting the museum, I saw the reconstructed studio, which was visible through a window that separated the viewer from the chaos inside. Every surface was strewn with books, papers, clothes, and miscellaneous junk, a paint-stained mess. Paintbrushes spiked up, like tufts of hardy grass, from jars caked with residue. The jars had once held instant coffee or sweet and sour gherkins; other brushes sprouted from old baked bean cans. These repurposed vessels grouped the brushes roughly by size, the only concession to order in the ruinous room.

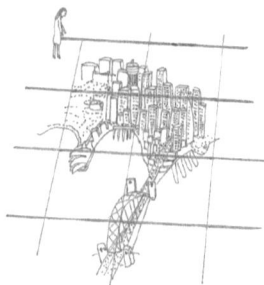

176. City Model

We hurry across the foyer of Customs House, but not too quickly for me to notice that the newest skyscraper has already been added to the model underneath the glass floor. In the model, as in the city outside, the new tower twists up in an asymmetrical spiral, a block behind the Quay. When we go back outside, the real building, with its sharp angles and off-kilter balance, looks more improbable in actuality than it did in miniature.

We continue along the incline of Phillip Street, up from Warrane, following the east bank of the Tank Stream. The hill strains my legs more than I expect, reminding me of the shape of the land underlying the city. Stopped at the traffic lights midway along we have a clear view of the new tower. As we wait here a shadow comes across, as if a cloud has moved over the sun.

Looking up, we see that it's a face, huge and distorted, above a giant body, and giant feet standing on the pane of glass that seals us in above. A finger looms, pointing at the new building, and the mouth moves, saying something that's beyond the scale of our hearing, until its echo comes. With the wind sweeping the leaves and trash down the street it says, 'the city is a crime scene'.

177. Curse You Red Baron Patch

The patch exactly covers the fox logo on the front of the backpack, replacing it with a smug Lucy from Peanuts. The patch, unofficially produced by a company called Moon in the 1970s, provides a Peanuts remix of sorts, pairing Lucy with one of Snoopy's catchphrases: 'Curse You Red Baron!' Beside the text, Lucy has a coy, smiling appearance, waiting for someone to fall into a trap she has set for them.

It's an understandable mix-up, as Lucy is usually the angry one, raging at the other characters, or she is set up inside her psychiatric help booth, dispensing blunt advice for 5c. Snoopy, on the other hand, never says a thing, apart from in his thoughts. Sitting on the roof of his doghouse he pretends he's a World War I flying ace, in pursuit of his Red Baron nemesis.

The patch was marketed to appeal to 1970s sensibilities, and its packaging presented its own slogans. 'If it's cloth and it's blah, now you've got a chance', reads the cardboard insert, alongside photographs of models in customised hotpants and swimming trunks. 'Moon Patches are all things to all people. They're right now. They're bright now.' Even in this extended right now, all these many years later.

178. Smell Survey

Inserted into the September 1986 issue of *National Geographic* magazine was a fold-out pamphlet, the largest ever experiment into the human sense of smell. The pamphlet included six scratch-and-sniff panels. After you scratched them with a coin to release the scent, you were asked to rate the results. Did the odour evoke a vivid memory? Would you apply something that smelled like this to your body? Was it floral, spicy, burnt, foul, sweet?

When I came across the smell survey among the magazines in Gould's Books I had long missed the deadline, but the survey was in mint condition, the panels unscratched. The survey's introduction quoted Baudelaire:

> I stupefy myself
> on the mingled scent
> of musk and tar and
> coconut oil for hours...
> from which I gulp
> the wine of memory

Motivated to embark on my journey of stupefying memory, I bought the survey. At home I picked up a coin and scratched away at the first panel, pressing hard in case the scent had faded over time. Lifting it to my nose, I inhaled deeply. A nostril-curling stink filled my senses. Sweat radiated off the page, an intense teenage-boy, high-summer, sports carnival smell, and I was, indeed, stupefied.

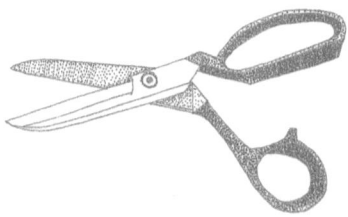

179. The Good Scissors

Throughout my childhood I believed that reserving a pair of 'good scissors' was a practice particular to my grandmother, who referred to them in the singular, as the 'good scissor', a quirk of her vernacular. The scissors had a specific position in the kitchen cupboard and their sharp blades could not be used for anything so minor as snipping a plastic toggle, opening a packet, or cutting paper. This would only blunt them for the rare times when they needed to be at their sharpest.

Eventually a television comedy skit alerted me to the fact that the good scissors were, in fact, a more widespread phenomenon. The joke on the show was that the good scissors suggested the presence of evil scissors, which were dangerously lying in wait somewhere in the house. It was funny, but also came as a shock, that something I had thought particular to my life story had turned out to be so commonplace.

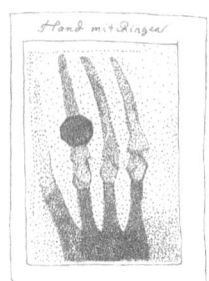

180. Radiograph

The first x-ray image was of a hand. The long thin shadows of the finger bones extended across the print, with one darker circle on the ring finger. *'Hand mit Ringen'* is written at the top of the page, in curling script, although not by the same hand as in the print. The x-rayed hand belonged to Anna Bertha Ludwig, wife of William Röntgen, as she assisted him with the first of his imaging experiments.

His discovery had come after a photographic screen in the laboratory glowed when he performed an experiment with cathode rays, alerting him to the fact that another energy was at work. He called it 'X' for its mystery, and the name remained even when the rays were well understood. Although the image of her hand was significant in demonstrating her husband's findings, Anna Bertha was disquieted by the results. It was too close, she said, to seeing her own death.

At the radiology place I stand against the square plate that will receive an image of my neck. There is a brief surge of sound as the machine activates. Something has changed, though I feel nothing but the tension of holding still. Later, when the images come through to my phone and I see the shapes and shadows of my bones framed within the screen, I think of Anna Bertha, and her unease.

181. Mermaid Weathervane

The mermaid is made of greenish copper, her figure positioned above the four points of the compass to make a weathervane. Her hands are outstretched, her tail extends into a curving fin. Above the garage roofs of the back lane, she floats outside of her usual element.

This narrow street has a patchwork of fences, a pink frangipani and an overhanging lemon tree. Here, most of the time, the ocean feels far away. But on some nights, when the breeze is brisk and cool, a taste of it comes. The wind changes its current, and so the mermaid turns.

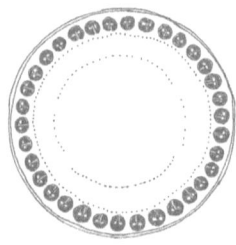

182. Telecom Dinner Plate

From the mismatched stack in the cupboard I pull out a Telecom dinner plate, thick and white with the logo in a strip around the edge. It had been part of a full range of crockery that had been printed for the national telecommunications company, for use in staff canteens and office tearooms. Teacups, mugs, saucers, milk jugs, and ashtrays were all printed with the design, an orange circle which contained two white shapes like periscopes, set back to back to form a T.

Designed in 1975, it was launched at the same time as the Australia Post logo, a red circle with a stylised 'P'. The 'P' is still in use, but the 'T' was retired and slowly sunk away from everyday recognition, remaining only as a secret message on manhole covers and the occasional, dispersed op shop dinner plate or saucer.

183. The 1986 Smash Hits RSVP Directory

In the 1980s every issue of Smash Hits magazine printed a half-page of 'RSVP' advertisements, pleas for letters from teenagers all over the country.

I'm absolutely sick of this. Every afternoon I come home from school to find an old empty letterbox. Will someone PLEASE save me from a broken heart and write???! (Denise WA 6170)

It must have been a difficult task to choose which ads were worthy enough to run, so in 1986, rather than choose one Madonna fan or Spandau Ballet obsessive over another, Smash Hits published the *RSVP Directory*, a 28-page magazine supplement entirely of RSVP ads.

I want a real weird, loony sort of person who just loves and simply adores Cyndi Lauper. Yep! Cyndi Lauper! Cyndi's the only thing I'm into! This makes it pretty easy. (Bobbie VIC 3167).

Among them groups of girls sought matching hunks or spunks:

If you have been unsuccessfully searching this page for a couple of trendy, weird and unpredictable girls to write to, then look no further! (Hunk Hunters QLD 4144)

Others were unfussy:

I'll write to anyone who's game enough to write to me. (Anne SA 5042)

Across time, I find potential kindred spirits:

My hobbies include op-shopping, night-clubbing and carrying my totally cosmic kettle around with me. I'm 16 and enjoy freaking out. (Michelle VIC 3170)

184. Black Cat Celluloid Charm

A handful of black cats are in a dish of buttons and charms at the antique market. Two dollars each, a dollar either way towards either good or bad luck, depending on which tradition you believe.

The black cats in the dish are identical, so there's no way to know which is which. The stern expressions on their faces give little away and I hover my hand over them, trying to steer towards the good.

With the cat in my pocket I step outside into the rain. The wind has picked up in the time I've been inside the hall. As I walk out into the cold and start down the wet steps, slippery with leaves, I wonder when the cat will prove itself one way or the other.

185. The Middle Aisle

The middle aisle of every Aldi supermarket is officially known as the 'Special Buys' section, but also, colloquially, 'The Aisle of Wonder', among other nicknames. Here new items appear every Wednesday and Saturday, the only predictability being their extreme specificity and inessentiality.

One week, LCD-illuminated dartboards. Another, miniature anatomy models. Or an inflatable backyard water park. Perhaps a wi-fi enabled pet feeder that offers '2-way communication via built-in microphone and speaker'. Or a tote bag with concealed cooler, with a discreet spigot for dispensing drinks in the base. Perhaps a unicycle, or a sleeping-bag onesie. A foldable keyboard? An air compressor? A vinyl record player and accompanying cabinet to store the Elvis LPs that are also on sale?

Most of the Special Buys are at least notionally useful, so that someone with a sensibly-stocked trolley might be tempted into contemplation of a portable solar panel, a dog sofa, or a set of flamingo-shaped silicon pancake moulds. Special Buys bring about a mixture of despair and desire, bundled into a supermarket fever-dream (on a ventilated gel-infused memory foam pillow, $39.99).

186. Boots

My teenage shoes were Dr Martens, boots which I wore proudly until they wore out completely, sometime in my early twenties. By then the creases in the leather had cracked, the tread was flat, and some of the air pockets in the soles had broken through. I'd bought them as an aspirational punk, careful to abide by the lace code, avoiding the red or white that indicated sympathies with skinheads, although whether this meant much in suburban Sydney in the 1990s, I was not sure. What I did know is that they made me feel invincible, as if I could walk forever.

The whole time I had never thought to find out who Dr Marten was, if he was really a doctor, or even if he had existed at all. These were less subversive considerations than demonstrating my identity through wearing purple shoelaces. But there had indeed once been a Dr Maertens, a German doctor and soldier who, after World War II, had used salvaged materials to develop an air-cushioned sole that turned out to be most popular with, as specified by the official histories, 'older women'. After that, of course, they would go on to become popular with punks. When I wear them again now, I wonder which identity I am closer to.

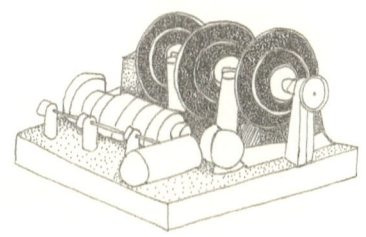

187. George the Talking Clock

The telecommunications museum is housed in a nondescript two-storey building beside Bankstown train station. There is no indication of what might be inside from its plain facade, but I'm curious and ring the doorbell. Nothing happens, so I try again, and just as I am about to give up the door opens.

The interior couldn't be more of a contrast. There are thousands of things inside, aisles of displays of past telecommunications objects: telephones, switchboards, pneumatic tubes, morse-code machines, teleprinters and, the guide tells me, George the Speaking Clock. 'You have George?' I ask, interested to see the machine which, from 1954, had announced the time, accurate to a hundredth of a second, to anyone who called the phone number for this service.

Advertisements had shown a figure with a clock for a face, wearing a dinner suit, but George was made up of gears, cogs, lights, and three round glass discs which carried recordings of an actor's voice reading out the hours, minutes, and seconds. When the guide turns on the power the discs come to life, rotating on their metal spindle. Cogs and gears activate and then the voice plays. 'At the third stroke,' it says, 'it will be ten twenty-seven and thirty seconds', with three short high tones to indicate the location of this precise moment.

188. Feather Fountain Pen

When I use the feather pen I think of being in Prague and leaving the Old Town Square, walking towards Staroměstská station. To the side of the square I stopped at an antique store. My footsteps creaked the floorboards and I moved slowly so as to not knock over the displays. The shop was a long, cluttered room that appeared to have no end, like I was in the tube of a kaleidoscope, one among many pieces that tumbled together to make the pattern.

The silver feather, long and straight and made of aluminium, felt almost as light as a real feather when I picked it up. Stamped in the centre of it was a brand name, MALTOFERROCHIN. SVATEK & Co. (Prague). I adjusted my grip and moved the nib in circles as if I was writing a message in the air, imagining the rooms in which clerks wrote with such pens, inside the iced-cake buildings of the city centre. Rows of wooden desks would be lined up underneath pneumatic tubes crossing the ceiling, through which, every so often, a capsule rocketed past. The clerk's black coats were draped over the backs of their chairs, their hats were hung up on hooks above their desks, their feather pens were light between their fingers and made their words come swiftly.

189. Hooded Hairdryer

Hanging in the window on two short lengths of gold chain is a perspex sign for Anna's Unique Hair Design, bracketed by the symbols of a hairbrush and a pair of open scissors. The salon is closed but I look inside, towards a screen of snake plants, their long thin dappled leaves drooping from lack of light. Pinned to the wall behind them are yellowing newspaper articles celebrating the achievements of a junior boxing champion.

My gaze travels further back, over the piles of magazines and the pens in a cup on the laminate counter beside a pink artificial rose. Lining the back wall is a row of hairdryers, the 1960s kind that look like space helmets. Here I stop – a woman is sitting in one of the chairs, staring back at me. She's wearing a brown dress from the same era as the dryers, brown with yellow shards. We lock eyes but she looks straight through me, as if I am transparent. I'm not sure which one of us is the ghost.

190. Virtual Fireplace DVD

There inevitably comes a day so cold that we switch the insipid heaters on to full power and wear puffy jackets inside. Finally, desperate for an illusion of warmth, we put on the TV Virtual Fireplace DVD. On the back cover, above the logo for Payless Entertainment Ltd, a description runs heavy on exclamation marks: 'Turn your TV into a realistic fireplace! Amaze your friends!' The crackling fire plays on a short loop, noticeable as there is an audible sniff at one point, as if the person behind the camera has a cold.

The Payless version is one of the many derivatives of the original video fireplace, an hour-long recording of a roaring fire which gradually died down to embers, released in 1982 by Video Naturals, a company from California that specialised in mood videos. Their catalogue included Video Fireplace, Video Aquarium, Ocean Waves, and Your Christmas Yule Log Fireplace. The concept has continued on into Netflix, where a fireplace series presents sixty minutes of various different kinds of burning logs (classic, birch, yule).

Our Payless DVD version does a reasonable job of turning the TV into a roaring fireplace. The licks of flame on the screen do play some kind of trick on me, even if the sniff comes to regularly break the spell.

191. Wine Bottle

Sitting cross-legged on the kitchen floor, with the door to the under-sink cupboard open in front of me, I am doing an inventory of vases, canisters, and stacks of anodised aluminium picnic cups. Reaching to the very back, my hand closes around a bottle. I expect it to be some kind of long-forgotten cleaning product but no, it's an empty wine bottle. Dead Horse Red, 1996, with an upside-down woodcut illustration of a horse on the label.

In that time, wine had been less-often sold with whimsical labelling, and Dead Horse had stood out. To explain the name the label included a jocular description of an exchange between the winemakers: one had wanted to call it 'Bloody Good Red', but the other said they'd have better luck trying to flog a dead horse.

It was a ho-hum, somewhat unconvincing story but the grim name suited me. It was wine for people who had a dead-horse part of themselves that came out at midnight, who lived in a top-floor apartment inside a high-ceilinged terrace house with mouldy walls and a perilous balcony and a record collection heavy on melancholy. The message in this bottle is that old time. I push it back into the dark depths of the cupboard.

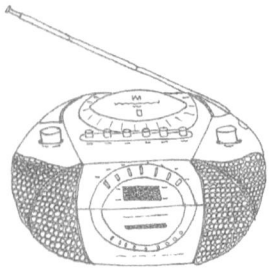

192. Antenna

In 2001 the First Theremin Concert for Extraterrestrials was performed by three members of the Moscow Theremin Centre, to be broadcast to sun-like stars many dozens of light years away, part of a broader communication known as the Teen Age Message. The program of the concert and its target stars had been chosen by teenagers, who believed that theremin performances of Saint-Saens's 'The Swan', and the finale to Beethoven's 9th symphony were accurate enough representations of human emotions to be sent into deep space.

The electronic warble of the theremin is still travelling towards its first destination, Ursa Major, which it won't reach until 2047. I think of it sometimes when I turn on the kitchen radio, an analogue set with poor tuning that I ineffectually try to fix by moving the antenna. As my terrestrial radio crackles, the theremin concert continues on its journey through space. Already it has been on the move for half my lifetime, continuing to travel, its energy growing ever more distant.

193. Dressing Gown

In *Woman in a Dressing Gown*, a British kitchen-sink drama from the 1950s, the gown's sagging, worn silk is the colour of a drab sky. Its dismal appearance is as unappealing as the burnt toast and brimming cups of tea the protagonist sets on a tray to carry out to her husband and son, attempting optimism despite the chaotic state of the house.

The gown is her softer, hidden life, one of sleeping in, leaving the dishes, and letting clutter build up. It is the malaise of her entrapment and her protest against it. Ultimately, though, duty wins out and throwing away the gown is her power move, with which she vows to overcome depression and regain her husband's love.

My own well-worn dressing gown, made of crimson wool, has been inexplicably hated by every one of my pets. In this remake of *Woman in a Dressing Gown* the qualities of the gown bring about psychic disturbance for the rabbit, who frantically circles it and nips at the hem, and the cat, who eyes it warily and backs away, not trusting that, inside it, I am still the person she knows.

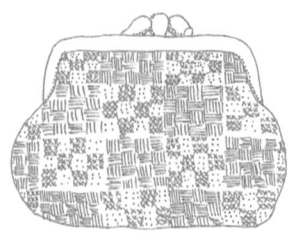

194. Welsh Tapestry Coin Purse

Waiting at the bakery, idly opening and closing the top of my coin purse, which is made of a purple and blue tapestry fabric with a brass clasp at the top, I think of Dora's reticule, and what Sigmund Freud believed it to reveal. Reticules, drawstring purses that were fashionable in nineteenth-century Europe, were, according to Freud, like jewellery boxes, substitutes for genitalia.

During one of their sessions she touches the top of the reticule as she is talking, opening and shutting it and touching its interior. This act Freud saw straight through: it was clearly a confession of masturbation, 'an entirely unembarrassed yet unmistakable pantomimic announcement' of it. It was a *symptomatic act*, he explained to her, a manifestation of her unconscious, which she would, of course, deny, because she was unaware what her gestures were revealing. 'Why should I not wear a reticule like this, as it is now the fashion to do?' Dora asked. But after that day she ceased to bring it to her visits to Dr Freud.

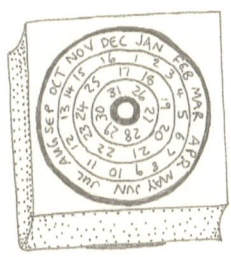

195. Calendar Stamp

The rubber stamp shop, narrow with shelves down either side, had stamps lined up in categories, a pictorial dictionary of figures, animals, and occasions, everything from owls to toadstools to false teeth. Behind the stamps a notice taped to the wall cautioned: 'Drug Dealers, please note that we do not allow our images to be used on drug bags. Kindly take your business elsewhere.' Below, on a workbench under the shelves, a cat was curled up asleep on top of an album of stamp designs.

Reaching behind the sleeping cat, I picked up a stamp with the image of a horseshoe with two sharp nails crossed behind it, and the words, 'wear a horseshoe and nail and have luck without fail'. Then a stamp of a potato, a top hat, a bed bug. Best of all was the calendar stamp, which had all the possible days of the year compressed into four concentric circles like a dartboard. Months on the outside, days on the inside, a whole year in my hand.

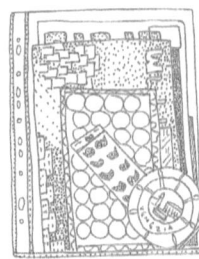

196. Plastic Sleeve

Inside the plastic sleeve are pictures that were once blu-tacked to the wall above my desk. I'd removed them before a house inspection, perpetuating the fiction that I would never affix to the wall a collage of a boy looking at the moon, a watercolour-pencil drawing of a cluster of Binishell buildings, a photocopy of the December 1985 cover of *Rip It Up* magazine featuring The Verlaines, a fruit-crate label for Fancy Apples, or a screenshot from an interview with Christa Wolf where she sits by a window, with the subtitle, 'Well, at that time I said: I feel different every day'.

Every inspection I make one of these collections in a plastic sleeve and put it aside. Later I find them, interleaved here and there, haphazardly filed among other papers. I am not meticulous like On Kawara, with his folders of sleeved documents quantifying the days of his life, in categories including *I Met* (people he conversed with, every day for 11 years); *I Read* (annotated newspaper clippings, 29 years worth); *I Went* (daily photocopied maps annotated with his movements, for 11 years). Inside uniform ring binders each plastic sleeve is a day, by way of a list of names, news stories, or routes drawn on city maps. Examine them all together and you might come close to reconstructing his life, or to realising how much else there is that can never be so easily contained.

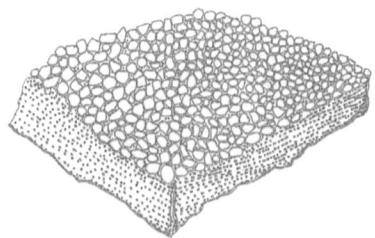

197. Pebblecrete

At certain times of day the only warm place is the patch of sunlight on the front steps, which, like the path that leads to the gate, are made of pebblecrete. Tiny brown and grey pebbles are embedded in cement, forming the rough, durable substance that paved mid to late twentieth-century suburbia, making paths and driveways and the edging for backyard swimming pools.

In some places around the path the edges of the pebblecrete are crumbling, lumps of it cracking off and coming free like icing off a cake. This makes it easy to pick up a piece and look closely at the pebbles, their irregular shapes, their fissures and cracks and the seams of colour running through them. After all the forces of heat, pressure, and time that formed them they are here, stuck in concrete, a surface absorbing the weak winter sun as the day wanes.

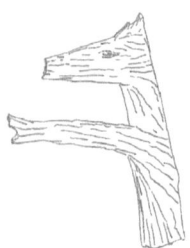

198. Anthropomorphic Stick

After a slow walk through the garden, visiting the daffodils, the lemon tree, the staghorn fern, and a full red rose that is the last bloom of the season, we turn back to the house. Against the back door I notice a stick, roughly the size and shape of a walking stick. The top of it is a broken-off section of branch which makes for a snout, with a knot in the wood like an eye.

The head of the stick looks something like the Mari Lwyd, the folkloric Welsh hobby horse figure made of a decorated horse's skull. Around Christmas the Mari Lwyd visits house after house, exchanging riddles with the residents to gain entry. The Mari Lwyd is both festive and macabre, with baubles in her eye sockets, colourful ribbons trailing across her ears, and a sheet for a body, underneath which someone hides to animate her.

Seeing me observe the stick my mother tells me how it had come down from one of the tall eucalypts at the back of the garden. From its fallen position on the grass, its expression seemed to demand it be picked up and given attention. There is a certain nobility about it for a stick, we agree.

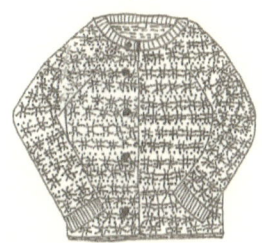

199. Mohair Cardigan

Bright and fluffy, patterned with multicoloured daisies, the mohair cardigan is the kind of comforting but preposterous garment that I suspect would look more appropriate in child size. I wear it every day in winter but rarely in public, shy of revealing this private self outside the house.

I'd longed for a mohair jumper as a teenager, in imitation of the London punks who had dressed in the striped or motley-coloured mohair jumpers sold at Seditionaries, a time and a world away from my mild suburban rebellion. By contrast this mohair cardigan is not subversive in the slightest, its tight-knit rows of flowers utterly cosy and unthreatening.

When I first put on the mohair cardigan I saw that it was missing one of the buttons, and searched through the button jar for one of the right size to sew in its place. The pale blue replacement is a clash with the dull bronze of the others. At first I planned it to be a temporary fix, but then I came to regard it like an on-switch, an indicator light, at the centre of this most unlikely of power-garments.

200. Printer Cartridge

Sitting cross-legged under my desk, stiffly bending down to reach into the mechanism of the printer, my awkward position makes me feel the burden of my life's worth of stuff. The papers, books, and objects in tight arrangements in this and every room, the bookcases and drawers without a whisker of space to add anything further, the teeming cupboards, the overflow piles.

I reach into the printer, unlatching the cover and feeling for the cartridge, which I decouple and remove. When I lock in the new one the machine springs back to life, clicking and churning. The task is complete but I stay under the desk, between a suitcase full of letters, an expanding file of administrative papers stretched to capacity, bundles of receipts, a box of yellow pencils, a can of compressed air, a bunch of artificial flowers, a velvet scrunchie, and a powerboard overloaded with plugs. Down here, with all this, I am a thing among other things.

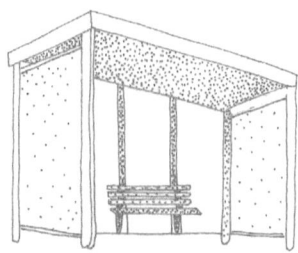

201. Bus Shelter

In the 1980s a bus shelter advertising company ran a trial to demonstrate the effectiveness of its product. Ads showed a girl wearing a striped sundress, her blonde hair tied back with a ribbon, and above her, in wobbly child-like writing, was the message, 'My name is Amy. I like slugs and snails'. There was no further explanation, but a few months afterwards another ad with the same photo appeared, with the message 'My name is Amy. Remember me?'

In the bus shelter where I wait after work I'm standing beside a student wearing headphones decorated with holographic stickers of Teletubbies. A pink light is cast over us from the advertising screen on one side. The ad is for a food delivery service and shows Paris Hilton and Bindi Irwin side by side, with the caption, 'Tonight I'm eating with my sister from another mister'. The more I look at it, the more estranged from reality I feel.

202. Knitting Needle

The mirror reflects me sitting with the salon cape draped around my shoulders, hair twisted up in a knot on top of my head. It is secured there by a long thin piece of metal, like it is an apple that has been run through by an arrow.

'Is that a knitting needle?' I ask, although it clearly is, pale grey metal with a cap at the end. The stylist tells me that a large-size knitting needle such as this works well to secure long hair. 'I feel like I'm in the legend of William Tell,' I say, sneaking a look around to the other chairs, at which other people sit reading magazines or looking at their phones. None of them have knitting needles. This kind of situation, in which I'm the conspicuous exception, happens often enough for me to suspect I somehow bring it about.

The knitting needle secures the as yet uncut hair on top of my head as I listen to the snip of the scissors. The ends of my hair at my waist would be four or five years old. The offcut years gather on the floor around me. The knitting needle arrow points towards the future. I watch myself in the mirror, caught in between.

203. Wood Slice

The xylotheque is made up of samples of different kinds of wood, labelled with their colonial names: ironbark, mahogany, bloodwood. Some sections and slices show irregularities, a thick hole bored by a wood moth, or cracks at the edges or through the centre of the trunk. These cracks, the accompanying information explains, are known as 'star shake' when they occur at the edges, and 'heart shake' at the centre.

The slice that shows the heart shake is a section of a tall hardwood tree, Tarunde'a, blackbutt. It has a crack through the middle, interrupting the concentric rings that mark time in bands of lighter and darker wood. A label identifies it, explaining how the crack forms, through 'uneven shrinkage' and 'variation in densities', a process I try to, but can only vaguely, understand.

I understand a heart shake, though, something that cracks through to your core, interrupts the concentric circles of experience. Counting the rings from the centre of the cross section, I imagine the haunted voice of Kim Novak in *Vertigo*, standing beside a slice of redwood trunk which has been labelled to show historical events over a thousand years. Touching it at the edge, she finds her whole lifetime to be only a moment.

204. Photo Envelope

Before digital photography, the process required patience. Wind back the film, take it to be developed, return to pick up the prints. This whole operation could take days, weeks, months, however long it took to reach the end of the film and then put it in for processing. During this wait I would become increasingly certain that my photographs had precisely captured the essence of their moments.

The photos came in printed envelopes with the slogan 'Quality Memories', as if there were other kinds of memories that were inferior. The envelope was decorated with an image of a child playing with wooden blocks as a Paddington Bear toy watched on. My own Quality Memories were nothing like this. They were photos of things I saw while walking around and the occasional wild night recorded in stark, unflattering flash, which gave everyone red eyes like we were secretly demons.

The photo envelope also included coupons for half-price enlargements, a grid for indicating reprints, and 'tips for better pictures'. All I needed to do was to 1. read my camera manual 2. get close to my subject. 3. place my subject off centre. Even so, no matter how close I came or how I positioned the camera, my photographs never quite matched up to my anticipation of them. The moment always escaped me.

205. Sasha Doll

Sasha Morgenthaler wanted her dolls to look like real people, distinct in identity even when they were mass produced. She designed them to have faces sympathetic to the mood of the beholder, which could be read equally as neutral or thoughtful, however you wanted to interpret them.

Wearing a knitted pinafore, my Sasha sat on top of the chest of drawers. With her wide eyes and unsmiling mouth, she appeared to be deep in thought. Maybe she was remembering other places and times beyond her ordinary suburban life with me. Her designer, the original Sasha, had been a student of Paul Klee, and part of a circle of artists and writers including Herman Hesse and Robert Walser. Later I would go on to encounter these artists, without realising I already had a link to them from the doll that would watch over me.

The most excitement my Sasha could hope for was when I submitted her to the hair treatment pictured as a comic strip in the instructions she had come with. First, wet a brush under the faucet, comb it through Sasha's messy black hair, then place a sock over her head overnight, and the next day the sock can be removed to find her sleek and restored. It was a seductive idea, that this was all it might take.

206. Cat's Eye Marble

Digging in the hard soil near the fence, once I get down far enough, I see that there are scraps of debris mixed up in it, between the fibrous tendrils of the tree roots. I pull them out as I find them. A shred of plastic, a 1¢ coin, a broken bottle, a piece of bone, and a cat's eye marble with a coloured swirl inside.

I put down the trowel and wipe the soil off the marble that has been so long underground, revealing the red-green spiral at its centre. A spirit, a flash of temper, inside the clear glass. I hold it up to the sky to look through it, to make its vision mine.

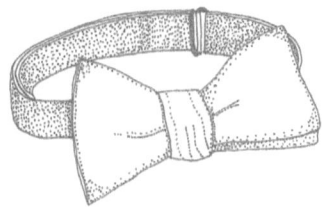

207. Bow Tie

A tax swindler, a confidence trickster, drinker of orangeade, wearer of bow ties, wanted by police, but nowhere to be found.

An unhappy marriage before the divorce court, brought to dissolution by the husband's insistence on wearing bow ties. He wears a red one to the trial.

A bank robber who wore the pink bow tie to do the heist, making away with millions of dollars, only to be found on a tour of ski resorts, spending his newfound riches, still wearing the same pink bow tie.

A valuable fox terrier dog, performer of tricks, with a grey face and white hind legs, answering to the name Trigger, wearing a black bow tie, last seen running in the direction of the port, never to be seen again.

208. Mannequin

When British archaeologists broke into Tutankhamen's tomb they found their fantasies of hidden treasure had come true. 'Wonderful things!' described Howard Carter, on looking into the tomb's antechamber, where he saw a throne and gilded couches, with smaller vessels and pieces of furniture stacked up around them. Objects laid away faithfully for the afterlife, never intended to be seen again by the living.

Behind the disassembled chariots was a wooden torso of the young king. Life-sized and contoured to mimic the shape of his body, it didn't have the same ornate appearance of other statues in the tomb, and more resembled the teenage boy that he was during his reign and at the time of his death. Carter decided it must have been used to display clothes or jewellery. For this reason, it is often said to be the first mannequin.

Maybe it was, but now this is thought to be unlikely, and that the figure had some other funerary purpose, lost to time. Maybe, some speculate, it is a home for the *ka*, the soul or life force of a person that lives on after death, for whom the elaborate tombs were furnished and sealed up with such care.

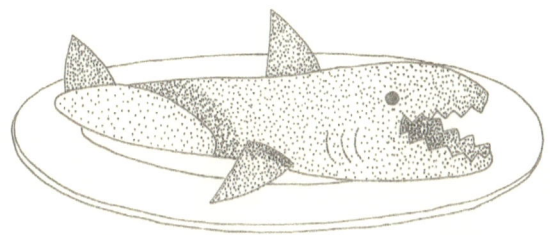

209. Vegetable Carving

The next post I scroll to is of the cover of a recipe book of garnishes and vegetable carvings. I swipe to examine a selection of pages, including the instructions for how to cut a cucumber to resemble a shark. Slices from the end of the cucumber make the tail, and the cutaway pieces are repositioned as fins. I think its eyes are made out of lentils. Beside it is a whale made out of a zucchini, with the end of a spring onion poking up out of it to resemble a spout.

Moving down to the next post the vegetable animals are followed by an advertisement for a day bed that claims it will relax all of the 30 trillion cells in my body. Grey square cushions, black aluminium frame. It is both difficult to comprehend that I contain so many cells and to imagine the day bed doing what it claims. I keep on moving down, sinking further into the infinite scroll.

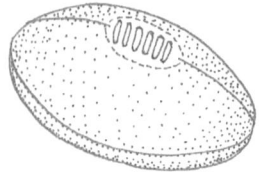

210. Football

Thick envelopes arrive in the mail, containing pages of instructions for S to follow. Among the requirements and cautions for radiation treatment are some unexpected directives. Patients are to secure a supply of lemon drops or 'other hard, mouth-watering candy'. We buy up packets of lemon sherbets, bright yellow lozenges packaged inside bags emblazoned with the brand name BIG LOLLY, and stack them up beside the things he will need for hospital.

'Are you nervous about it?' I ask S as we walk past the primary school. It is lunchtime and kids are swarming over the concrete play area behind the double layer of wire fencing. He starts to reply but as he does a yellow football comes flying over the fence, bouncing across in front of us, then onto the road. The kids rush up to the fence to watch it escape, lacing their fingers through the holes in the wire.

As I am saying 'it's gone...' S has already darted out to pick up the ball, which has come to rest in the middle of the road. He returns to my side, examining the yellow football. 'Lemon sherbet,' he says thoughtfully, pitching the ball back towards the playground. We watch it sail up over one fence, then the other, before it hits the ground and the kids descend upon it.

211. Buoy

Far away from shore, midway to the horizon, are two orange buoys which come in and out of view as the surface of the ocean undulates. Here, sitting beside the clifftop boardwalk, it is easier to talk bravely. My friends ask me a question about what they will soon be facing: what has brought me comfort in the times when people I love are dying?

I pause, drawing in some of the expanse and energy of the ocean before I answer. 'Sitting with them quietly,' I say, 'not needing anything more than being together.' A flash of memory comes of being with Helen in the hospice, before I'm back to the clear cold bright day.

I'm about to say more when a jogger rushes up to us. 'Have you seen the whales?' she says, pointing out to sea. 'They're far out, past the buoys.' Beyond the two orange specks we see a splash, then another, bursts of white against the deep blue, whales on the path of their northern migration.

The jogger continues on, good news dispensed, unheeding of her interruption. We are silent for a while, watching the ocean for more signs of the whales, which are our forces of life, behind the buoys, which are what guides us.

212. Door Key

The key hangs on my keyring along with the others, as if it is just as useful. A plain brass key stamped RELIABLE, a charm which I have carried with me for so long now that I can't think of discarding it.

Key to the house of my early twenties, the time when I stretched out towards the self I hoped to become. Key to the back door of a terrace divided into two apartments, upstairs and down. Up in my part of the house the elevated aspect made me feel as if I lived in a treehouse. The rooms had high ceilings and sloping floors and a section of the floorboards in the bedroom lifted up to reveal a secret underfloor compartment with dust and wires inside.

House of the anodised apple, of Dead Horse Red, and the key that keeps my connection. I often wake from dreams that I have returned to live there, as if I can't resist returning, or I haven't yet found the way to unlock its hold over me.

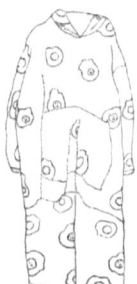

213. Onesie

A car, a dented Ford, pulls up slowly and crookedly at the service station, right in front of the automatic doors. Inside are two people dressed in matching onesies made of pale green fleece, patterned with cartoons of smiling and frowning fried eggs. The passenger is barely awake, her head nodding down onto her shoulder, into the folds of the hood, which is bunched up around her neck. The driver gets out, revealing the full extent of his garment, tucking his hands into its deep pockets.

At the entrance to the store he nods to the guard, who has been stationed at the door every night for as long as I can remember. The guard is an elderly man, not the usual kind of security presence, but a great force of civility, greeting everyone with so much courtesy that you feel an expectation of good behaviour. Onesie will be no trouble. He goes straight to the snack foods, picks out one bag of corn chips, then two, three, four, bundling them into his arms until he can hold no more.

214. Esoteric Healing Guidebook

On the bus I sit near the front, swaying as it stops, starts and turns its way through the back street route. Putting my elbow up on the luggage rack beside me, my attention goes to the two stray objects inside it: a volume knob come loose from its device, and a paperback book with a rubber band around it, a guide to esoteric healing. There are few other passengers, and no one reacts to establish ownership of the book when I reach out for it.

Taking off the rubber band I fan through the yellowed pages, stopping at the subheading 'Thoughts'. I read on: 'A camera has been invented enabling the photography of thoughts... Thoughts are radiated from the mind and appear in the photographic images as a diaphanous mist.' I look up from the book and out the window, to where a man is walking along the pavement, a white cloud of vape smoke billowing behind him, curling around his shoulders. The smoke begins to dissipate, melting into the air. 'We send our thoughts into all the corners of the earth,' the book continues.

215. Bert Smithson

The carved wooden figure, about six inches tall, has all the key features of Bart Simpson slightly amiss. Head too small, long pants instead of shorts, downcast eyes, black school shoes rather than sneakers. His toothy mouth stretches wide like that of a fairytale monster, all the better to eat you with. With this rough, handmade appearance, the figure is more like a Bart Simpson from a child's drawing.

'Perhaps it's a meat tenderiser,' S suggests, pointing at the top of the figure's head, where the wood has been cut crosswise to approximate a spiky haircut. It did indeed have the texture of a tenderiser mallet, but this was even more unlikely than the existence of a hand-carved Bart Simpson effigy in the first place.

His approximate appearance needed an approximate name, so I called him Bert Smithson and put him on the kitchen table between two ceramic cookie jars, one in the shape of a penguin, the other a teddy bear. The jars contain bits and pieces – business cards, novelty drink coasters, wind-up teeth, a kazoo – things that have no other place to belong.

216. Turtle

From the centre of the pedestrian bridge I watch the river, Goolay'yari, flow by underneath. There's always something moving along with it, mats of casuarina needles, strips of bark, plastic bags and bottles, dog-chewed tennis balls. Down under the murky water, embedded in the riverbed, the sediment is polluted with heavy metals. All that can be done is to leave it to rest undisturbed.

The tide moves slowly, a reminder of enduring things. The river's course has been changed, straightened out and diverted around the airport, but it continues in the same direction, towards the bay, Kamay. From the bridge I notice something on the surface, an artificial flash of green and blue being carried with the current.

As it nears I see it is a toy, and closer still, a plastic figurine of a Teenage Mutant Ninja Turtle, floating along on its back. It comes into view just long enough for me to identify it, then continues underneath the bridge and away. When it is out of sight I turn my attention down, plunging under the surface, towards the soft toxic mud that lies below.

217. Three Flying Ducks

When I lived in the house with the Reliable key, I would often walk by an abandoned house that, my neighbours told me, had been that way for a long time. No one knew for sure who had owned it or why it was left to decay. Sometimes when I walked past I'd step over the fence and push through the weeds until I reached the windows. One of the boards that covered them had come loose and here I'd look through, following the sunlight as if it were a torch beam.

Light had travelled millions of kilometres from the sun to end up here, filtered through a grey gauze curtain, illuminating the dust that lay over everything. The moths in the ashtray. The ratty arms of a thread-bare sofa. A bare room with peeling wallpaper. Over on the far wall there were three lighter patches where ornaments once must have hung, the outline of three flying ducks, wings outstretched, suspended in flight.

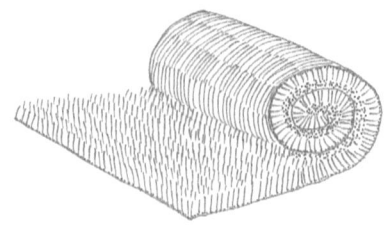

218. Artificial Grass

The playground has smooth artificial grass, a square of dark green that almost tricks the eye. People are sitting here with plates of gozleme and cups of sugarcane juice, or they hold up the dress or the candle they have just bought to show their friends. Typical market objects, the same kinds of things that I once bought here too.

Back then the playground had been a patchy, eroded lawn, worn away by the games of primary-school kids during the week and further by the visitors to the Saturday market. I'd sit on the scruffy grass to eat a container of oily noodles that, thirty years later, I still expected to find for sale for four dollars from a caravan set up by the side gate.

Of course it wasn't going to be the same, although my memory makes it difficult to see it as it is now. All the details match up until I come closer. Fast fashion, phone cases, vegan donuts. As I thread my way around the groups sitting on the artificial grass, I pick up on the same spirit of the moment as I remember.

219. Airmail Paper

Before I left home I looked through my box of blank notebooks to choose one to take away with me. I decided on a pad of airmail paper, the pages featherlight, thin as onion skin, from the days when airmail letters were charged by weight. The pad had a cover illustration of an ascending Concorde jet on the front, and behind it, the same size, a fainter illustration of a seagull.

When I arrive at the house I bring my bags inside but don't rush to unpack them. I sit at the desk with the airmail pad in front of me, looking out over the field below. Paddocks extend towards a line of acacias, blooming yellow in this cold season.

This is how I come to be writing a note from Yuin country, where it is now approaching sunset. A willy wagtail dances on the fencepost, seeing out the last hour of light. Here I would be far away from my worries if I didn't always carry them with me. How can I do everything, what might happen, is everyone I love okay? But when I open the window in front of the desk, locking in the brass arm wide, I set them on the wind, and they are quick to fly away.

220. Greenlites Waterproof Matches

When I turn off the light switch as I leave the house I expect my eyes to adjust, but there is no ambient light outside, just the stars faint overhead. The night is complete in its darkness. On the porch I feel for the candle and fumble with the Greenlites, striking match after match against the side of the box until one eventually flares into flame, a brief spot of yellow warmth that quickly burns itself out.

Greenlites matchboxes had labels that featured illustrations of camp-fire scenes: people fishing by the shore of a lake, skiers warming a coffee pot, a couple sitting together on a beach, and a miner wearing a hard hat, lighting a cigarette. All this outdoor activity was to prove the Greenlites claim, that under all conditions, even when wet, their matches would still light.

Although waterproof, they were not invulnerable. When I bought them I thought I was securing a lifetime's supply of Greenlites, paper-wrapped by the dozen, deadstock from the 1980s. Working through the boxes, meeting again and again the miner, the skiers, and the camping lovers, fewer and fewer matches strike a flame, the green matchheads crumbling, softened by time.

221. Granny Square

Hours of patient stitching are bound up in the granny-square blanket, which I carry over my shoulder as I walk to the river. The coloured wool is bright against the sand as I lay the blanket down. Cheerful and comforting, or at least putting on a brave face, their blocks of contrasting colours are like the squares of a calendar, each day a distinct pattern. Sitting on it I watch the ripples that rush across to the trembling tideline. The surface of the water is endlessly changing, alive with slowly advancing and morphing lines. The crocheted squares are order, and the shimmery river is flux.

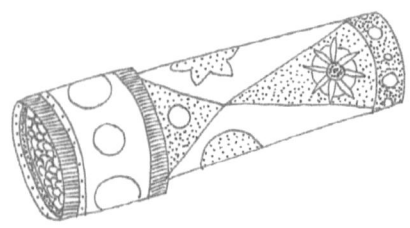

222. Kaleidoscope

The $2 sale basket outside the country-town newsagency carries dolls and kaleidoscopes, packed in tightly together. Weird siblings, roughly the same size, the dolls have stiff plastic bodies and mops of blonde hair, and the kaleidoscopes are cylinders of patterned paper with glass lenses at the end.

In the 1980s a resurgence of interest in kaleidoscopes was championed by an American woman named Cozy Baker. She found them beautiful, each one a world unto itself, and collected more than a thousand of them. At home she kept kaleidoscopes in every room: on top of the fridge, lined up on the windowsills, beside the bath. She wore a miniature kaleidoscope as a necklace, and would look through it while waiting at the traffic lights and in any other everyday situation that was in need of transformation.

Out on the street the Skippy Food Bar contorts into crystalline shapes. The blue sky and the pavement interweave in origami folds, melting into new configurations as I move the kaleidoscope. A fractured yellow shape fills the frame and when I look up away from the illusion a man wearing hi-vis and a perplexed expression, grasping a Chiko roll, fills my vision.

223. Knitting Pattern

In the secondhand bookstore I flip through a box of 1960s knitting patterns, most of them from the Patons Classic series. The first classic is the Raglan Pullover, plain and dependable, one row knit, one row purl, all the way down.

The pattern is illustrated with a zany, *Jules et Jim*-like fashion shoot. On the cover models wear matching pullovers of the same pea-soup green as they pose against rows of leather-bound books. Captured mid-smirk, one model points out something in the open book he's holding, which, like the tomes on the shelves behind them, has marbled edges to the pages and a gold-embossed cover. The other model looks at it with her eyebrows raised and mouth open in surprise, so he must be pointing out a particularly thrilling section of *The Australian Law Journal*, which is the only visible title in the bookcase.

A third model joins them for the next pattern. Now wearing mohair jumpers and black-framed glasses, the trio hold the books crookedly as they pose, their exuberance at odds with their staid surroundings. When I turn the page I expect a stern librarian to enter the scene next, modelling the most sensible pullover of them all.

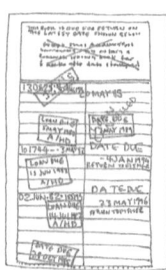

224. Date-due Slip

Rain pats at the windows as I sip tea from a cup with two black swans painted on it. My braids snake over my shoulders, their ends tickling the pages of the library book I hold open on my lap: *The Poems of Laura Riding*. I check the table of contents, scanning the titles, and then turn to 'Autobiography of the Present'.

Other readers have sat with this book and this poem, behind other windows, in other weather. Like me they have taken up the method for living in the poem's first line, 'Whole is by breaking and by mending', thinking of their own breaks and their own repairs.

The only clues to these readers are the stamps on the old date-due slip glued onto the inside back cover, capturing a twenty-year slice of irregular borrowings. Each is another past present, never to come again in exactly the same way. 30 Aug 1976, 14 Jul 1982, 23 May 1996. With each date I imagine the sound of the stamp crunching down, establishing that day on this record.

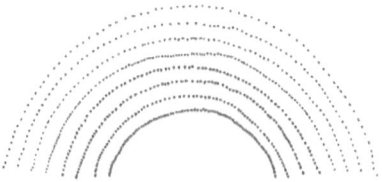

225. Rainbow

It is only from a particular viewpoint that a rainbow appears, and even then it exists only so far as we can see it. A rainbow is a perception as much as an object, an optical illusion turned into a description.

In the blue painting a rainbow spouts from the mouth of a golden fish, arching from its throat into the sky. A human figure, hunched over with effort, has pinned it down, their foot stamping down on the fish's tail to prevent it plunging back into the ocean. The rocky shoreline where the two struggle is between both their worlds.

The fish's rainbow is a pale stream of colour, an escaping enchantment. In this fairytale the fish bargains with the fisherman who catches it. If the man returns the fish to the sea, it will grant him what he wishes. The man comes to the fish with increasing demands until he asks for control of the sea itself, and the fish will not fulfil a wish of that magnitude. As much as the fisherman wrestles with the fish, the rainbow will escape, ungraspable.

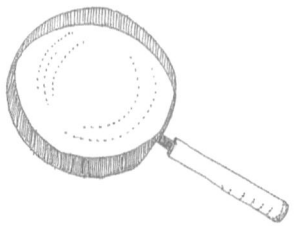

226. Magnifying Glass

Inside the glovebox the most useful things are on top, like breath mints and headache pills, but underneath are more unpredictable objects. I find a stem of bay leaves picked from a tree outside the Portuguese Ethnographic Museum in Camperdown, a small plush toy of Ernie from *The Muppet Show*, and a magnifying glass.

The glass is not what I'm looking for but I pull it out anyway. So used to seeing it as an icon in the corner of a screen, I had almost forgotten it was an actual object. Through its curved lens the back of my hand has a shiny, fish-scale look, the veins blue and strong under the skin.

With the glass in my pocket I am a sleuth, following the muddy track which climbs the hill towards a stand of gadi trees. Beside the granite outcrop at the top I look for the rock shaped like a dog's head. I had left myself a note here, three years ago, folded it up and wedged it into a crack behind the dog's ear. Now I am back but the note is gone. There's no sign of it ever having been there, and no amount of detective work will recover its message.

227. Automatic Door

When the automatic doors don't open I feel invisible, standing at the entrance to the shopping court at the edge of the carpark. Waving at the sensor does nothing, and then I see in the gap between the doors that the bolt is pulled across.

On the other side of the building the door responds, and once I'm inside I realise that the shopping centre is almost entirely vacant. The skylights in the central lightwell illuminate the dusty shop windows and the pine-clad walls and ceilings.

I follow the ramp up a level, passing a closed cafe with a frothing blue milkshake painted on the door, then a shop piled high with boxes, and another one empty apart from a pair of muddy boots on a piece of newspaper in the centre of the floor, until I'm back at the same inert automatic doors I had tried five minutes ago from the carpark. Through the glass, like looking into a mirror, is me from five minutes ago, stubbornly waving at the sensor.

In a panic I look away from my double, further up the ramp to where, beneath a cobwebbed exit sign, a third automatic door stands ominously closed.

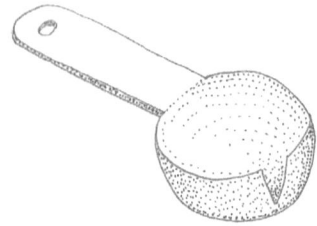

228. Tick Removal Spoon

The plastic spoon at first looks like a medicine scoop, the kind that measures out vitamin powder, apart from the V-shaped notch at the tip. It is this part that you fit around the tick. Then, by performing a continuous forward sliding motion, you simply detach the tick, neatly and safely.

Instead, I freak out and do exactly what you're not meant to do, which is yank out the tick using your fingernails. Later I look ruefully at the tick spoon, wishing I'd had the calm presence of mind to use it. Such a solid practical object, distinct in its one and only application.

Looking up the instructions for future reference, although this has been the one and only time I have ever had to remove a tick, I read the testimonials for the spoon on the product website, which come in the form of scanned physical letters. All these postally inclined thankful owners of long-haired dogs with their decorated notepaper. One page has an illustration of a ferret inside a love heart, another of a bear sniffing a daisy. They are thankful. They are relieved. They will now be giving tick spoons to all their family and friends.

229. Tin of Leaves

Summary: a rectangular metal tin with a hinged lid with embossed cameo figure, once containing chocolates (c.1930s, label on base reads, 'This beautiful casket contains one pound of Nestlé's "Winning Post" choc assortment'). Now contains a collection of eucalyptus leaves of various species (spotted gum, stringybark, ironbark), dried, curled, and insect-damaged. Collected by Berry on Wodi Wodi country, August 2022, while walking the Haunted Point Loop at Bundanon, during the writing of *Calendar* (Upswell, 2025).

See journal no. 52 (Feb 2022 – Mar 2023), p. 87: 'I pick up the leaves that light my path, they make themselves known to me, I carry one until I find the next, and then when I'm back turn out the collection from my pockets onto the desk. A leaf library, the story of my walk'; p. 90, 'Leaves packed away in the cameo tin, something for me to find again in some future year, a way to return to this memory.'

230. Gocco Machine

In among the op shop toys and puzzles there is a Print Gocco machine: I recognise it from the family on the box. Mum, dad and daughter joyfully print birthday party illustrations together, with the help of the hinged contraption at the centre of their red gingham tablecloth.

The Gocco condensed the screen-printing process into a gadget that would produce both the screen and the prints. The best part of the process is making the screen by pressing down the detachable plastic lamp, lined with reflective foil and loaded with flashbulbs, into the top of the machine. The bulbs burn out in a second with a flare and a crackle. The thrill of this is only enhanced by the fact that the parts are in limited supply, and every flash feels as if it could be the last Gocco screen ever made.

'What's this then?' asks one of the ladies at the counter. 'We're nosy,' says the other.

'It's a home screen-printing machine,' I say, 'made in Japan, they were popular in the eighties.'

As I'm speaking another shopper comes up, keen to see what I have found. She is carrying a rubber brontosaurus under each arm, and we can't help but feel a little envious of each other.

231. Silver Bear

Back at home I put my bags down in the living room and go through to find S's note on the kitchen table. *Welcome Home*, with a pencil drawing of the silver bear, sitting on a raft which is floating along a river.

Of course the bear is in the usual position, on top of the bookcase beside my desk. A metre tall and sparkly silver, fitting neatly between the bookcase and the ceiling, a polystyrene teddy bear in a seated position, wearing overalls, covered in glitter. One of those objects that I found for sale and thought no, no, how ridiculous, I don't need that. Here is a chance for me to exhibit maturity and restraint, I had told myself. Head high, I walked out of the reuse centre empty-handed. Only to walk out again, five minutes later, with my arms around the silver bear.

232. Paperweight

The photograph of Colette is taken in a mirror over a mantelpiece, on which is lined up her collection of paperweights. They are heavy glass millefiori domes, miniature universes of starbursts and bouquets. The mirror reflects them so they appear to stretch back towards Colette, who is sitting in a low armchair or perhaps a chaise longue, a book open on the desk in front of her, pen in hand, sleeves rolled up. The writer's world is a microcosm, the photograph suggests, compressed and intricate.

An equivalent photograph of me writing would show me sitting on an ergonomic desk chair covered by a granny-square blanket, notebook open on my desk, pen between my fingers, the paperweights just about indistinguishable beside all the other things surrounding me. There are two of them, both made of resin. One has plastic cherries inside it, and inside another, a real bee is positioned on top of an artificial daisy. The bee rests on the mat of pollen at the centre of the flower and I feel sorry for it, forever trapped inside the plastic dome.

233. Egg Mug

Each mug in the cupboard aligns to a particular mood. My favourite is printed with watercolour illustrations of birds' eggs, delicate planets of brown and blue. The gannet, golden plover, chiffchaff, and house sparrow are everyday birds of the northern hemisphere that I know best from their appearances in books, flying past, or singing a brief note of song. Or I think of their local equivalents, the lapwings that stalk the university lawns at night, or the same species of house sparrow, which, like the cane toad and myna bird, was introduced to control agricultural pests, before it became a pest itself.

For all my love of the Egg Mug I rarely use it, afraid of breaking it by dropping it or hitting it against the tap while doing the washing up. I tell myself it's made to be used, to accept its impermanence, that it is better to enjoy it in use than be so afraid of breaking it…but this sensible script rarely plays loud enough. Strongest is wanting to preserve the Egg Mug as if it were as fragile as a blue-speckled song thrush egg, or the wren's little egg, cinnamon brown, rather than a sturdy coffee mug made to withstand the microwave and dishwasher.

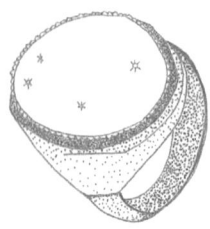

234. Mood Ring

At first, the mood ring was marketed as a tool for self-awareness. Its changes in colour revealed deep secrets, subconscious feelings, and buried emotions, allowing insight into the wearer's emotional state. World-famous celebrities wore them, from Sophia Loren to Muhammad Ali, benefitting from the precise emotional weather report the ring provided: states of blue (calm), violet (passionate), yellow (anxious), or black (stressed, bad karma).

The pragmatic understanding of the mood ring was that, like the Fortune Teller Miracle Fish, which indicates a person's moods by twitching its head or tail as it sits upon their palm, the mood ring was made of a substance that responded to heat. The magic stone was a layer of heat-sensitive liquid crystal set under glass, which responded to fluctuations in hand temperature. Even knowing this it was tempting to ask more esoteric questions of the mood ring, and believe there could be easy and immediate ways of accessing hidden self-knowledge.

I knew all this, but much as I'd enjoyed outsmarting my teenage mood ring, by putting it in the fridge to make it anxious, or warming it under my hand to produce a shade of passionate violet, I felt a panic when the crystal eventually wore out, turned black, and could no longer be coaxed back into life. It was difficult not to feel as if I'd lost vital energy, that my aura had dimmed.

235. Bonsai

My mother and I are fussing over the bonsai pine tree, picking off the discoloured needles from its foliage. As we do this we talk through one of our shared stories, of the time when someone stole the bonsai she used to keep at the front of the house. It had happened on Mother's Day, and the story culminates in our imagining the thief going on to present the stolen bonsai to their own mother.

The bonsai nursery we sometimes visit together had also been targeted by thieves, so the oldest of the bonsai are locked up in a fortified greenhouse. These are the trees with gnarled trunks and graceful shapes: a maple over a century old, an azalea that, in spring, is covered in flowers like a little pink cloud.

As interesting as the bonsai themselves are the specialised tools used to prune them. The pincers, saws, picks, and scissors on display indicate the high level of skill it is possible to attain. With the right amount of time and patience I too might one day carefully wield root rakes and twig shears. Every intricate craft makes me feel this way, seduced by its meticulous knowledge.

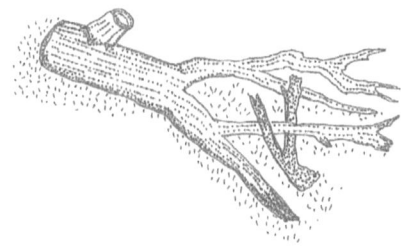

236. Log

In the lockdown years my most companionable object was a log. A thick overhanging branch of the neighbour's elm tree, lopped and left by the fence, forming a diagonal across the corner of the yard. It was strong enough to take my weight and in just the right position to catch the morning sun.

Every day fell into the same sequence: making tea, putting on the mohair cardigan, and going out to sit on the log, where I'd read for as long as the sun lasted. As I read the cat would appear from under the house, blinking and trailing spiderwebs, lightly stepping over the lawn towards me. Every time she would peer down into my mug of tea, hoping that something interesting might have appeared inside.

No matter what I was reading, I would find in it a line that carried a particular message for the present. With the mug of tea beside me, and Soxy stretched out on the grass nearby, I marked a passage in *Villette*: 'The charm of variety there was not, nor the excitement of incident but I liked peace so well, and sought stimulus so little, that when the latter came I almost felt it as disturbance, and wished rather it had still held aloof.'

237. Bubblegum Cards

When I open the set of Namennayo cats trading cards a brittle stick of pale pink gum falls out, forty years past its best-before date. The pictures on the cards are of the kittens wearing biker gear or school uniforms, difficult to understand without knowing the backstory.

One day, on a visit to the dry cleaners, an artist named Satoru Tsuda came across four stray kittens and decided to rescue them. They were tiny and required round-the-clock care, but soon grew to be strong and friendly, and also the same size as the dolls that Tsuda's girlfriend collected, and thus able to fit into their outfits.

Tsuda's photographs of the cats as delinquent schoolchildren, a rock band, and a biker gang became suddenly, immensely popular. In interviews Tsuda told the story of how he trained the kittens to sit up on their back legs and familiarised them with being dressed up. He would work quickly to bring the photograph together, he said, so as not to outlast the kittens' comfort or patience. The rebel kittens' fame was brief, but long enough for their images to be printed on enough posters, bandanas, badges, and trading cards for them to remain in circulation for decades afterwards, all the time moving further away from being something readily explicable.

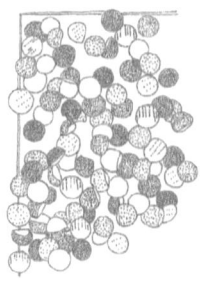

238. Dot Sticker

For filling in the questionnaire (no, no, yes, yes, no) we receive a round coloured sticker from hospital reception. Today's is royal blue. With it affixed we are free to find our way through the corridors to the correct waiting room. Yet another row of beige moulded-plastic chairs angled towards a ceiling-mounted television broadcasting the news (former PM questioned about secret portfolios, retail giant's profits drop, e-scooter accidents on the rise). We join the others who are sitting waiting, looking listlessly at the television, stickers on our collars.

When S is called into the ward I walk down with him to the isolation room at the end of the corridor. Yellow radiation warnings mark its doorways and I can't go any further. Behind my face mask, at least, no one can see the curl of my lips as I try not to cry, retracing the path to the street outside.

Once I'm out I am eager to move away from the hospital, to get back to the car and give in to my tears. Across the street, outside the demountable building that houses the Covid clinic, is a bus stop with the sign covered in a confetti of admission stickers. The stickers polka-dot the sign, each of them marking an exit from the hospital world. I peel mine off my collar and add it to the other colours.

239. Inflatable Cheese

The inflatable cheeses dangle from the ceiling of the deli, a long and crowded shop that appears to extend back indefinitely, into a vortex of olive oil, pasta, sweet biscuits, and jars of pickles. The inflatable cheeses are hooked onto the end of the fluorescent lights which illuminate the high shelves below. In the aisle I'm in the way of a mother and daughter and I stand aside as they pass, stepping back towards the wall of amaretti and rusks, into an alcove created by a display of packets of *pan di stelle* biscuits.

I wait as they unsnag their trolley from where it has been caught on a stack of packaged jam tarts, watching the inflatable cheeses sway ever so slightly from the disturbance of the air below. In this pause a sensation prickles over me, bringing me back to my body. The part of me that trailed behind, lingering in the hospital corridors, has caught up. I feel my breath and my heartbeat, that I am alive, existing, and the shiver of the present is moving me in its current.

240. Sunday Paper

In the photo in the newspaper I lean up against a bricked-in window, trying my best to smile. Earlier in the week I had posed for this photograph under a sky heavy with grey rainclouds, my hands resting against a gritty sandstone windowsill. The article was about residual architectural features – bridges that go nowhere, doorways marooned halfway up the sides of buildings, faded signs – details I am enough of an expert on to act as their representative.

I hadn't expected the photo would be on the cover until I walked past a Sunday paper draped over a front fence, freshly delivered to a house still sleeping. For a split-second I didn't realise why the person in the photo looked so familiar. In the newsagency there were more copies, a stack of them beside the greeting cards. 'That's me,' I said to the unfailingly cheerful newsagent, as I held up the cover. 'Ah,' he replied, 'but you look better in person.'

241. Dream Map

For three nights the sleepers assembled in a field, lying out individually, just beyond arm's reach of each other. They were to sleep among the fairy rings, mushrooms growing in a circular formation that some people believe carry enchantments.

In the morning the sleepers discussed their dream experiences – dolphins, a church, a spiral path – and sketched them out on tracing paper. Then the dream maps were combined into one, overlapping circles and pathways, tunnelling in, moving through, their multiple landscapes.

I'm dreaming alone but in the morning I try to sketch out something. All I need to do is to hold onto enough of the dream to record its shape. It wants to escape me but I call it back: cars, an aquarium, a walk around an oval that's also a lake, the sense of something about to happen that never quite does. A path that curves and doubles back.

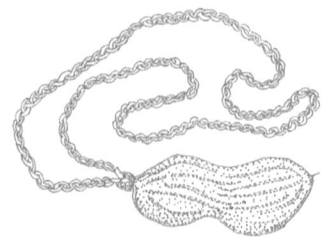

242. Silver Peanut

Whenever I wear the silver peanut necklace, someone asks me, 'is that a peanut?'

'Yes,' I say. It couldn't really be anything else. A silver peanut hanging on a length of chain, a faithful representation in all respects, the same size, shape and texture, only hard and gleaming instead of the soft pale brown of a usual peanut shell.

Why do people want to confirm what it is? Perhaps for the same reason I am drawn to wear it, the unlikeliness of something as slight as a peanut being singled out as worthy. A charm for minor things made significant, of inner softness. As hard as I squeeze it, it will never crack.

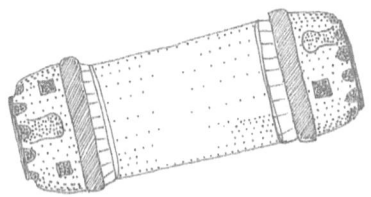

243. Pneumatic Capsule

In this hospital waiting room, I fix my eyes on a contraption on the wall which I realise is a pneumatic tube station. On a trolley beneath it is a stack of capsules, sections of clear plastic tube with red caps on either end, awaiting pathology specimens.

Although now mostly found only in hospitals, pneumatic tubes were once thought to be the transport mechanism of the future, an efficient method for circulating goods and information. Capsules holding money, mail or objects, or even train carriages full of people, could be moved quickly and smoothly, propelled by the rapid and ready forces of compressed air.

In the 1920s a job advertisement for a city department store might read, 'Smart girl, accustomed to pneumatic tubes, required immediately'. She would send a capsule with the docket and the customer's cash through the tubes to the cashier, and then receive the change in reply. In Paris even up until the 1980s you might have posted a letter in a slot marked *PNEUMATIQUES* and have it sent through the pneumatic postal system. A network of tubes extended through the sewers, carrying letters in metal capsules, through the push and pull of the city's hidden circulation system.

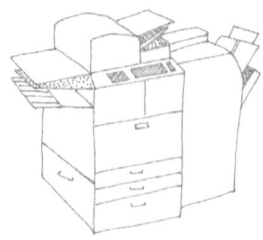

244. Photocopier

Something is wrong in the sticky heart of the photocopier. A warning is flashing on the screen, directing me to open the door at the side, then another inner door, then to press a lever to reveal a configuration of rollers. The problem pages are stuck wrapped around them. I reach in carefully, pull at the warm sheets of paper to extricate them, making me momentarily part of the machine's workings: rollers, static electricity, heat, and my tentative hand.

The electrostatic process for producing photocopies was invented with the aid of a lamp and a handkerchief, almost a century ago. Soon after it was named xerography: *xero* for dry, *graph* for writing. Copying, like writing, could be a creative act. I realised this first in my high-school library when, with the sweep of the scanner light, I copied page after page from long-unborrowed art books. In *Kitsch: The World of Bad Taste* I was attracted to many of the objects used as examples of tastelessness: the Mona Lisa bath towel and spectacle case, the costumes in Cecil B DeMille epics, or kitsch souvenirs like Eiffel Tower-shaped pepper grinders and brandy bottles. Once these were copied, flattened into black and white, I could use them for my own purposes.

245. Flight Commander Suit

The Flight Commander suit used to hang on the wall above my desk, on a wire clothes-hanger poked into the air vent. A child's dress-up outfit made of pale brown corduroy, the texture of its fabric had stood out from the rack of children's clothes at the op shop where I'd found it. Stitched onto the chest was a patch that read FLIGHT COMMANDER. It was a spacesuit for travel in a shuttle made out of egg cartons and margarine containers, towards a bedsheet moon base.

Over time it became so much a part of the room that I barely noticed it. It would only come back into focus when someone visited. The suit was inevitably the first thing others saw. Their eyes would go to it immediately, they would want its story, and rather than the truth, which was simply that it amused me, I'd invent a different one every time.

As a child I wanted to be an astronaut so much that I wore it every day.

I wore it during my appearance on *Play School*.

It is a symbol of escape. I sometimes imagine that I'm wearing it and floating in space.

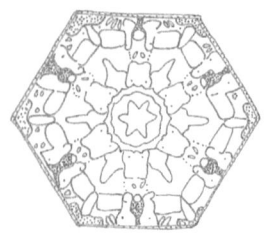

246. Snowflakes

Every winter, on his farm in Vermont, Wilson Bentley would stand out in the falling snow with a black velvet board until it was dusted with snowflakes. Moving quickly, he would then retreat to the open shelter in which he had set up a microscope connected to a camera.

Careful for the heat of his breath or his skin not to melt the snowflakes, he would look over them with a magnifying glass. After choosing one he would use a whisker of wood to transfer it to a glass slide, nudge it into position with a turkey feather, fit the slide into the microscope, a photographic plate into the camera, and take the photograph before the crystal melted away.

He collected over five thousand, finding that, among them, no two were alike. Even if they had broadly similar kinds of overall shapes, their interiors showed infinite variety of patterns: lines, dots, loops, and shapes in endless differentiation. Stars, daggers, petals, and pearls. Chess pieces, tridents, turtles, birds in flight, hippopotamus heads, grazing deer, a table set with bowls and bottles, an endless inventory of forms.

247. Flower Press

As we walk on Guringai country the wildflowers are in bloom as far as we can see. Hillsides of waxy pale eriostemon and pink boronia, spiky red proteas and yellow drumstick flowers. My sister and I move slowly, stopping to take photographs, and as we do so I remember our flower presses.

The presses had layers of cardboard and blotting paper inside, sandwiched between wooden covers. We'd place our chosen flowers within the layers, then fit the top cover over it and turn the screws to tighten it up. Every few days you were meant to twist the screws another turn: when I did this I felt thorough, like I could be trusted to follow a process through. After a few weeks the flowers would turn thin and papery, colours faded, ready to be peeled off the press.

Adults now, we follow a path of slick clay soil beside which frogs make squeaky, rubbery calls. The flowers are in bloom all around us. At the wide flat rock with the engraving of the whale we pause, quiet and humbled.

248. Jar of Buttons

Once people kept button diaries, holding onto a button from every garment they wore. Reading about this, I wished I had a diary of this kind. Without one, all I can call to mind of the buttons of my life are the big deep whirlpool buttons on my grandmother's blue coat, the smooth green buttons on my school uniforms which started the year shiny, but soon became scuffed and discoloured, and the odd blue button at the centre of my mohair cardigan.

My button collection is only of strays, the ones I find in the house or that come away in my hand as I do them up. If there's no time to sew them back on I add them to a jar that once held Zwart wit Zout, Dutch salty liquorice powder that tastes like it might be dust from a meteorite. Inside the jar are fabric-covered coat buttons, pearl shirt buttons, blue and green buttons from cardigans and dresses, and always a few of mystery origins. A diary of missing pieces, telling no particular story.

249. Car Air Freshener

In the taxi a cardboard leaf dangles from the rear-view mirror, swinging over the view of the backstreet route to the airport. Kind morning light falls across the houses. A black cat in a window, magpies pecking the oval, a painted mural of Prince on a corner wall. The beaten-up truck for Whirlwind Removals, already on the job.

The maple leaf is labelled 'New Car', a sharp and sweet scent that attempts to mask the deeper odour of cigarettes that has sunk into the upholstery. The combination nudges my memory non-specifically, towards every smoky car or room I've been in where air freshener struggles against it, always unsuccessfully, no matter the efforts of Peach Blossom, Winter Ice, Fresh Linen, or Spring Breeze.

250. House & Garden Magazine, May 1977

The bookshelf that extends along the long side wall of Monarch Cakes holds magazines, a lifetime's collection of *Architectural Review, Architectural Digest* and *House & Garden*. As I make my selection I overhear the conversation from the table behind me, an impassioned discussion about the age at which you can consider yourself old. 'When you start thinking of sleep as a reward not a hindrance,' one person says, confirming that I have been old for my entire life.

House & Garden, May 1977. The cover features a completely white living room, everything from the modular lounge and the deep-pile carpet to the full-size artificial palm trees that reach to the ceiling. The only colourful thing is a giant-size pop-art painting of a slice of watermelon hanging on the wall. Printed across the lounge suite are the headlines for the articles inside: Trompe l'oeil in the Home, Houses by the Sea, Picnic Recipes.

'Trompe l'oeil in the Home' is missing, the pages torn out. The 1970s rooms I have flipped through on my way to this disappointment – with their psychedelic wallpaper, shaggy rugs, and bulbous light fittings – would have been difficult to live in, already too much alive. As I look at advertisements for flocked wallpaper and Nordic saunas I see the man who renounced sleep has stood up and is on his way to the counter. He pauses and turns to his companions. 'Whatever I know, or you know, it's all relative,' he says. 'Who can say we even know anything at all.'

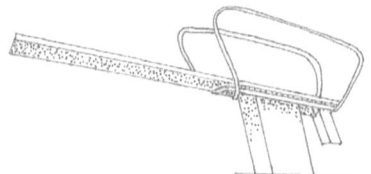

251. Diving Board

I'm back at work teaching, and as class progresses my metaphors for the writing process begin to stack up. The first is a springboard, then a conversation, then juggling, then a toolkit. Then a pantry, where you carefully select the ingredients and seasonings because it would be unpalatable to choose them all. I joke about bringing all the metaphors together and making an exquisite corpse from them, as an ultimate metaphor for writing being many activities in one.

As the class continues a memory runs in the background, activated by the springboard. I can feel the board's resistance with every shift of my weight, an uncomfortable sensation of instability. The gritty texture of the board rasps my uncertain feet. I can't bring myself to jump and my classmates are queued up behind me, getting restless, but I can't face the ignominy of turning back. The sports teacher marches up the board behind me and when I'm within her reach she gives me a shove, hard enough that I lose my footing. Suddenly underwater, water burning in my sinuses, I wonder what she believes she is teaching me.

252. Woollen Suit

The suit is reddish-brown, a skirt and a sweater, from fifty, maybe sixty, years ago. It is such a distinctive colour that I wear it only once a year, choosing its day carefully. The first time I wore it was to a writers festival at which Douglas Coupland was one of the speakers. I lined up to have him sign my worn and well-thumbed copy of *Life After God*, though my head was empty of anything significant to say. As it turned out, the suit said enough. 'That's a great suit,' he said, 'like a baked bean.'

This year I wear the baked bean outfit to a party in the mountains. Musicians run the sounds of kitchen equipment through synthesisers and people stand around outside wearing puffy jackets in the cold night, eyes watering from the wet wood smoking on the fire. In the house are objects from the same era as the suit: a round glass lamp with the image of a sunset painted onto it, a casserole dish with a pattern of yellow mushrooms. The dining table has a leg of ham in a foil tray and a pink-iced cake as the centrepiece. I slice up the cake as beside me a group of students debate about what art is. 'It is fiction,' one says. 'It is possibility,' says another. 'It's anything and everything,' says a third, as static crackles in the speakers, and a gust of bitter smoke blows through.

253. Stereoscopic Slides

On the counter of the antique shop is a lightbox with photographic slides displayed on it. Coming closer I see that they are what once would have been called 'glamour' shots: women in swimsuits posing beside swimming pools, or wearing tight uncomfortable evening gowns and leaning against 1960s cars. Each is double, two matching images mounted side by side inside a cardboard frame.

To take a stereoscopic photograph a special camera with multiple lenses was required to produce two almost-identical images. Viewing them side by side, one image for each eye to focus on, gives the illusion of depth when positioned at the correct distance. Then the optical and cognitive adjustment comes, the eyes straining until the images overlap and resolve into the combined, three-dimensional image.

I rescue one of the models from her double life, choosing a slide of a woman in a sky-blue dress, gripping onto a camera on a tripod as if this time, she is going to be the one in control of the image.

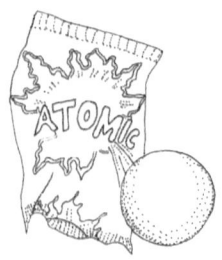

254. Gumball

Atomic Fireball candy was one of many mid-century, American-designed domestic objects that took inspiration from the atomic bomb. Atomic-themed diners, dishwashing detergents that blasted through grime, and furnishings printed with the starburst shape of atoms all attempted to recast the bomb as a novelty. If an obliterating force of annihilation could be made cosy enough to be brought into the home, perhaps it could make it easier to live with the looming threat of it.

Children could be convinced to ingest the fireball in the form of a hard bright red candy. The same explosive graphic is still printed on the wrapper, the seething purple and yellow flames a warning and a challenge. As S hands me one he alerts me that the guy in the candy shop, with his tattooed arms bulging out from his muscle shirt, had said they were strong, very strong. In fact they were the most intense form of cinnamon candy in existence. 'Okay,' I say, unwrapping it, believing I have the strength to withstand it.

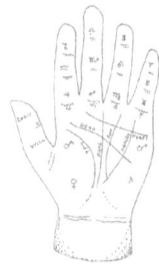

255. Palmistry Hand

One night in Amsterdam, February 1941, a young woman named Etty Hillesum was the object of a chirology lesson. A palmist and psycho-therapist, Julius Spier, led these sessions, in which whoever was the object of study would have their hands painted with ink in order to make prints for the students to study. Etty pressed her inked palms against sheets of paper, enough so all students had a copy. They then set to work decoding her heart, head, and life lines, compiling her psychological profile from the evidence in her hands.

Soon afterwards, on Spier's suggestion, Etty began keeping her diary to develop an awareness of her inner life. In one of her first entries she wrote, 'My ideas hang on me like outsize clothes in which I still have to grow'. But already there was not much more time. She wrote of her moods, her daily reflections, and increasing Nazi persecution, against which she held hopes for future writing: 'If I should ever write – but what? – I would like to brush in a few words against a wordless background.' Her diary itself became this writing, a record of her life between the night of her palm reading and her death in Auschwitz less than three years later.

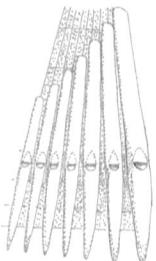

256. Pipe Organ

At the book fair an announcement comes that the books are now ten dollars a box. There's a rush on the empty boxes piled up at the side of the hall, underneath the row of portraits of past Vice-Chancellors. At the tables people intensify their search for worthy titles – *Great Rivals in History, Street Games, Vanishing Landmarks of Cairns, Exotic Styling, Letters to a Young Poet* – scanning quickly along the rows.

The crowded scene at the book tables is offset by the grand hall with its stained-glass windows and vaulted roof. Overhead, on the wooden roof beams, are carved angels holding books that symbolise their subjects: Astronomy with a star, Poetry with a harp, Music with a lyre. Down below them, people browse these same categories, marked by signs in plastic frames.

Three loud, quick pipe-organ notes sound out and everyone looks up, surprised. Under the phalanx of pipes a thin white-haired figure sits overshadowed by the grand instrument they are in control of. The sound descends in cascades. After resting in low, solemn chords the notes move up high and fast, climbing again. The music is a duel between the divine and the malevolent, a struggle mirrored in the search going on at the trestle tables. When a minor chord sounds and the organ falls silent, my hand alights on the book *The Hidden Power of Everyday Things*.

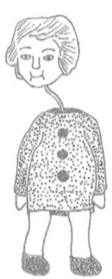

257. Bobblehead

My ability for remembering the locations of even the most minor objects means I quickly find the tin of bits and pieces which contains the bobblehead doll. It isn't a contemporary bobblehead, the kind you might see nodding on a car dashboard, but a celluloid doll from the 1940s, a figure in a red shirt-dress, with her head on top of a long, thin, sturdy wire. At some point, curious about how it worked, someone must have pulled the wire up more than was intended. Her head hovers like a *rokurokubi*, the Japanese ghosts with long, stretchy necks that enable their heads to float free from their bodies.

To add to her disquieting effect, her face is that of a mature woman, something like Queen Elizabeth II, while her body is attired in a girlish dress and black school shoes. When she was on display in the kitchen, visitors found her so disturbing that I packed her away. Taking her out from the tin, I find her effect undiminished.

258. Odradek

What is Odradek? I've read the Franz Kafka story that introduces Odradek many times, but can't say I know for sure. Odradek is described as a star-shaped wooden scrap that seems to serve no purpose, but is unusually alive. Something like a spool, while also being unlike anything in particular, it rolls on the points of its star, propelled by a mysterious life force, always evading attempts to catch it.

Odradek will sometimes reply if you ask it questions, or produce a weird rustling laugh if it has no other response. It will sometimes disappear for months at a time as it moves around the houses and apartments where the story is set, on an average street, the very kind of street that you or I might live on.

Keep a lookout, listen for the laugh. For it is very likely Odradek still exists, and may appear by the stairs, or in the hallway, or just rolling out of sight by the door, a glimpse of something you can never catch or properly understand.

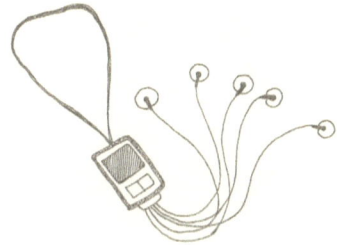

259. Holter Monitor

The earliest versions of the Holter heartbeat monitor, back in the 1960s, contained reel-to-reel tape, but this version is digital and small enough to slip into a pocket. In the morning we unhook its cords from the electrodes on S's chest and wind them up neatly so I can drop it off later that morning.

It is strange to be walking around with his heartbeat captured in the Holter. The plastic box contains a day of his life in heartbeats, a hundred thousand of them, fast and slow, regular and irregular. Detached from his body, detached from events, soon to be converted into data.

On the way to the hospital I cut through the Newtown backstreets, my usual route past the faded mural with fairies and mermaids annotated with their everyday, unfairyish names like Toni and Carol. Even in the side streets people walk fast, gripping takeaway coffees or having AirPod conversations, the usual morning hurry to get going and get things done. Our heartbeats make our way among the rush.

260. Stress Ball

Printed on the stress ball are two roaring dinosaurs, a T-Rex and a Triceratops, fighting against a flame-bright orange background. It must be the split second after the asteroid hit, a wave of fire before obliteration. It would be a scene to put my own stress into perspective if it didn't make me consider equivalent scenarios for future annihilation.

Stress, from *distress*, from *estresser*, from *strictus*, which means, among other definitions, to squeeze. In this way the idea was already in the name, centuries before the production of the foam balls printed with smiley faces, corporate logos, or fighting dinosaurs, easily crushed by a tight, tense grip.

261. Wet Concrete

The concrete surface glistens, freshly poured and smoothed. Around it a bunting of orange flags is hung between traffic cones, marking the corners of this new stretch of pavement. The workers have packed up their cement mixer and gone. Now is my chance to inscribe something, like CHAOS or YOUR IDEAL MAEVE or LEGS, my favourite pavement messages that I look out for on my walks around the neighbourhood.

Smooth shining surface, like grey cake icing, like the skin on a soup, like something you might want to poke at. As I reach out towards it a group of people round the corner, and I quickly resume walking as if defacement of the wet concrete had never crossed my mind.

An hour later, when I come by again, someone has beaten me to it. The bunting is pushed aside and a dog's paw prints stamp across the surface of the concrete. Under them someone has scrawled WE DO. An answer to an unknown question, solidifying in the cool evening air.

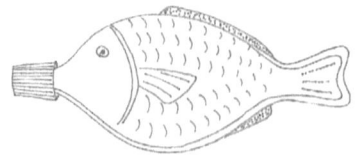

262. Sushi Fish

The first time I encountered a soy sauce fish I believed it to be an item unique to one particular suburban shopping mall sushi stand. It was such a good idea, I thought, before waking up to the fact that it was actually a terrible idea. A plastic fish that exists entirely for the purpose of dispensing three millilitres of soy sauce, and then what? Landfill. Or, worse, the ocean, which before too long will contain a greater weight of plastic than it does fish.

I ran my finger over the details moulded into the plastic of the sushi fish, over the scales and fins and its bulbous eye, screwed its red nose back on tightly, and added it to the detritus at the bottom of my bag. Alongside hairpins, paperclips, 5¢ coins, and cigarette lighters it would roll around in there for as long as it took me to realise that it wasn't something so special after all.

263. Sprout of a New Generation Painting

On a New York street in 1966, outside the Warwick hotel, a crowd gathered, hoping to glimpse The Beatles. A news crew was there too, recording interviews with the young women standing with restless patience, ready to seize their chance to see the most famous band in the world. Some had brought binoculars to better see into the hotel windows. One had brought an oil painting she had made of Paul McCartney, his face in semi-profile under his moptop haircut, wearing a black suit, rising up out of a landscape.

'The name of it is *A Sprout of a New Generation*,' she tells the reporter. The camera zooms in on it as she continues: 'It shows Paul McCartney coming up from the earth, growing like a sprout.' When the interviewer asks if she thinks she has any chance of meeting her favourite Beatle, she admits if she did it would have to be luck. She didn't have the connections, but she was a true fan. 'I'd speak to him like a decent human being,' she says, her voice determined.

264. Computer Monitor

This hospital waiting room has a painting of river rocks on the wall, a wooden magazine rack standing empty by the water cooler, and single-file rows of chairs so no one can sit close to anyone else. The only other person waiting is a man with a thick crest of silver-white hair, looking at his phone. A two-second burst of a David Bowie song blares out before he rushes to quiet it.

Then S is called and I follow, taking up my usual sideline position in the doctor's office, sitting so I'm tucked away behind the computer monitor. Its blank back is a mirror for my mood as the doctor waits for the images to load. I can tell when they appear because he leans forward, concentrating.

'Nothing untoward,' he says. He turns the monitor around so we can see the row of four grey human shapes, like figures captured by a night-vision camera. A pattern of darker patches indicates where the radiation has settled. We inspect these outlines as if we might be able to further understand them and are not completely reliant on his interpretation. The doctor turns the monitor back in his direction and gives no more explanation. We take 'nothing untoward' away with us, as we leave the hospital, returning to the day outside.

265. Puzzle Jug

There were two objects in the first package S gave me, back in the early days of our relationship. One was a Welsh love spoon, with a squirrel for a handle and 'protect' etched in underneath. The other was a miniature porcelain jug with a neck latticed with holes. 'It's a puzzle jug,' he had said, pointing to the side of it, on which was written a challenge in verse: 'try how to drink and not to spill, and prove the utmost of thy skill.'

Foolishly I filled the jug with water and tried to sip from it. Of course the water flowed out the holes and down my arm. My mistake was thinking it would magically work out just because I wanted it to. 'What's the secret?' I asked, but S just said, 'try again, look carefully, I know you'll figure out the trick.'

266. Bobby Pin

In the furrow of the bark we can see the thin silver edge of the coin where we had left it at the start of the year, before we knew what we would have to face. The coin was our wish and it was time to come back to retrieve it.

Between then and now the tree has lost its leaves and new ones are bursting out in festoons of lime green. The creek is high and birds dart down to snap up tadpoles from just under the surface. When they fly off, ripples move out in concentric circles.

The coin is in too deep to reach and we search through what we have with us that might help. The bobby pins holding back my hair offer their tight wire grip. We take turns going fishing with one, although it is ill-suited to the task and the coin evades us, continually slipping to the side. My determination rises the more impossible it seems to be. Eventually I pincer the coin and draw it out. Tarnished from its seasons in the tree, it is our circle come back around.

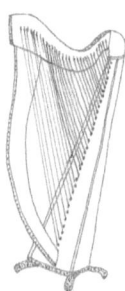

267. Harp

In Melbourne, on Wurundjeri country, we are walking in suburban Hawthorn. On a street where cherry trees are in bloom with white blossoms, we turn off onto a path beside a blonde-brick apartment building. Each has windows which extend the length of the wall, providing a view into the rooms inside.

A completely white bedroom, no decorations, white bed linen, no objects, only someone lying down with their hood pulled up and a laptop resting on their chest, staring at the screen. The apartment upstairs has hundreds of photographs stuck to the wall above the couch and a TV on, playing a recap of the AFL grand final. Beside it is an apartment with the blinds down so the only clue there are people inside is the slivers of light at the edges of the windows.

Last is a room with a harp, its polished wood frame queenly beside the functional bulk of a treadmill. From a sagging black leather couch behind them a big poodle watches me, alert. Waiting for me to come home, if this were my apartment, and at the end of the day I'd climb the stairs, turn the key in the lock, and make my decision between the treadmill and the harp.

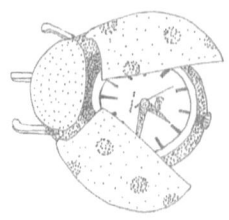

268. Gold Cicada Pendant Watch

The market in the supermarket carpark is the same as I remember it, open at dawn then all over by midday. Dealers, bargain hunters, teenagers, tourists. Cherry-blossom trees in flower, a gold coin to enter.

At one stall is a gold cicada pendant, smooth as a droplet, with wings that part to reveal the watch face underneath. The seller doesn't stop me from opening the display case and picking it out to examine it. He is engaged in a spirited conversation about some other collectable with one of his regular customers but he is tracking me with his sixth sense, which extends across all the objects on his stall.

With the cicada in the hollow of my palm I can see that the brand name on the watch is Genius, written so the tail of the 's' stretches back to the bar of the 'G' to make an underline. The wings are scratched and tarnished and the watch movement is stuck, and this makes me falter. When I return it into the jewellery case a hand immediately reaches out from behind me to snatch it up, and I realise I have made a mistake, that I did want it after all.

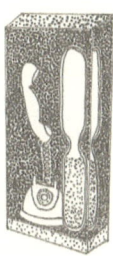

269. Telephone Timer

On the kitchen table of the apartment where we are staying, I line up the things from the market. An aluminium acorn with a sewing kit inside it, a slide photograph of a city crowd in Martin Place in 1962, a bottle opener in the shape of a leg in a high-heeled shoe advertising Arnos paper fasteners, and a telephone timer.

The telephone timer is a block of lucite with an hourglass inside, with enough sand to count three minutes. Landline telephone calls used to be billed in intervals of this length, and so the sand trickled through, counting out the limited time you had to arrange something, apologise, or deliver good or bad news, whatever needed to be said.

I flip the timer, the sand starts to fall, and I race against time to finish the story of the cicada watch. As I continued through the market regret came over me, and I had to know for certain if the cicada was gone. I turned back to see if, by chance, my rival had put it back. I didn't dare feel lucky until I was close enough to see it, a gold droplet beside a handful of tie clips in the jewellery case. This time I picked it up and didn't let it go.

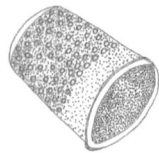

270. Thimble

When I took the top off the metal acorn a thimble was wedged inside it. 'It's the wrong one,' the stallholder told me, taking the acorn back to extricate the thimble. A plastic spool was underneath, with lengths of black and white thread wound onto it. A metal cap on the spool sealed a further chamber, inside of which were three gold sewing needles.

'You'll need a smaller thimble,' she said when I bought it, which gave me something to search for. Another stall had a wooden tray with pieces of rusted and discoloured metal, green with verdigris, irregular shapes, pieces of buckles, buttons, or coins. A label identified them as 'English Metal Detector "Finds" Roman, Viking, Anglo-Saxon, Medieval and Later'. The stallholder told me he buys it by the bag, before going on to describe Roman buckles, clearly a favourite topic. The soldier's body and clothes would quickly decompose, he tells me, but the buckles take much longer. Detectorists find them by the dozens as they sweep the fields.

I ran my fingers through the buckles and unearthed a thimble, which must have been from the 'later' category, and certainly not worn by a Roman or a Viking. But it fit snugly inside the acorn, as if this was where it was always meant to be.

271. Pinball Machine

On the scoreboard of the Supersonic machine is an illustration of a jet taking off into a sunset-orange sky, between the Statue of Liberty on one side and the Eiffel Tower on the other. Under the glass is a network of ramps, flashing lights, bumpers, and scoring instructions that resemble the markings on an airport runway, with numbers arrowing off in different directions.

Once you have taken enough initial notice of something, it exerts a magnetism for a while, coming often to your attention. So it was with the Concorde, which I had first seen on the travel agency sign, then on the airmail notepad, and now, here, in pinball form, preserved from 1979, in an espresso bar where, at the back of the room, quartets of serious nonnos and nonnas play games of cards.

My pinball strategy, which is also the most ineffective one, is to focus only on the flippers and to flick them in a panic, using frenetic activity to make up for lack of skill. Using this method it is only by accident that the ball can go on a successful tour of the board. Either chance is on my side and the ball goes on a journey, bouncing between the bumpers, activating flashing lights and extra lives on the scoreboard, or, despite my frantic efforts, the ball sinks, disappearing into the machine.

272. Lilliput Dictionary German-English

The Lilliput dictionary, three centimetres wide, is covered in blue vinyl with the title embossed in gold, a serious reference book shrunk down into miniature. It is far from being the world's smallest book, but it is about the smallest a book can be and still be readable to the naked eye. Almost undetectable, it is easily hidden in your hand apart from the fact that you have to bring it up close to your eyes to read the minute text.

I ruffle the pages, preparing to choose a word. The capital letters of German nouns make them into solid entities, of a stronger material than the lower-case words. I stop at *Kopf*, for head, a word which makes me think of someone clapping their hand to their forehead in frustration, unable to bring something important to mind. Its list of compound words suggest further: a *Kopfschmerzen* (headache) from too much *Kopfrechnen* (mental arithmetic), requiring a rest on a *Kopf-kissen* (pillow).

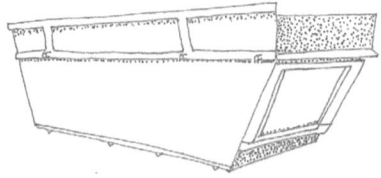

273. Skip Bin

On the day we return home I see that a skip bin is outside the house by the bus stop and workmen are loading it up. They are removing a year's worth of salvaged street discards from the house's yard. Furniture, toys, mirrors, prams, plant pots, a slow parade of rotting wood, peeling paint, and rust.

The workmen carry the objects over to the skip and release each with a crash before going back to get the next. As is usual when the bin comes, the woman who lives in the house, who I often see out walking with her trolley, is nowhere in sight.

The neighbours gossip and I just nod, rather than admitting sympathy with some of the impulses that lead to holding on to such broken things. The urge to arrest the easy come, easy go of consumer culture, the continual offer of something new or better than what already exists. Deciding something is useless and might never be worth anything to anyone again is to condemn it. Wanting to rescue things, save things, keep a hold of things that no one else cares about, that part of it, at least, I understand.

274. Diamond Ring

From an old newspaper article I imagine it, one night in 1931, a woman putting on her coat and diamond ring, a weapon sharp enough to do the damage. A thunderstorm was sweeping through the city, on its way towards the ocean, and the heavy rain saw to it that no one would be out on the streets.

No witnesses. She pressed the diamond to the windows, enjoying the ripping sensation of it, carving lines, circles, crosses. She scraped the diamond across the windows of The Kollar King and the store that specialised in superheterodyne radio receivers. On the window of the furniture store that sold fold-up go-karts, she scratched her name in block letters.

LONE WOLF

Her ghost still haunts shopping malls. I could be waiting for the elevator, looking towards the window of the jewellery store, where a display of rings with small mean diamonds shines under the lights. A person in a blue-grey coat comes up to the window and presses their finger up to the glass, moving it across, writing something, then drifts away into the crowd of shoppers. I go over to read it, unsurprised by the message.

LONE WOLF

275. Sheet Music for 'Venus on Earth'

The frame is leaning up against the laneway fence, wet from the rain, which has soaked the cardboard backing but has yet to reach the page displayed inside. At the centre of the print is a woman wearing a diaphanous gown. She hovers in a pink blush of watercolour shadow as a group of admirers – among them a painter with an easel, a horseman holding a crop, and a soldier – hold up champagne glasses in a toast to the beautiful apparition.

The print is sheet music for a waltz, I realise, when I take it out of the frame. The notes cluster on the staves, chords up in the high notes, runs of semiquavers that cascade down, and a two-line lyric, a plea for Venus to visit earth, promising a fountain of champagne if she does. I try to hum the tune but my attempt is not how a song to lure a goddess should sound.

In the corner of the cover is a stamp from a shop in Toowoomba, with 'Teresa Duggan' written in ink beside it in looping handwriting. Looking up her name in newspaper archives I find her a century ago, a pianist on a country-town circuit, bringing Venus to earth at garden fetes, suppers, waltz competitions, and euchre tournaments.

276. Gamebook Novel

Going for a walk in your new neighbourhood you notice a white house on a street corner, decorated by a papier-mache model of a black and orange moth attached to the windowframe.

As you come closer you see there's a trestle table set up in the front garden with an array of objects displayed on it. Some kind of yard sale, although there's no one overseeing it, just a black cat slinking off into the long grass as you cautiously enter.

At the table you look over the objects, wanting but too nervous to touch, until you decide on one.

If you pick up the music box turn to number 72.

If you pick up the Glomesh cigarette case turn to number 104.

If you pick up the coin purse turn to number 194.

If the door opens, and a woman wearing a mohair cardigan comes out, turn to 199.

277. Tulip

Carrying a pot of supermarket tulips in the crook of my arm, I think of the story of Oscar Wilde on an absinthe binge, seeing tulips sprouting from the floor of the cafe where he had been sitting drinking.

At the bus stop on Broadway, with the pot of tall purple flowers in my arms, I have my own vision. A painted banner draped over the row of buildings across the street: 'why let houses rot?' This was a long time ago, during the 2000 Olympics, but it still hangs there in my mind's eye, whenever I look at these buildings. Then, after the squatters were gone, a family of white cockatoos nested inside one of the parapets above where the banner had hung. I'd watch them swoop over the road and land at the broken edge before disappearing inside.

The roof is sealed up and below are unremarkable offices and shops, but I hold on to the memory. The cockatoos are flying in to roost, and the squatters' banners are stretched across, protesting what the city was, and what it was to become.

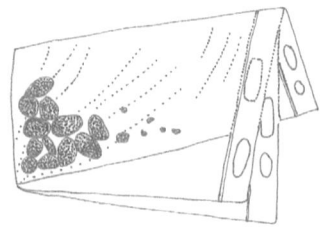

278. Snap-lock Bag of 'Shoe Rocks'

Maybe it was because the sun didn't set, only hovered at the horizon for a few hours in the middle of the night before rising again. Or that travelling to the opposite side of the earth had performed some trick upon my perception of time. A day could hold a visit to a black sand beach, a walk across a lava field the colour of the moon, and a climb into a cliff with a crack which water rushed through, cold and keen. My thin sneakers slipped against the wet path and the people behind me, in their proper hiking gear, had little patience for my slow progress. I stood to the side and let them disappear into the cliff face.

In the midnight light I sat on the deck of the cabin I'd rented for the night, looking over at the patches of snow on the mountains, eating a packet of potato crisps. I'd arrived at the town too late for anything to be open. The crisps were all I had brought with me but at least their salty taste was suitably elemental for this landscape of rock and water.

The shoes were in a bad state, so I wrapped them up and returned them to my suitcase, swapping them for another pair. When I unwrapped them again, back at home on the other side of the world, I found pebbles, tiny smooth pieces of lava that my shoes must have collected as I was walking. I tipped them into a snap-lock bag and labelled it 'Shoe Rocks, Iceland, 2017'.

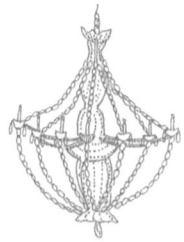

279. Chandelier

A chandelier might evoke a palace as it hangs in a living room or a bedroom, like diamante earrings worn with an otherwise plain outfit. Their shimmery excess might suggest a majestic life inside a more domestic one.

Suburban lighting shops sparkle with these crystal chandeliers, competing for attention in the window displays. Some have tiers of pendants like icicles, others resemble candelabras, their globes shaped like flames, their metal and glass configured into classic or asymmetrical shapes. In the dead of night, all together in the shop window, they glitter like treasure, their light spilling into the street, for lonely drivers and insomniac walkers, and often for no one at all.

280. Paper Cup

The edge of the paper cup softens as I nibble it, a vestige of a nervous habit of chewing pencils and my fingernails. Nervousness is also a vestige, from the days before I figured out all I needed to make conversation was some stories to tell. How the ceiling in the classroom was leaking and all I could find to catch the drips were teapots. Of baulking at the plastic hideousness of the Halloween display in the supermarket, of the skulls leering from their boxes and the racks of plastic skeletons.

The wine we've brought with us is called Devil's Run and I sip it slowly from a paper cup printed with zebras. I had already poured it when I realised the zebra cups were meant for the kids, rather than the plain adult ones. No matter. We talk about how it feels to ride a bike in the rain, to paint a mural, to recall old email addresses when you chose a silly or poetic alias instead of your name. Mine, I remember, was 'howodd'.

This talk flows on until a Mick Jagger type comes up and interrupts, abruptly overriding us to talk about his days as a nightclub DJ. The moral of his unprovoked story is that it is hard to cue up vinyl records in the dark. He finishes the tale and turns towards the kitchen bench, where he fixes on the bottle of Devil's Run as if recognising his name on it. I watch him pour the rest of the bottle into his own paper cup, then gulp the lot of it down in one swig.

281. Treasure Box

The treasure box is a tin with a hinged lid, about ten centimetres across, printed with a pink and yellow pastel illustration of a sweet shop run by cartoon mice. In the mouse's shop window is an array of lollipops, candy canes and gingerbread, a scene designed to appeal to a love of tiny things, a Polly Pocket sensibility. Printed inside the tin is the interior of the shop, where a mouse family browses the sweets and the mouse shopkeeper wraps up a packet of biscuits.

I have kept it with its contents, from a time when my treasures were: three opals inside a heart-shaped case, two sticks of red sealing wax, an Opticolite folding magnifier. An American quarter, an iron-on patch of a butterfly, a mouse made out of Fimo modelling clay, and at the bottom of the tin a ceramic nameplate with a painted illustration of a girl sitting cross-legged, holding a doll that looks almost identical to her, intent upon it.

282. 'Honey Bee' Pinafore

The dress hangs awkwardly, with two long pieces of white fabric for the front and back, as if it were only ever half sewn together. Handwritten on the price tag is '1980s pinafore', which is curious enough for me to take it to the mirror at the back of the hall and try it on over my clothes.

It is confusing until I realise the back piece secures with a fastening around my waist, then the front section ties over the top with a sash. There are two deep pockets on the skirt, and in the corner of one I find brittle buds of dried clover blossom, so I can imagine wearing it on a summer night, warm and slow. Moths bump up against the lamp, a screen door bangs shut next door, crickets are turning the air into soundwaves. Putting my hands in my pockets I find a fresh chain of clover flowers, and a scrap of paper with a rebus drawn on it: eye, heart, U.

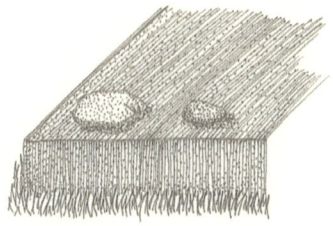

283. Visiting Stone

On the way out the door I pick out a stone from one of the plant pots by the front door. Even though it is the act of placing that is significant, rather than the origin of the stone, I like to charge one up on the journey to the cemetery, as it takes on warmth in my pocket.

Walking down the rows, I look for the overgrown succulent plant spreading across from the neighbouring grave, encroaching over the plots to either side. If the plant wasn't such a good landmark I would bring the secateurs and trim it back, I think, as I do every time I visit.

This time, like every time, I add the stone to the row of them on the ledge under the black granite monument, and sit cross-legged on the grass at the end of the grave. Most of the stones I recognise from my plant pots. I don't come often, once a year perhaps, but the stones stay in place, each of them a recognition that I returned here, that I remember.

284. Certificates of Marriage

Out from one of our bookcases I pull at the edge of a long thin booklet with a blue blotting-paper cover until I see enough of it to recognise it. A booklet of marriage certificates, unused from the 1960s, four holes down the left side, for the rings of the binder in which they once would have been filed.

Inside the blue cover, under the edge, I can see from the torn-off margin that one of the certificates has been removed. The remaining nine are blank, awaiting names and signatures. I flip through them all, although they offer no further clues. Someone must have stolen the entire booklet, even though they only needed one, for whatever good or no-good reason.

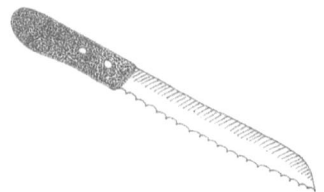

285. Bread Knife

Of all the advice I've ever received, helpful or unhelpful, particular or general, from friends, parents, therapists, self-help books, internet searches, tarot readers, or strangers with something they believe I need to know, I recall very little directly. It either is absorbed immediately or slides quickly out of my head and away, but there are a few tenets I remember.

Perfection in its opposite, believing that anything we might desire is possible in one way or another. So the backyard might temporarily become Paris, with a washing-line Eiffel Tower. Who is to say it isn't real enough? Or the idea that if I patiently do all the small things that make me feel stronger, they will add up to something greater. Or following the wise friend who saw me slicing bread, pinning the loaf under one crushing hand, sawing down into it with the bread knife. He directed me into a lighter touch, saying 'let the knife do the work'.

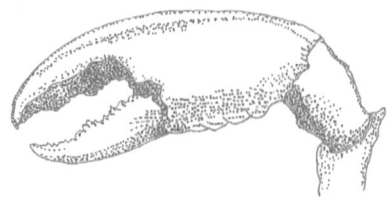

286. Lobster Claw

Hotel C, Venice, 1981. An artist pretends to be a chambermaid, her camera and dictaphone hidden in her cleaning bucket so she can record what she encounters in the rooms. Her photographs of mundane objects make them into evidence for future viewers to assess. How much can a folded newspaper on a bedside table, socks drying on a radiator, or a hairbrush in a drawer reveal?

As she reads letters, tries on shoes, and examines the contents of wastebaskets she attempts to piece together the lives of the hotel guests. The test is how much you can really know of anyone from objects alone. Not as much as you would think. Things keep their secrets. The broken drinking glass on the edge of the bathroom sink. The balloon floated up to the ceiling. The lobster claw in the folds of the sheets.

287. Panda Nightlight

The nightlights were made in the shape of different animal characters. Teddy bear, elephant, rabbit, a dog in a kennel, a kangaroo, and a panda gnawing on bamboo, with black circles around its eyes. Plug them in and they would come alive with a muted glow that defied the long night.

By the time the children who had been comforted by them were grown up, the nightlights were ready to be rediscovered. I built up a collection, a dog, a panda, a teddy bear. Some nights all I wanted to do was turn off all the lights in the house, switch on the panda and listen to *Trust* by Low, lying in bed feeling cosy and hopeless.

In other sharehouses I came across other nightlights, the rabbit or the elephant, performing the same kind of vigil over wilful or inadvertent surrender. Nights of aimless self-destruction, or calculated abandon, with just enough light to see outlines of things.

288. Relief Map of Sydney and Environs

At the entrance to the map store are two identical relief maps, vacuum-formed out of plastic, leaning up against an empty bookcase. The store is closing down and everything must go, but although people stop to touch the relief maps, running their hands over their contours, they are expensive and no one thinks seriously about buying one.

The mountains encircle the harbour and the plains, a ring around the suburban sprawl. Red lines of roads extend out like blood vessels, but the life is in the furrows of the valleys and the waterways that wind through them. On this colonial map of firm lines and imported names, the rivers mark the thresholds between countries, the mountains are geologic time.

The more I look the more the mountains become a creased fabric, the more the red and orange city smoulders. I'm here within the glow, somewhere underneath where 'Parramatta' is printed in capital letters, in a room that contains the world many times over.

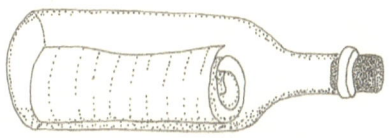

289. Message in a Bottle

1949, springtime, and a man is going for a walk along a San Francisco beach, feeling down on his luck. Washed up on the shore he finds a bottle with something inside. Written on a long thin strip of paper is a message:

To avoid all confusion I leave my entire estate to the lucky person who finds this bottle and to my attorney, Barry Cohen, share and share alike. Daisy Alexander – June 20, 1937

He doesn't think much of it at first, until he finds out that Daisy Alexander is a real person, and she had been extremely wealthy, an heir to the Singer sewing machine fortune. She died a decade before, without a will, and considerable efforts – conversations with her pet parrot, calling in a clairvoyant – had been dedicated to trying to determine the location of one. She also had, according to those who knew her well, a fascination for ocean-going bottles.

For a while, before the note was declared invalid and most likely a hoax, he dreamed of the day when the inheritance would come in, and how things would change for the better. Even long afterwards he kept the bottle, never quite giving up on what it offered.

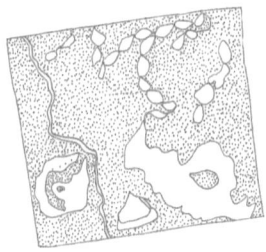

290. Sunprint

Against the sheet of blue paper I lay out a shell, a leaf, and a thin root with a jagged twist like a spark of lightning. I have to work quickly. As soon as the square of paper is exposed to sunlight it begins to fade around the shadows of the objects on top of it. When I set them down, no matter how deliberate I am about arranging them, they make minute adjustments of their own, settling once my fingers have withdrawn.

Like memory, a sunprint holds only certain details. A part for the whole, distorted shadows rather than actual objects, suggesting figures or moods other than what they are. Like writing, the sunprint requires careful arrangement and a capturing of time. For it to exist there must be life; what is left is its trace. If I could write in the way of a developing sunprint, it would be by fixing shadows, converting light and movement into words, bringing objects and time together.

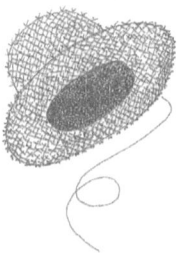

291. Straw Sunhat

To demonstrate the force of the steam issuing up out of the vent, one of the volcanologists tosses a straw hat into the updraft. It is a hat with an unfinished brim, the ends of the straw forming a ragged, ruffled edge, the kind that is good for working outdoors in strong sun. Once it meets the vent it dances on the air currents, kept aloft by the invisible, billowing gases escaping the earth underneath it.

The dancing hat is part of the footage the volcanologists shot of incidental moments on their expeditions. A tent set up inside a crater, cooking eggs in a frypan placed on top of a lava flow, foil suits that protect them from the intense heat and molten debris of an eruption. In these circumstances, a frypan becomes breakfast at the hell mouth, a roll of tinfoil a shield against a furnace, a straw hat something alive.

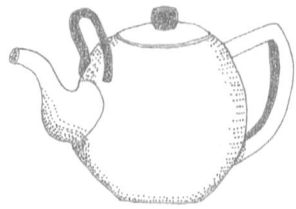

292. Lapidary Club Aluminium Teapot

There's a sudden clatter from the kitchen and I find the big aluminium teapot on its side on the floor, the lid rolled off towards the corner, fallen from its position on top of a row of cookbooks. I pick it up and set it to rights. The teapot, when full, is so heavy that it has a handle on either side in order to carry it, intended as it is for mass gatherings where twenty cups of tea would be poured in quick succession.

It had come from a garage sale at the Lapidary Club, when the new members sold off the old fixtures from the clubhouse. Years before I had been a member of the club, spending six months worth of Saturdays endlessly polishing the same nub of obsidian, never getting it quite smooth enough for my instructor's approval. He'd been a member since the club's heyday in the 1960s and had instructed generations of casual lapidarists.

The obsidian became smaller and smaller, and I started to sleep in on Saturday instead, letting my membership lapse. At the garage sale I recognised the former decor, all up for sale, the old biscuit tins, the vinyl chairs, the wall plaque with the legend 'Old rockhounds never die, they just petrify', and the aluminium teapot that had once held enough for everyone.

293. Gachapon

The ratcheting *gacha* is the turn of the handle, and the *pon* is the thunk of the capsule dropping down into the hatch. What is inside? The egg comes apart into two halves to reveal:

A model of a crow pulling a piece of bread out of a bulging grey rubbish bag.

Or a skeleton designed to hang upside down off the edge of a cup, hooked on by the fold of its bony legs.

Or a tiny loaf of bread standing up on four stout legs.

Or Rodin's thinker performing a gymnastic move on his pedestal, balancing on his hands, legs outstretched.

Or a 'corn engagement ring' featuring a plastic corn kernel on the band instead of a diamond.

294. Garden Queen Watering Can

The watering can is a particular shade of bold orange that reached everyday popularity in the 1970s. A strong searing colour, marigold or pumpkin, fire or sunset. A colour for salt and pepper shakers, canisters, lamps, tablecloths, and toothpick holders. Secondhand, I gather them up like they are the pieces of a puzzle I am reassembling.

The Garden Queen watering can has a figure embossed on the side, a cartoon monarch wearing robes and a crown, grasping a flower. When I use it I imagine the plants it might have watered before my front-step succulents and geraniums.

Monstera and philodendrons, planted in pots on either side of a wood-framed window with the net curtains pulled back, each side tied with a sash. The gardener watches the clouds move quickly over the sky for a minute, before she picks up the Garden Queen and continues her circuit, watering the monstera, the philodendron, the spider plant and the devil's ivy, all the occupants of her room.

295. Focal Photo Frame

If the frame was made out of wood or metal, it would be an example of delicate craftmanship, fine in its carved details, notched and scalloped in an intricate design. A frame which, scaled up, might be thought of as grand. But I've always been content with the ersatz version of things.

When sold new these frilly plastic frames had inside them a piece of paper with the brand name – Focal – and motifs of yellow flowers. I often came across the frames with the original price sticker on the glass, showing that they had never been used. My theory was that, with the frilly ornamentation around the paper insert, designed with contrasting sans-serif font and stylised flowers, the Focal frame was a complete object in itself and didn't require any more intervention.

The plastic frills make a distracting border for most photographs, but it was right for me and Helen standing side by side, her holding a blue paper parasol and me a red bird whistle. Both of us are laughing, so happy to be together that we are undiminished by the decorative excesses of the florid plastic lace surrounding us.

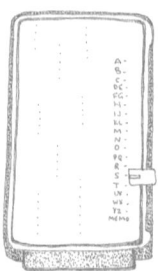

296. Telephone Index

As we often do, my mother and I talk about how hard it is to go through things, let alone throw things away. Our lives and memories are bound up in the things we have kept, and sorting them can only happen slowly.

Every time I visit her things have moved around slightly; something else will have shown up. This time it's the Teledex which used to belong to my grandparents. The case held alphabetised cards with names and phone numbers under a brushed aluminium cover with the alphabet printed down the side. As a child I'd enjoyed sliding the selector bar up and down, clicking from letter to letter. I was forbidden to do this in case I broke it, so I had to watch for when the adults were otherwise distracted.

Clicking through the Teledex, I open the case at every letter, moving through relatives and friends now passed away, all the way through to the blank card at XYZ. When I push the slider back up to the top of the case, I am overeager in doing it and it detaches, falling off into my hand. They had been right not to trust me.

297. Souvenir Treasurefold Wallet

A wallet is one of those objects, like shoes or a favourite jacket, that becomes so ubiquitous that it can be difficult to realise it has worn out. So it was with the Treasurefold. Only when a rip appeared in the side did I see how worn out it was, with cracks at the corners and broken threads in the stitching.

The Treasurefold was produced as a souvenir of Winnipeg, Canada. Most of what I knew about the city came from the film *My Winnipeg*, a shaky, scratchy dream portrait of the city which presented it as a place where people are perpetually sleepwalking. Sunk in a permanent winter, it is impossible to ever leave the city, as much as you might want to, because to live there is to be stuck in a vertiginous cycle of collective memories. Incessant snow, frozen horses in a frozen lake, a mother's face looming hugely in the train window, peering in at her son who is trying in vain to escape.

The wallet was made of Valhyde, a trademarked mixture of leather and vinyl, used exclusively for the making of Canadian souvenir gifts. These objects, stamped with a red-brown maple leaf and names of key cities and localities, included wallets, key holders, and bookmarks printed with 'here's where I fell asleep', the best clue I had that Valhyde was a product that came from a dream place, rather than a real one.

298. St Anthony Medal

When one of us had lost something in the chaos of our rooms, our keys for example, or some crucial sensible thing, something we were holding only a moment ago, Natasha would call upon St Anthony. She knew all the saints and the right time to appeal to them.

On the phone I complained to her that I'd lost the ring I liked to wear, the marcasite one shaped like a teardrop. 'Pray to Saint Anthony,' she said. 'How?' I asked, unsure how to go about it. I hadn't yet figured out that a prayer was an appeal that could take whatever form best served its message. 'Say "Help me, Saint Anthony,"' she said, amused by my cluelessness. 'Help me, Saint Anthony,' I called out, hoping no one else in the house would hear me. A few days later the ring surfaced, whether from saintly intervention or just from the surface churn of things.

After Natasha died her parents gave me a box of her jewellery. Some of the things inside I'd once coveted, like the dangling earring of the fish skeleton, and the ring with the row of smiling cats. More than anything I wanted to talk to her again. At the bottom of the jewellery box, there was a St Anthony medal, his haloed image stamped into the cheap metal. I picked it up, held it gently, asked it to help me.

299. Blue Nun T-shirt

The shirt featured an image of a nun in long robes, carrying a basket of grapes, with the slogan in flared lettering: 'one sip and you're converted.' It would be verging on forty years old, unworn from the peak popularity of Blue Nun in the mid-1980s, when it was marketed as a wine that was a perfect accompaniment to any meal. I left the antique market with the smugness of a person having come upon a rarity for five dollars.

When I took the shirt out of the packet I realised there was no way I could wear it. If it had been 1985, I would have had better luck as it was a t-shirt that would best fit a child. I held it up in front of me, perplexed at its small size. What child would wear a t-shirt advertising a low-alcohol sweet white wine that could be paired with beef as readily as fish? The reason for its miraculous preservation was suddenly apparent.

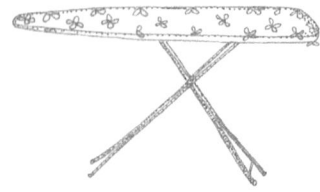

300. Ironing Board

As S sets up the ironing board to use as a drawing desk, I think of Ruth Park and her descriptions of life with her husband, D'Arcy Niland. Both were writers and worked at home, finding space and time for writing in and around the care of their children. Niland used the dining-room table, and Park the ironing board or another provisional arrangement, sitting with the typewriter on her knees, or sometimes working in bed with it on her lap.

Park describes this time as one when 'writing was life itself'. It was their shared vocation, and the work that sustained their family life. Niland died young, in 1967, and decades later Park remembered their working arrangements in her memoir *Fishing in the Styx*. Looking back over her life, she stood by her decision not to insist on the table for herself. She stressed the reciprocity of their relationship in other ways, and their harmony as partners. 'We set off sparks in each other,' she wrote, remembering the love of her life.

301. First Memory

On TikTok people are re-enacting their core memories, although a memory specialist interviewed about the trend says that really, there is no such thing. No memory is immutable, there is no inalterable core. Whenever you remember something you lay it down afresh, so you can't help but shift it slightly every time.

My first memory is being given a blue toy car with a Minnie Mouse figurine inside it. I was little more than a baby, in hospital having tests of some kind, or so I was told later, when I was old enough to understand that the story of the car was a memory, an experience of something both present and absent.

It must be well distorted by now. It returns like I'm looking through the bottom of a glass, making the scene blur and bulge. The room has a high narrow bed with a green sheet over it. I'm crying until a nurse reaches up to a shelf and brings down the Minnie Mouse car to soothe me, tells me I can keep it. Did it really happen that neatly? The memory is as unreliable as any, but finds its anchor with this object.

302. Trash and Treasure

The legendary flea market is on again, setting in motion the customary sequence of events. The wait outside the hall, the rush once the door opens, the fractional, essential advantage in being near the head of the queue. The crush of people and things, the forces of chance and swift action.

At the redbrick church hall the only thing that has changed is the sign taped to the wall. *Trash and Treasure* has become *Recycled Treasure*. Everyone in the queue is friendly enough but we size each other up as we chat. The woman in front of me is on the lookout for brass vases, she says, as she eyes the canvas bag hanging empty from my shoulder. She is dressed in gym gear, practical and ready to pounce.

A minute after nine the door to the hall opens and the queue surges in. The woman runs for the vases, I grab a cardboard cut-out of a rabbit, two flower presses, a length of green and white spotted fabric, and a foolscap notebook. People continue streaming in the side doors, joining the throng, all of us in search of something, anything, everything.

303. Foolscap Notebook

When I first became aware of it, foolscap-size paper had almost been phased out, replaced by A4 as the new standard. Foolscap pages were long and narrow and their weird name fascinated me with its merge of syllables. Fool's cap, named after a watermark of a court jester wearing a pointed cap with bells. Over time the words had run together, and foolscap became a way to describe a particular size of paper whether it had the watermark or not.

In 'The Writer's Technique in Thirteen Theses' Walter Benjamin confirmed that 'a pedantic adherence to certain papers, pens, inks is beneficial'. Therefore the best kind of notebooks are foolscap and plain-ruled, with thick cardboard covers. I am forever on the lookout for them, secondhand and unused. The foolscap notebook has space to go further, to extend beyond, as I write towards the end of the page, which pulls me down towards it, drawing out the words.

304. Carved Pumpkin

There are specific tools to carve pumpkins with, and specific pumpkins grown to be carved, sold in the weeks leading up to Halloween
along with the plastic skeletons and packets of artificial spiderweb.
We have real spiderwebs on the windows and a regular pumpkin does
well enough. S hacks away at it with a kitchen knife, giving it a toothy
grimace. The tealight candle inside makes a sweet roasting smell once
it has been burning for a while.

We put the pumpkin out the front of the house, on top of a plaster
plinth. It is too late for children to come to the house to trick or treat,
not that they usually do anyway, unsure whether it is decorated or
actually just spooky. The pumpkin grins for the street cats that skulk
under cars and the bats in the fig trees. We eat chocolate eyeballs,
watch *House of Dracula*, wait for midnight.

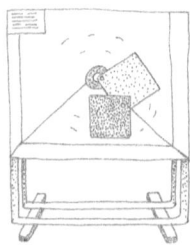

305. Chaos Machine

In the evening, with the weight of the day settling, I make a detour. Past the squash courts which shriek with the skid of rubber soles against the shiny floor, and the medical sciences school with glimpses of anatomical models through the windows, then the Physics Building with the names of legendary physicists carved into the sandstone facade.

In the central hallway of the Physics Building is a tall perspex box mounted on aluminium legs. Inside it is a mechanism of two coloured squares, connected at a corner. They are as big as dinner plates, one cheese-slice yellow and the other dark blue. The label on the corner of the cabinet declares that 'very simple systems can exhibit chaotic behaviour'.

I turn the crank on the wheel on the back a few times before letting it go. The squares begin to spin, pulling away from each other, twisting and flipping. The perspex box shudders as the movement inside grows in intensity. The squares spin with an excess of energy, turning over each other in an erratic dance, slowing down then speeding up again in haphazard bursts of motion. Trapped inside the box is a science of unpredictable change and strange attractors, a concentration of invisible, ever-present forces.

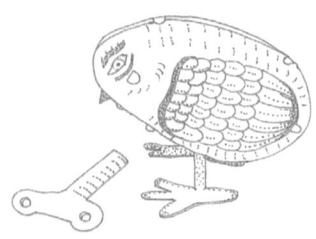

306. Wind-up Chicken

Put the key in the slot on the underside of the tin chicken and wind it up until you can wind no more. Turn the toy upright and it will start to peck in a sudden fervour, hopping in circles, an artificial chicken pecking at invisible grain with a rapid-fire click like a staple gun, intensely searching the surface of the desk or the table or the floor or wherever you set it going, relentless for half a minute or so until you notice it is starting to slow, the pecks are becoming fewer, and it's impossible not to feel just a little bit sad at its diminishing energy, its inevitable wind-down, as if by some magic it might have been gifted with perpetual motion from the act of you winding it up. But it gives out only one more peck before it falls still.

307. Ox-tongue Plant

Every weekend, a handpainted sign appears by the roadside, advertising CARNIVOROUS PLANTS. The tall red hungry words are an invitation or perhaps a warning.

At the front of the house are the standard, non-carnivorous plants, and it's only in the back garden that you can see the carnivorous display. Here there are thousands of pitcher plants, a forest of red funnels. 'A bad place to be a fly,' I said, the first time I visited, as the gardener showed me his collection with quiet but evident pride.

There are other plants for sale, ones easier to grow than the pitchers, and that first time I chose a succulent with long fleshy leaves like straps of leather. 'Ox-tongue,' the gardener called it, explaining how to propagate it by cutting off one of the straps at the base with a sharp knife. 'Leave it to dry out for a day, then put it in soil, and more tongues will grow from it,' he instructed.

Now its longest tongues are up to half a metre long, and I have started to wonder if it will outlive me, and what will happen to it when I'm no longer here to care for it. I think of the begonia on display in the Freud Museum in London, a descendant of Freud's own plant. Heart-shaped leaves, patterned with white spots, extend at the end of gnarled stems. People stop to look at it expectantly, as if there's something it might reveal.

308. Psychedelic Wrapping Paper

Keep anything for long enough and no matter how humble or functional, time will estrange it. It will take on additional qualities, surreal, decorative, poignant, or ridiculous. Consider this piece of wrapping paper folded into a square, printed with a magenta and green turtle, strolling through a forest of purple daisies, with heavy-lidded eyes, sleepy or stoned.

Or another sheet printed with funfair scenes of children riding in a rollercoaster, rowing in a teacup, and driving in dodgem cars underneath drifting balloons. A line of text in the corner gives the date of manufacture as MCMLXXV, like in the credits of a film.

Another sheet, carrying the greeting *Best Wishes,* illustrates coming-of-age rites. All the important adolescent milestones are here: going bowling, changing a tyre, going ice-skating, tap-dancing on top of a grand piano.

Another has a mustard yellow background against which the same friends are shown in various outfits, alternately turtlenecks, flares, minidresses, striped tights, and overalls. A different musical instrument matches each outfit: a trumpet, a banjo, a guitar. In the background, other versions of themselves dance to the music of their multiples, in this territory populated entirely by themselves.

309. Toilet-roll Doll

The bathroom had only two decorations: a shower curtain patterned with penguins and the toilet-roll doll, dressed in a lacy mauve gown and bonnet as if for a garden party. Her skirts spread around the roll of toilet paper, which performed the supportive action of a crinoline petticoat, her plastic legs anchored in the centre of the cardboard tube. I often inspected her, as I inspected everything in the house. Whether tacky or precious, most of the objects had been acquired long before I was born, and I was curious to absorb the knowledge that was carried within them.

When the time came for the house to be cleared out, its things sold or redistributed, I doubted anyone else would want the toilet-roll doll. 'Can I have this?' I asked, brandishing the doll in the doorway of the bedroom. My mother looked up briefly and nodded, consumed by the task of sorting her parents' things.

The doll found a new place, by the door of my room, propped up in a vase that contains boxes of pencils and a length of ornamental rope. She catches my eye whenever I enter or exit. Her dress has turned grey and its lace become brittle with age, a miniature Miss Havisham, waiting for her party.

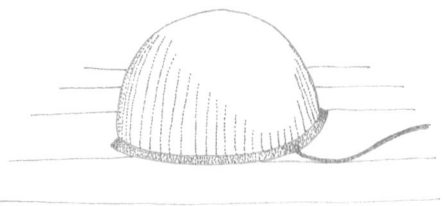

310. Red Nose

While the elevator is coming I look out the window beside it, which has a view over the flat corrugated-iron roof of the lower wing of the hotel. On top of it is a row of air-conditioning units, a ventilation fan, and a red dome a couple of metres across, tied onto a fire escape ladder with a cord. At first I think it's a skylight, but it's not set into the roof. It is faded and scratched as if it has been there a long time. Then something clicks in my memory and I realise that the dome is a giant red nose.

When Red Nose Day began as a charity fundraiser you could buy a range of novelty noses. Some were the clown kind that you could wear over your own nose. More popular were hard plastic domes which you could tie onto the front grille of a car. Rarer were the building noses, which were of a scale large enough that they could be affixed to the facade of an office or a factory. Or attached to a highway motel that would, thirty years later, have almost all its 1980s features renovated out of existence. But there's often something left behind.

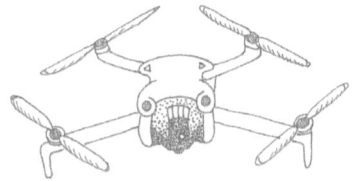

311. Drone

The cat detects it first, flattening her body to the ground, looking up to the sky with her eyes wide. I follow her line of sight, up through the branches. A mechanical whirr increases in volume and then the drone appears. Soxy has already run for it, disappearing under the house, not knowing what is happening and not waiting to find out. 'It's okay,' I call after her, wishing I too could follow my instincts to slip away whenever I felt something wasn't right.

The drone is watching me, or at least it seems to be, hovering directly above where I sit on the blanket on the lawn. I remember envisaging drones delivering pizzas and mail, back when they were a new technology, too naive then to realise they were more likely to be used as spies and weapons.

I remember a story from earlier in the year, from the war in Ukraine: an elderly woman in her apartment in Kyiv heard a drone nearby and went out to the balcony to throw a bottle of preserved tomatoes at it. She hit the drone and it fell into the street below. She went out to smash it up further, so it was of no use to anyone or anything.

312. Stamp Album

Many of the most collectable postage stamps are misprints, like the US stamps from 1918 mistakenly printed with a biplane flying upside down. One sheet of a hundred were printed this way, and gradually these stamps were dispersed among collectors. Some were kept in mint condition, others were posted by mistake. One slipped out of its frame, was sucked up by a vacuum cleaner, and had to be retrieved from out of the dust. Even just a single one of them might now be worth a million dollars.

This story gave me aspirations for my own collection, which was made up of stamps I'd soaked off my father's business correspondence. Skateboarders, military uniforms, bowerbirds, a leafy sea dragon, a hairstreak butterfly. Much of the rest of the album was filled by assorted world stamps that were sold in packets of 100, images of athletes, animals, and technological innovations from around the world. I was sure that one day, among these, I would come upon an undetected rarity. A mushroom growing upside down or a satellite out of orbit, a million-dollar misprint which would change the course of my life and its fortunes.

313. Encyclopedias

The encyclopedias were designed so the spines of the 22 volumes, lined up in order, spelled out WORLD BOOK. Within the set was the assurance of comprehensive knowledge, everything it was important to know contained within the span of the collection.

In the meeting room, as the presenters figure out the tech for the slide-show and pour glasses of water, I stare at the books which line the walls. Most of them are clothbound tomes that perform the function of furniture more than anything else. On the top shelf the set of World Book encyclopedias stands out with their sky-blue spines. One day someone must have stared at them for long enough to figure out the anagram. They waited until the room emptied, climbed up on a chair, and set to work rearranging. Ever since then, the books have spelled out BLOOD WORK, and no one has changed them back.

314. november99.doc

Searching my computer files, I type in 'Cordobes' and press enter. One entry shows up, *november99.doc*, an account of November 23rd, 1999. The voice of my younger self is garrulous, sharp like a toothache. The day unfurls from a sleepless early morning, with a book sale at the Women's Library, then back home for oven chips. The phone rings with an update for that night: 'we were going to Cordobes instead. This was a much better plan.'

But not a surprising one, as we often went to Cordobes, a pizza restaurant with wood-panelled walls hung with paintings of parrots and cockatoos. I'd watch the chef construct the pizzas, taking handfuls of capsicum, mushrooms, and olives, piling up the toppings improbably high. It was difficult to eat them politely, but it wasn't the kind of place where anyone cared about that. It was often as raucous as the parrots on the walls.

On this November night we order gelato, drink wine, play Streetfighter, then stumble out across Newtown. We drink more wine in the park and attempt a shambolic game of cricket against the cemetery wall until the police move us on for causing a disruption. 'People have been complaining,' they said, ordering us to leave.

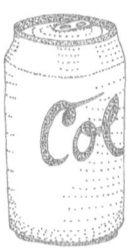

315. Can of Cola

A poster in the anarchist bookstore: a soldier in a gas mask and the slogan 'World Domination Goes Better with Coke'. A rumour: in the early days, when it was sold as 'the ideal brain tonic', cocaine was its active ingredient. Another rumour: leave a tooth in a glass of Coca-Cola overnight and by the morning it will have dissolved. Good for: removing oil stains from driveways, scouring burnt saucepans, remembering the Olympia Milk Bar.

My last purchase from the Olympia was a can of Coca-Cola, which I kept, undrunk, as a souvenir. The proprietor was a reserved man who had inspired considerable mythology with his quiet endurance as the city changed around him. The council had decreed the broken windows, sagging ceiling, and poorly lit interior of the milk bar to be unsafe and forced it to close, but he sat at the desk at the back as he had always done, listening to the radio, waiting out the hours. When I caught his attention he opened the door only just wide enough for us to make the transaction. The can was bright as a bauble as it passed from his hand to mine.

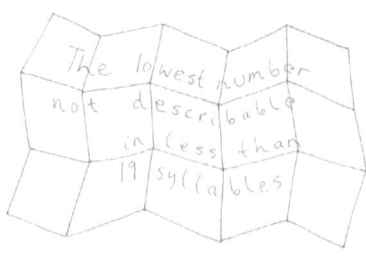

The lowest number not describable in less than 19 syllables

316. The Berry Number

'I have an object for you,' S says, coming up to me with a mathematics dictionary. The page he holds open has complicated formulae, with italicised xyz's, sigma signs, brackets, and exclamations.

Listed between Bernstein polynomials and Bertrand's postulate is the Berry paradox. It is a paradox of description, based on the fact that any number can also be described in words; 10 is 'ten', for example, and 3628800 is 'three million six hundred and twenty-eight thousand eight hundred'. The Berry number is the lowest number not describable in less than 19 syllables. But 'the lowest number not describable in less than 19 syllables' has 18 syllables, so the description cancels itself out, making the Berry number an impossibility.

G. G. Berry had been a junior librarian at the Bodleian Library at the turn of the twentieth century. No relative of mine, despite the name, and by the few accounts of him in the public record he was a humble man with a deep love of paradoxes. When he met people, he handed them a card. On one side was printed: 'The statement on the other side of the card is true.' On the other: 'The statement on the other side of the card is false.' This endless loop was how he hoped to be remembered.

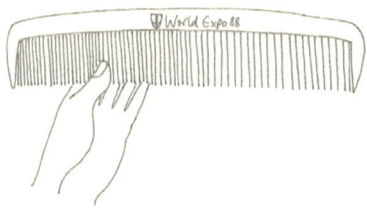

317. Giant Comb

Across the top of the pink plastic comb, embossed in flourishing script, are the words 'Giant Comb'. It's nothing more or less than exactly that, a comb as long as my forearm, the lowest tier of fairground prize, what you get for feeding the laughing clowns just enough.

On the other side of the comb, 'World Expo 88' is stamped in gold ink. The Expo had been held in Brisbane and featured international pavilions and a selection of entertainments: a monorail, the talking car from the TV series *Knight Rider*, acrobats on skis, laser light shows, dress-up screenings of *E.T.*, and a computerised pen-pal service.

All these attractions were in line with the Expo's theme, Leisure in the Age of Technology. In the near future, when technology had liberated you from the need to work, you could play virtual golf while a robot did the household chores. Everything that needed to be done would be taken care of. Everyday objects like the comb would be free to be parodies of themselves.

318. Tightrope

A group of people are gathered in the park, wearing tie-dye t-shirts and army disposal pants with patches sewn on, eyes and suns and other talismans. Strung between two trees is a tightrope, low to the ground to make for an easy dismount. One of the group steps up onto it and steadies herself, gradually straightening her posture, focussing. When she notices me watching I turn away, not wanting to cause her to lose her balance.

Later in the day, I am browsing through an image archive of photographs from the 1930s, and come across a photograph of a tightrope walker in an outdoor performance. It looks cold, with an overcast sky and one bare tree with thin branches like forks of lightning. The children who have gathered to watch face away from the camera and up towards the high wire, which has been suspended between two tall poles specially constructed for the feat. The tightrope walker wears a clown suit and carries a long pole to aid his balance. In every one of his steps he holds the crowd's expectations.

In the foreground is a row of children sitting on a bench, their legs dangling. All are watching the man on the wire apart from one girl. She is turned away, looking instead at the camera, maybe bored, maybe nervous, unable to trust that the tightrope walker won't fall.

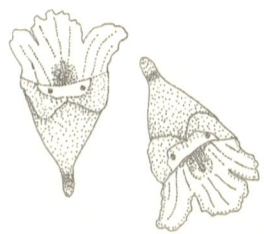

319. Jacaranda Flowers

The trees have blossomed so quietly and suddenly, all unexpectedly. In odd and unusual corners, one comes upon their blue perfection.

Tree of elusive tint, known variously as: a graceful and living cone of floral grandeur, a lovely mauve-coloured cloud, as joyous a thing as ever carried a headful of buds and blossoms. Disporting its myriad of little bells, the sun filtering through its azure mesh, they wave one painted hand as if in invitation to rest beneath their delicate loveliness.

Underfoot is spread a carpet, a soft yielding carpet, for is it not formed of the little flower faces, which, upturned trustfully, are soon to wither and die, as numerous unheeding feet pass and crush them.

Only the real tree poet can strew our paths with sonnet, song, and story such as are today falling from the uppermost limbs of the adorable jacarandas.

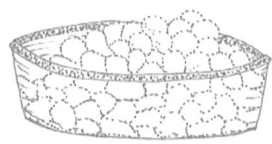

320. Hailstones

Hailstones bounce up off the road and quickly the path and the lawn turns white. The stones are too small to cause damage but there is a great density of them, and when the hail passes I follow my impulse to pick up a handful, enough to fill a container. The cold makes my fingers ache, a chill moving up my arm like the storm has entered my veins.

The green-grey storm clouds move out to sea, and I put the container at the back of the freezer, behind emergency containers of casserole, ice-encrusted flatbread, and an assortment of legacy objects: a mezcal worm inside a jar, a few slips of paper with names written on them, and a boiled sweet kept as a souvenir from Novelty Automation in London.

The hail I collected looks clean enough, a hard bright white. But like all rainwater it contains forever chemicals, which never break down and are present, now, in all the earth's skies and waters, and in our blood, toxic and inescapable.

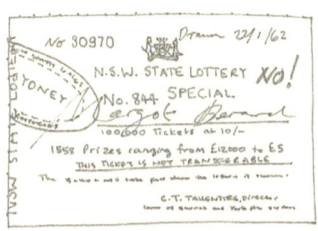

321. NSW State Lottery Ticket No. 844 Special

Someone kept this lottery ticket, writing the date and the result on it in pencil – *Drawn 22/1/62 NO!* Even though it offered 1558 prizes ranging from 12,000 to five pounds, this ticket had not won any of them. Sixty years later I pay two dollars for it, because a ticket holds a promise, even if it is a past kind.

The bookstore where I found it has a set of plastic stacking drawers heavy with papers. Each contains a different type of ephemera: catalogues, letters, pamphlets, and 'misc.', the things that don't fit anywhere else, like the long-expired lottery ticket.

Ephemera, meaning 'for one day', was used to describe a fever that surged up and burnt bright and the next morning was gone. It went on to become the word for papers that were not meant to be kept beyond their immediate use. Tickets, cards, menus, packaging: like the fever, they were temporary. That they are not meant to last, but sometimes do, is the source of their power.

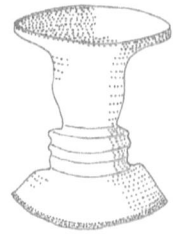

322. Rubin Vase

If I hover at the edge of sleep I focus on the patterns behind my eyelids, the sparks and shadows that are my own electricity. Soon enough an object will form, like a cloud resolving into a shape. At first it is a railway carriage, but as I stare at it the more it looks like a chandelier, and then it changes again so that it is more like a stepladder, stout and capable.

Following the patterns I watch them shapeshift, attentive to the way their edges prickle. The edges are where the object begins to change first, so it is no longer a ladder, it is a flying saucer, and now a tent, and now a letterbox. Like the Claymation figures in *Prometheus' Garden*, where things erupt into other things and can't stay still or stable, I see an axolotl, a frying pan, a manhole cover, and a vase that is also two faces watching each other closely and seriously. See the vase and I lose the faces. To see the faces the vase has to disappear into the space between them, and this dark gap is the gateway to sleep.

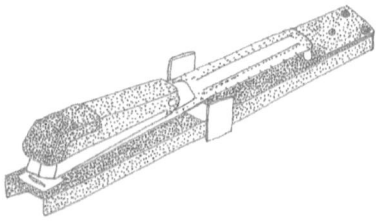

323. Long-arm Stapler

The stapler has 'Stanley Bostitch' printed on the top, two pairs of syllables that themselves are like the crunch of a staple. I use it on the zines which I am collating while sitting cross-legged on the floor, leaning over so my shoulders ache, lining up the pages and pressing the nose of the stapler down over and over.

The long-arm confirmed my destiny, like some other destinies have been sealed by a guitar or a cricket bat or a box of paints. In the biopic the actor playing me enters the office supply store and the camera zooms in on her hand closing over the box with the stapler inside. In an earlier scene she was shown counting out the thirty dollars she'd saved up to buy it, which, then, had been almost half a week's rent.

Throughout the rest of the film the stapler is often called into use. The room sometimes changes but it contains the same level of disorder and the same mood of expectation when I lay out the photocopied pages on the floor. Collate the pages, fold, and staple, eventually notice the inevitable mistake. Until then I blithely staple them, crunch after crunch.

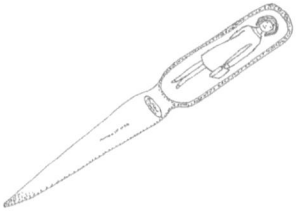

324. Letter Opener

I'm wrecking the tip of the letter opener by poking it underneath the staple, pushing up the crimped edge so I can remove it and fix the page order. The blade works too well for me not to use it, despite the tip blunting more every time.

The letter opener solved the mystery of the Fuller Brush Man, a puzzling reference from 1950s American TV comedies. These assumed everyone would know the Fuller Brush Man. Of course they would, apart from children on the other side of the world many decades later, watching these shows unable to guess what he was or did.

The figure of the Fuller Brush Man is embossed into the handle. He wears a bowler hat, a wide-shouldered suit, sharply creased trousers, and a necktie, and carries the briefcase containing the brushes. On the other side is another Fuller Brush representative, with a bouffant hairstyle, wearing a shift dress, carrying her case by her side. She would knock on the door, sit on the couch, and open the case to show me the miracle hair or carpet brush that would, she guaranteed, make my life so much better in ways I could have never thought possible.

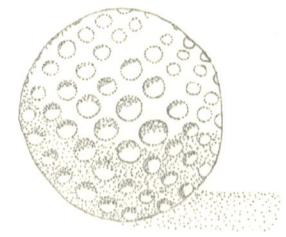

325. Golf Ball

The golf ball was by the riverbank, glowing white beside the track at the edge of the golf course. This unofficial path has been worn down by walkers brave enough to risk a ball flying off course, people who resent how the golf club has restricted access to the river. Though I have no need of a golf ball I pick it up and pocket it. As I continue walking, following the path, the ball grows heavier and heavier.

The ball is growing heavy with premonition. Casting forward into the time when the golf courses are wild, with the lawns grown out into long grass and the trees extending tall and wide, some with fallen branches or their trunks split in two. The watercourses will be wetlands again, with marshy edges and waterbirds in the shallows, noisy with the creaking calls of frogs.

At the bottom of the pond will be golf balls, hard and dimpled, embedded in the sediments. There will be more balls buried in the soil, down under the compacted undergrowth, all of them bad shots when such things mattered. The players had laughed and reached for another ball. There was always another, then.

326. Wanted Poster for 'Boffy'

On the long wall by the station exit are lost cat notices in the form of a Wanted poster. 'Wanted: Very Naughty Cat, Guilty of Running Away.' Boffy could be very close by, lingering just out of sight, 'pursuing a life on the mean streets rather than staying in his loving home', as the poster went on to describe, underneath photographs of a black cat with a contrite expression.

Further on past the Esperanto school, along the row of terrace houses, there are more posters for Boffy. The bins put out for collection are overflowing with household stuff, shoes and folders and saucepans, spilling out onto the pavement. I dodge a pale-pink slide shoe and a small and stained cushion that I recognise as an iPad beanbag. On every power pole Boffy's guilty look accompanies me to the corner.

By the high half-brown hedge of conifers where the printing workshop used to be something moves across, low to the ground. It is Boffy until it resolves as a black plastic bag, alive with the wind, travelling swiftly towards me. It wraps softly around my ankles, rustling, wanting my attention.

327. Faux Tortoiseshell Sunglasses

The winning bid on the pair of faux tortoiseshell sunglasses once owned by Joan Didion was US$27,000. Everything in her estate auction sold for thousands. Books, furniture, her cast-iron cooking pots and bundles of blank notebooks, all charged with the aura of literary celebrity.

It is a stretch to find the extraordinary in any of the objects, precisely photographed for the online catalogue. The descriptions note the condition, mostly fading and minor wear, consistent with use, of candleholders, a cane chair, cushions. The forensic attention of cataloguing sanitises even the most worn of the objects, a pair of tan leather wastepaper baskets with blotches staining the sides.

Clicking away from the wastebaskets, I examine a pair of her faux tortoiseshell sunglasses, photographed from every angle. I zoom in, examining the reflections in the lenses, which are carefully adjusted so the glass shows only a blank. But in one of the shots I can just make out the reflection of the camera that took it, and the hands holding it, the unintended detail I had been looking for.

328. Novelty String Ball

It is difficult to remember the first object I desired, or that I noticed my desire of, the first object beyond the necessary, that existed for no good reason other than to provide a temporary delight.

A toy of some kind? Maybe something like the Koosh Ball that I had been convinced would complete me. I was too young to understand how my desire was being trained, with a ball made of thin rubber threads, knotted together in the centre like a pompom, just the right size to huddle in my palm. The sound it made when I tossed it from hand to hand, the rustling koosh which provided its name, was its whisper that with it in my life I was no longer lacking. Until the next thing arose with the same promise. The Koosh is the spirit of every new and useless thing that tries to move me towards wanting it.

329. Mascot

You have a new memory. Okay. Let's see it. When this happens the algorithm usually turns up my own face from two, or five, or however many years ago. My face naive without knowing what I now know, about what the intervening years will bring.

On this day. It turns out that Photos wants to show me a reel of photographs from a year ago, set to noodling guitar music, of a mascot for an automatic door company. The cartoon magician wears a tuxedo and a blue cape and has an orange button for a head, a friendly smiling pumpkin which he presses down on with one gloved hand, releasing a shower of sparks.

The app must have misrecognised the Magic Button mascot as a significant other or relative, important enough to celebrate the anniversary of meeting up with. In his suit, shooting sparks, an encounter worth remembering.

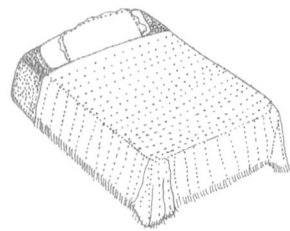

330. Chenille Bedspread

In the spare bedroom at my father's flat, the bedspread is a mustard yellow with fringing around the edges and a nubby, tufted surface. Pulled smoothly over the bed, it seals it into one neat expectant block.

The room has in it only this mustard bed and a nightstand with a desk fan stored on its side on the lower shelf. Everything is some shade of brown, the wooden door with a brass doorknob, the carpet a golden fleece. I peel the bedspread back and crawl in under it, listening to the sounds of the hot night. Here, in Maroochydore, Kabi Kabi country, the sounds are different to home. Traffic, a fleet of sirens starting up, the police coming to put a stop to the drag racing which goes on in the Bunnings carpark. My father had warned me about this, after the show about beaver conservation ended and I said goodnight.

Sound comes over from the televisions in other apartments: voices, gunshots and explosions, surges of music. So many crises sounding at once, coming in through to me on my chenille island.

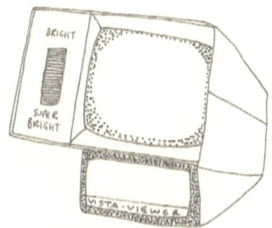

331. Hanimex Vista Viewer

The Vista Viewer resembles a miniature television, the screen angled upwards on a plastic base. Two settings, BRIGHT or SUPER BRIGHT, are activated by a switch on the side. When a slide photograph is inserted into the slot in the back of the viewer the image is illuminated, appearing enlarged and translucent on the screen.

My father and I pass the viewer back and forth. Scenes from the 1960s, my mother standing in the shallows on a tropical beach, a view across the ocean towards a row of islands, fish under a glass-bottomed boat, difficult to make out under blotches of discolouration that have bloomed over the film. The slides were stored at his brother's place for decades, my father tells me. This box was the only one not destroyed by the lime powder put under the house to drive away the rats that were eating the food for the racing pigeons.

The next box of slides is closer to the present, overlapping with my lifetime. It takes a moment to recognise myself as the child in the short dress, sitting with legs stretched out on carpet as red as tomato soup. In the photo I'm looking towards my father who is lying beside me in a stripe of sunlight. He is holding something I can't quite make out, both of us intent on this mystery object.

332. Stoneware Sugar Bowl

In the cupboard was a stack of beige melamine dinner plates, divided into segments, with 'Rosti, Denmark' stamped underneath. These plates were from my childhood, as were the Quaralex drinking glasses that tapered down into a star-shaped base. I recognised, too, the speckled earthenware sugar bowl, which had a strip of brown glaze around the rim like a darker seam of sand. The name of the design was 'Stone Manor', which I had imagined as the name of a castle made out of the same speckled pottery.

They were divided up when my parents split, all those decades ago, half of the Rosti plates and the Stone Manor set each, apart from the solitary sugar bowl which my father must have taken. He had been the one to have sugar in his coffee, two spoons of it at least. When no one was looking I'd go to the sugar bowl and take a teaspoon from it, desperate for sweetness. Between my teeth the sugar was cold and granular and never as satisfying as I expected it to be.

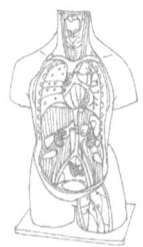

333. Anatomical Model

In a corner room of the library, where the wall clock is stuck on 12 and there is a stack of plastic tubs containing educational toys – polyhedron dice, giant transparent beads, wooden pizza counting sets – there is also a collection of anatomical models. Pieces of them are lined up on the long shelf under the window: legs cut away to reveal the muscles, a giant eyeball displaying its layers. On a table in the centre of the room is a model torso. Most of the organs have been removed to lie strewn across the table, along with segments of plastic skeleton. A skeletal hand drapes over the side, beckoning.

Up closer I can see the numbering in thin black numerals over every piece. I unhook a bean-like kidney from its position inside the torso and turn it over to see what's inside. More details, more numbers. Every part contains more parts. I return it and scan upwards, following the veins and arteries, red and blue. In the neck the thyroid gland is a very pale blue, shaped like an open book set across the neck. Touching the model here I have a flash of my dream from the night before, of a swarm of butterflies of this same colour.

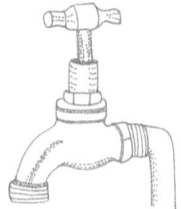

334. Garden Tap

'None of this was here six months ago,' my father says, as we drive on the new road, past a hulking grey shopping centre. On the other side of it are fields behind wire fences, draped in advertisements for new developments with names like Harmony and Aura.

'No one comes to these places,' he continues, 'but they build more anyway.' I look out towards the empty carparks, where there's only one security car lapping the internal road around the buildings. In summer it's different. People go in to escape the heat, to sit on the sofas in the furniture warehouses, close their eyes for a while, until someone asks if they need any help. Their answer is always no (but more honestly, deeply, yes).

Beside the empty mall are car yards and more stores selling household fixtures. Outside one is a giant garden tap, the usual brass kind with a bar for a handle, but two storeys high. From the spout is a sign in the shape of a blue drop. I ask if this, too, is new. 'It wasn't even here yesterday,' my father says.

335. Advent Calendar

I arrive back home on the first day of the advent calendar, which is a cardboard cut-out in the shape of a building six storeys high. Glitter sparkles on the window frames, above the shutters of the numbered rows of windows.

I prise open the first set of shutters, revealing an illustration of two children pulling a sled with a pine tree balanced on top of it. They look down mournfully at it as if they don't have enough strength to get it home. This is something to take on, the scene of the heavy tree a better prediction than my horoscope – 'you may feel in a daze today' – a caution which is nothing but generally applicable.

The unexpected object in the advent calendar can set a mood or theme if I want it to. Every day of my year has been this way, waking up not knowing what the day's object will be, but by night, going to sleep, I see it as a shadow behind my eyelids. I turn the story I have written with it over in my thoughts.

336. Rabbit Nail Clipper

It was mid-summer, humid, and sweat ran down my neck as I moved through the flea market in the grounds of the Kitano Tenmangu Shrine in Kyoto. My eyes ran over the objects arranged on tables and in boxes, reading them as shapes and textures, like running a film in fast-forward in search of the right scene.

At first I thought the red plastic rabbit was a toy. Picking it up from the table I saw that for a mouth it had a pair of sharp metal teeth, upper and lower, and that it was actually a nail clipper. The nail file on the base of the figure confirmed it, as did the distasteful sound of a few old clippings rattling around inside when I turned it over.

By pushing down the long lever of the rabbit's ears the metal teeth close, chomping together, the action that would clip your fingernail if you dared. This made the rabbit menacing enough for me to buy it, although I've never used it for its intended purpose. When I press down the ears, and the rabbit's teeth bite together, it looks at me askance with its plastic eye, as if it senses my apprehension.

337. Royal 240 Typewriter

The Royal is panelled in artificial wood, convincing enough until you come up close. The idea of a wooden typewriter interested me enough to respond to the Gumtree advertisement. We organised a time and the seller met me at the end of his driveway. Together we went to a garage in which typewriter cases were stacked to the ceiling. He had 400, he said, at the height of his collection.

Every typewriter has slight mechanical imperfections that make the text it produces as unique as a fingerprint. Typing the story of my day on the Royal – sitting in the cemetery among the yellow daisies, walking down to the harbour, following the breezeblock and iron-lace fences – I found that the Royal has an 'r' that prints darker than the other letters, and an 'a' set slightly above, as well as other more subtle distinctions of density and spacing that only a forensic investigation would reveal.

Typewriters are idiosyncratic machines. When they came into popular use in the 1880s it was thought by some of their inventors that they might prove effective in communicating with the dead. Typewriters performed well at seances, even if their communications from spirits were delivered in a surprisingly business-like manner.

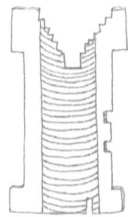

338. Linotype Matrix

The printing museum is housed in an unassuming shed beside the harness-racing track. No racing today, the only movement is the jacaranda flowers falling from the trees. All activity is concentrated inside the museum, where the presses and typesetting machines hinge and rattle as the printers demonstrate them one by one.

First the typesetter shows me the linotype machine. He switches on the lamp above the keyboard and begins to type, fingers moving quickly over the keys. As he does, flat brass bars drop down from a receptacle at the top of the machine. These bars, he tells me, are the 'matrices'. The moulds for the letters which form the line of text which is then cast out of molten lead.

'Thomas Edison described the linotype as the eighth wonder of the world,' the typesetter says, as I watch the matrices move through the machine. After the demonstration he gives me one of them as a souvenir. I examine the thin, notched section of brass, how at the top is a V-shaped row of teeth, like the jaws of a cartoon alligator, and on the side, very small, indents containing the letter 'b'.

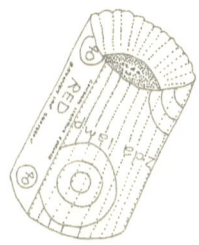

339. Light Bulb

A Pretenders song is playing loudly and people sing along to it as they look around. I find myself humming too, examining the miscellaneous electronics at the back of the shop. Among the foot spas and donut makers I focus in on a red lightbulb, packaged in a corrugated card-board tube.

The package has concentric circles like sunspots, moving from yellow to red on a black background, a design forty years old at least. It gives me the memory of standing at the base of a ladder, holding it steady, waiting for my mother to hand the expired bulb down to me in exchange for the new one.

Then another more recent memory, from the night I visited Morrin and they gave me some of Helen's ashes. Back at home I paused, holding the container, thinking about her life, her death. Standing in the middle of my room, concentrating on the weight in my hands, I opened out my thoughts. There was a soft, almost inaudible crack as the lightbulb burnt out above me. 'Helen?' I said, my voice small in the suddenly dark room.

340. Valhalla Poster

The Valhalla was an arthouse cinema, a capacious, run-down art-deco picture palace at the quieter end of Glebe Point Road. The main theatre was cold and musty and the seat cushions were lumpy with worn-out stuffing, but that was all part of the faded glamour of it. There was always something more interesting happening on the screen to distract you from these discomforts.

You'd see a certain type of cult movie at the Valhalla, ideally at a late-night screening, *Koyaanisqatsi, Blue Velvet, Blade Runner* or *Down by Law*. These screenings were listed on the Valhalla program, a poster published twice yearly and reliably displayed in every inner-city sharehouse. Inside the rows of calendar squares would be the film's title and maybe an image of Jack Nance's luminous *Eraserhead* hair, or the sinister silhouette of a trio of droogs from *A Clockwork Orange*.

Blu-tacked to the kitchen wall, the Valhalla poster measured its own time, six months of films to soak up nights or afternoons. Staring at the poster I would imagine the boundaries of the squares dissolving and all the films merging, the droogs running wild through a city street in *Koyaanisqatsi* with the angels from *Wings of Desire* watching on from a rooftop, observers of the chaos below.

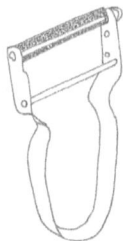

341. Potato Peeler

She peels a potato, holding it firmly in her left hand, dragging a knife over it with her right. Her arms, covered by the sleeves of a grey cardigan, rest on the square of newspaper that is spread out on the cork-topped kitchen table to catch the peelings.

She starts slowly, pensively, her thoughts impenetrable. Already for almost two hours we have been watching her efficient movements around the apartment, her daily routine as she cleans and cooks, greets the man who comes every afternoon, and has dinner with her sullen teenage son. She clicks the light switch off immediately upon leaving any room, as she moves briskly through task after task. Are we to imagine her mental world is as precise as her movements?

Nothing and everything is happening. Her face is impassive as she turns the potato over, looks back down at it, then speeds up her peeling until it is bare. She drops the potato into a tub with a few inches of water in it, then reaches for the next one.

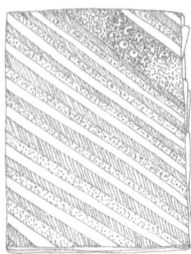

342. Recipe Scrapbook

Taking out the scrapbook from the shelf of cookbooks I have to be careful. The cover has come away from the spine and the pages are torn and stained and barely holding together. On the inside cover is a list of recipes written in my neater, early-twenties handwriting: Blueberry Brownies, Parsnip Soup, Beetroot Risotto. It was an aspirational list, because at the time I compiled it I knew how to cook only two survival meals: gluggy pasta alfredo made from a packet, and avocado on toast.

The scrapbook had blue pages that were already fading to a grainy purple-grey when I bought it secondhand, and residual scraps of newsprint marked the pages where articles had been glued in then ripped out. I made it my own, starting with a recipe for Anzac biscuits from the back of a packet of oats, then another for 'Ethel's orange cake' printed from the rec.food.cooking newsgroup in 1993, then 'easy rosemary flat bread', clipped from a magazine, and so on, my future stretching ahead of me in a succession of risottos, soups, cakes, and biscuits. Rhubarb Pie. Salsa Verde. Pan de Muerto. Marble Cake.

343. Wallpaper

At the end of the hallway a wall was papered in a design of silvery palm leaves, glinting in the afternoon light, an artificial garden.

In this bedroom the yellow wallpaper seemed to be hiding something under its pattern, an uneasy force or message that was struggling to escape.

In the smaller bedroom the wallpaper was red like the heart of a poppy.

In the living room, the wallpaper was loose against the wall and trembled with every loud footstep or voice.

Even outside the house, everything looked as if it had been carefully painted as a sort of wallpaper, all the details perfect but unreal.

344. Souvenir Oil from the Mikhail Lermontov

One night in 1986, off the coast of Aotearoa, the captain of the Mikhail Lermontov made an ill-fated shortcut. The waters to the north of Queen Charlotte Sound were too shallow to clear the bulk of the cruise liner. Rocks tore at the hull and the ship took on water rapidly, listing heavily to the side. The passengers were rescued safely but an engineer died, remaining trapped on the ship when it sunk completely a few hours later.

In the months that followed divers made their way over the wreck, in an operation to drill through to the tanks and drain them of the oil and fuel that would otherwise rupture and spill. They carefully traversed the wreck, through the casino and the bars, past the incongruity of the submerged swimming pool, towards the fuel tanks.

After the oil had been removed from the vessel some of it was made into souvenirs, packaged into bottles labelled with a photograph of the ship and the details of the disaster. At the antique traders at the Avondale Racecourse, the plain black and white graphics on the bottle caught my eye as Erin and I examined the teddy bears and the teaspoons. What was this unusual tincture? A liquid brown and viscose, with a smell like tar and engines.

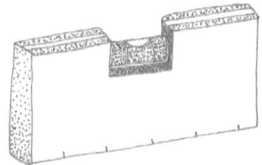

345. Spirit Level

While the band is playing I look over the warehouse with its worn, stained floorboards and vines trailing from hanging baskets. Around the huddle of people listening, the walls are hung with paintings of teddy bears striding over postapocalyptic landscapes. A bookcase holds encyclopedias and tools, with a spirit level on the top, its bubble slightly off centre.

The party is in the bubble, aside from regular time, a distillation of the past in the present. I had been the youngest of this group of friends. When we met I was learning my own way, searching for clues and disguises. We'd sit out in the courtyard, drinking instant coffee, with the asparagus ferns feathery in the garden beds around us. The traffic noise was loud as it streamed to either side of the teardrop of land that divided the lanes of the highway, which was just wide enough to fit two rows of houses in between.

If I borrowed Vic's purple jacket with the black and white spotted lining I felt bolder, taller, more inclined to be brave. What could I offer in return? Things I found in op shops, like ceramic hands, ruffled dinner shirts, and a green flocked board with 'pray without ceasing' in gold lettering. Our devotion was to late nights, forgotten things, and worlds of our own making.

346. Black Screen of Death

Nothing revives it. No reconnection of the charger, no lingering press of the power button. The screen is inert, unresponsive, as the wind roars through the trees outside. The sound of someone letting off illegal fireworks in the park is also the sound of my nerves crackling.

In one of her Saturday newspaper *crônicas*, Clarice Lispector wrote an ode to her typewriter titled 'Gratitude for the Machine', expressing the desire to give her typewriter a gift. This is difficult, she reflects, as there is nothing her typewriter wants.

The laptop wants me to realise my helplessness in the face of its black screen, which holds my anxious reflection, sitting there in its thrall. Electricity, a vague prayer, yet another long press of the power button, my head in my hands. Whatever this adds up to, when I lift my head again I am staring at the craggy headland of the login screen, as if it had only been hiding, waiting to see what I would offer up to entice it back.

347. Second-place Rosette

Rosettes were given out for sports events and I wanted to win one, but the harder I tried, the worse I performed. Even in the concessional event for the less sports-inclined children I failed, falling midway through the sack race, stricken in the centre of the oval. 'Get up!' my relay partner screamed, but lying tangled inside the scratchy hessian I was overcome by futility.

After the sack humiliation I tried to avoid races. It was difficult. A key aspect of schooling was pitting us against one another. Whatever competitive spirit spurred on others to want to be the fastest or the best, I just didn't possess it. Even so, the rosettes on their stiff cardboard, their hierarchy of blue-red-green for the three top places, attracted me.

After failing in the sack race, I found my event. The red cardboard rosette, its yellow '2nd' in the gothic script of certificates and haunted houses, proves it. A hole at the top marks where the safety pin had affixed it to my shirt and on the back are the particulars. 'Name: Vanessa. Date: Oct 1984. Event: Egg & Spoon.' The secret of my success was to let the egg lead me, as if it were the one running the race.

348. Swimming Pool Watch

On the trestle tables set up on the footpath everything for sale is something ancillary – clip-on earrings, pin dishes, bookmarks – until I spot the white wristwatch. It has no numbers on the face, just an image of a pool like in a David Hockney painting. Instead of the usual minute hand it has a figure in a bikini, lying stretched out as if floating on the water's surface. The stallholder notices my interest.

'It's to make you relax your attitude to time,' she says. 'I used to wear it in the eighties, when I worked in an office. It was a basement with no windows but when I looked at the watch I'd relax and ask myself, what is time anyway?'

I stay quiet, sensing she has more to say, and after a moment she continues.

'I worked in the office by day and as a cabaret performer at night. I'd wear a tight black dress and carry a long cigarette holder, get up on stage with mascara trailing down my cheeks and berate the audience. In those days,' she tells me, 'everyone had more than one identity.'

349. Karaoke Box

In the shopping mall, between the travelator and the lifts, is a row of forlorn amusements: claw machines with piles of chocolate bars or soft toys inside, and two booths, like oversized phone boxes, for singing karaoke. In one of them, behind the soundproofed glass, is a woman wearing a white lace dress, holding the microphone in both hands, moving her weight from one foot to another, waiting out an instrumental break.

She is in the sad songs booth, by far the more popular of the two. Happy songs hold little appeal for people to sing alone in the shopping centre, at the midpoint between the two supermarkets. There's rarely anyone in that one, and sometimes, a wait for the other. Today, outside the booth, only the woman's shopping trolley is waiting, loaded with lumpy bags of groceries. She keeps her eye on it as she starts the next verse, as if it is the cause of all her troubles.

350. House Number

The first message of the morning is an alert for a development application '0 metres north'. Exactly in the place where I stand frowning into my phone, reading that the plans have been lodged for 'demolition of existing dwelling'.

Our house with the gutter sagging and gate askew, the moth decorating the window and the ox-tongue plants lined up along the pebblecrete. The house I've lived in longer than any other, that has come to feel most like home.

Over all the time we have lived here, the space the house occupies in my psyche has grown, so I am more likely to say 'the house' than 'my house'. It is an entity unto itself, made up of fibro panels, patterned carpet, and geometric bathroom tiles with the optical quality of an Escher drawing. On the front wall, facing the street, is the house number in wrought iron, hanging on two metal hooks. I imagine that, when the house was built back in the 1960s, it would have been the finishing touch. I think about the house empty, leaving it for the last time. Unhooking the number, taking it with us.

351. Lava Lamp

'How do we disassemble all this,' I ask, gesturing around me, to the rooms packed full like bulging suitcases. S reminds me that it doesn't have to happen straight away, and he's right, but I'm taking stock anyway. Under the kitchen table: dust, an almond, the dried end of a spring onion, a rusted hairpin, a wicker basket with cables inside, a cassette player, a fire blanket, a Roller Santa Bear toy in its box (insert four D-size batteries to activate), and a lava lamp.

Lava lamps had been designed for mood, as domestic conversation pieces in the 1960s. Dinner party guests could watch the 'rising, dancing, twisting, fascinating fluidity' of the molten wax rise and fall, creating a 'rich feeling of sophisticated luxury and wellbeing'. They were also excellent to watch when stoned, an unintended effect that ensured their success.

Clambering out from under the table, I pull the lava lamp with me, trailing dust. When I switch it on the light illuminates the pink fluid inside the cylinder and the pink wax settled stiffly at the bottom. After a while the wax melts and rushes up to the top of the cylinder to begin its hypnotic cycles of bloop and ooze. As it travels, the wax never forms the same shape twice. I watch it for a while, wanting it to mesmerise me.

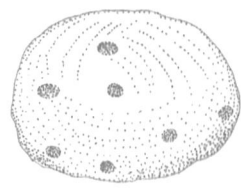

352. Fruit Bun

After the planning alert on the house, I realised the portents had been accumulating. Over in Stanmore the Olympia Milk Bar had closed down, and hadn't I written, years ago, that 'this will mark the day I leave Sydney to its shiny metropolis future and move somewhere else'? The Olympia was boarded up but I hadn't moved an inch, just bunkered down further, weeds growing out of the gutters, dust gathering.

Next Luigi's closed down. He was retiring, taking his sourdough technique, inherited from a long line of Italian bakers, with him. Many mornings I waited in line at his bakery as the nonnas counted out their coins in exchange for dozens of rosette rolls. Behind the counter the walls were decorated with photos of Luigi and his kids, a clock featuring soccer players, and a print of the pair of Raphael cherubs looking bored and contemplative, surveying it all.

The fruit buns from Luigi had been perfectly soft and elastic to the bite. Now that the bakery was closed the two in our freezer were perhaps the last in existence. I cut them in half and put them under the griller to toast, an offering towards acceptance of change.

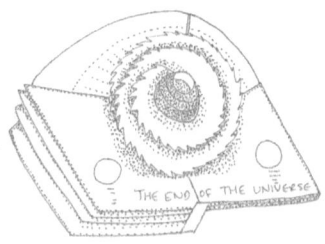

353. Pop-up Book of the Universe

There are two ways the universe could end, as described in the pop-up book of the universe. Either slow and drawn out as the universe continues to expand, or a sharper, devastating contraction, an implosion. The more likely of the two scenarios forms the pop-up at the centre of the page. An immense black hole, made up of merged galaxies of dead stars, is constructed as a dome encircled by fiery rings, an ominous red and black eye with a comet tail swirling out from the back of the page. This is all that's left in the universe before it goes on to further expand into cold dark nothingness.

This, the text reassures us, will happen so far in the future that it long exceeds human existence. If the thought of a slow, cold ending is too confronting, it points out that some scientists believe there might even be another universe on the other side of black holes, although there would be no way to withstand the radiation inside one to travel through and find out. In the book we can come close, peer in through the hole at the centre, through the layers, towards a cardboard staircase of green blocks. This is the potential other universe, visible only through the portable black hole that folds neatly away, compressing down underneath the back flap of the page like a bird tucking its head under its wing.

354. Cologne

The pharmacy offers a list of services on the door – faxes, watches, school bags – and inside the products on display are similarly anachronistic. In one cabinet is an arsenal of Felce Azzurra talcum powder in blue-striped containers, in another, 4711 cologne with its ceremonial aqua and gold label, as if you were receiving a prize by choosing it.

I dab some 4711 onto my wrist with the tester, and the smell of it is the bottle on my grandmother's dressing table, in her bedroom with the blinds always drawn, so it was always either dark or artificially lit, the room perpetually asleep. 4711 cured headaches, she told me, another one of those beliefs I thought for a long time to be peculiar to her alone.

4711 was intended from the start to be curative, a 'miracle water' rather than a fragrance. Its secret recipe was purported to soothe minor ills, foremost among these nostalgia for an Italian spring morning, which is what the scent was intended to evoke. All day after I dab it on, the lemony smell on the cuff of my shirt smells like another place and time, a springtime breeze, a dark room.

355. Terrarium Coffee Table

When we move the piles of books surrounding it, the coffee table comes back into view like the surprise return of a sultry starlet on a daytime soap opera. Under the smoked-glass tabletop is an octagonal terrarium made up of clear glass panels. Inside, on top of a layer of moss and woodchips, strands of artificial ivy are coiled, variegated green and white, almost realistic enough.

A circular label on the side identifies it as a product of Octarium Glass Creations, Pacific Highway, Tanah Merah. Here glass, mirrors, and artificial plants were configured smaller or larger or in different shapes depending on furniture requirements. Top of the range was a six-seater dining table set on two octagonal terrarium pillars.

Inside the coffee-table terrarium, the ivy neither grows nor withers, but on the glass top things are constantly piling up and being cleared off. Today: a balled-up handkerchief with a print of a blue giraffe on it, a melamine dish holding hairpins, and an empty teacup with a crescent of pink lipstick on the rim.

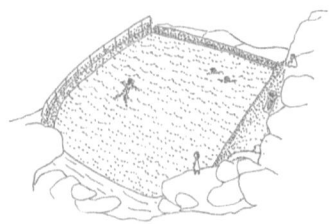

356. Ocean Pool

The longest day is gloomy and overcast, as if resisting itself. On the horizon, grey sky meets grey sea. The ocean pool, cut into the cliff face, is almost empty of swimmers. Only two leathery old-timers going up and down, up and down. I'm afraid of how cold it will be, but I'm here on the solstice to swim the year out, so I make myself plunge in.

A length of the pool for every month, counting as I go. The movements of my arms are the moon running through its phases, my legs the earth on its orbit. When I catch up to the present I lie back to float, for the one minute more of daylight today than there was yesterday, and than there will be tomorrow.

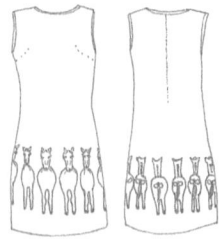

357. 'Heads and Tails' Dress

Hanging on the wardrobe door is the Vested Gentress dress, with a print of horses around the hem, winking at me from under their curly eyelashes. The horses are lined up one after the other, tufts of grass between them. On the front they are standing facing forward, barrel bodies supported by spindly legs. The back of the dress shows the horses from behind, their long tails with gingham bows sewn on at the top.

Most of the garments made by Vested Gentress featured prints of comic animals: frogs on lilypads, pink elephants, a cat holding a golf club in its mouth. One dress was patterned all over with mice and a cat asleep on the pocket. Another had a solid, long-eared dog looking down at a parrot which was standing under its nose, pointing the tip of its wing up in accusation. On another a tortoise ran on its back legs, chasing after a hare, inverting the usual order of things.

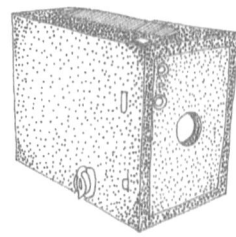

358. Box Brownie

Holding the Brownie camera up to my chest, I look down to where the view is mirrored onto a small glass panel on the top of the box. A greyish image of the house behind the row of hackberry trees hovers in the frame. I press the lever, opening the shutter for a fraction of a second for light to alchemise the film.

The Brownie was the first camera of daily life, easy and cheap enough to use to record everyday scenes. This camera was a century old and had surely captured houses before, and people standing posing, like I do for S to take another photograph, later that day, in Centennial Park. The camera has seen this before too, other rose gardens, other flocks of geese, other people trying to hold still and compose their expressions as they face into the sun, trying to defy its brightness.

359. Christmas Tree

Imagine living in one of these houses along the highway, where the cars never stop day or night, roaring ahead or veering towards the off-ramp. The only thing that might make it better is to decorate one of the roadside trees, changing the decorations with the seasons, as a spectacle for passing motorists.

This Christmas there is a leopard figure carved from wood and painted green, with tufts of red wool in both its ears, hanging suspended from one of the branches. A tapestry of the Last Supper hangs midway up the trunk, and fake gifts made from polystyrene broccoli boxes and red packing tape are tied below it. Dangling on wires from the streetside branches are two chandeliers with icicle lights strung between them, vinyl records, a plastic helicopter, and a toy guitar with 'Get Down This Christmas' scrawled on it. It sways in the wind, turning slowly, displaying its message in all directions.

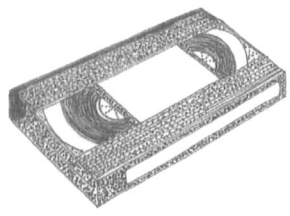

360. Videotape

The last quiet week of the year, in which the hours seem to be on pause, muddles my sense of time. I'm living many days at once, a videotape overwritten with multiple recordings, all of which have left their traces.

A week ago, dabbing cologne on my wrist.

A year ago, swinging too high in the tyre-swing in the park, hoping no one is watching me.

Ten years ago, at the drive-in cinema, unchanged since I was there as a child for a *Star Wars* and *E.T.* double feature. Only the palm trees were taller, the asphalt more cracked.

Twenty years ago, when I was fearless enough to walk around at night, picking flowers from front gardens, welcoming the details popping out at me like spooks from the shadows.

Thirty years ago, blu-tacking gig flyers to my bedroom wall.

Forty years ago, sitting on the bright red carpet, playing with a rubber-stamp printing press, the first indication of what I would grow up to be.

361. Grillmaster

'Is that a Grillmaster?' I ask S, pointing over to where a stove, identical to the one in our kitchen, is marooned on a corner in a Paddington backstreet. It has the same domed silver dials, and the same printed panel giving suggested temperatures for five types of cake (scones, patty cakes, sponges, butter cake, fruit cake) and, simply, 'meat'.

Our own Grillmaster arrived after the former stove had expired with a lightning spark and a sharp bang. The lights went off; I pinched my arm to check I was still alive. The next morning I watched as the replacement arrived on the back of a ute, surprised at the age of the appliance, a relic of the 1960s more suitable for a museum display than for twenty-first-century use.

'They made things to last in those days,' one of the men installing the Grillmaster said, handing me the hotplate covers, with were printed with sunflowers, another one of its retro features along with the chrome dials and the cake instruction panel. Things have a way of finding their place; I was indeed the ideal recipient for the Grillmaster.

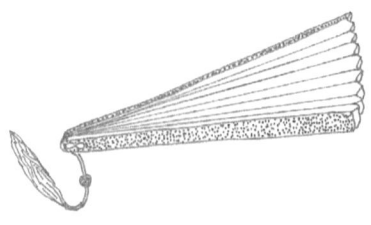

362. Folding Fan

Begin to open the fan of memory and you will never come to the end of its segments. The red and black fan that I would take out to goth clubs, another printed with tropical fish, another with an image of Jesus floating in a blue sky, another a Japanese promotional fan advertising air conditioners. The tissue-paper fan S painted for me, on which I'm wearing a pink dress and flying through the sky on a blue bird, holding a gold lantern. At the edge of the fan another, smaller, me is wearing the same pink dress, holding the same gold lantern, sitting on the back of a mouse. So I always have another way to travel.

363. Gold Foil

On these afternoons of long light, sunlight shines in at a certain angle to reflect off the sheet of gold foil pinned to the wall. When I see this I am tricked for a moment into thinking it is lighting up of its own accord. The foil glows like it has something ready to impart.

Printed in the centre of the foil is a life-size drawing of a rat. When I bought it, picking it out of an ephemera album of chocolate foils and fruit crate labels, I thought it was an unlikely packaging decoration. Perhaps the rat is some lost lucky symbolism or talisman, I thought, before realising the foil had probably originally wrapped some kind of rodent bait. Whatever it had once contained, someone had thought it worthy enough to keep.

Gold foil, shiny rat. On my wall it draws the light and catches my attention. Close up I can see creases, the impressions of its former folds, and closer still, the circles traced by the fingers of whoever had so carefully smoothed it out again.

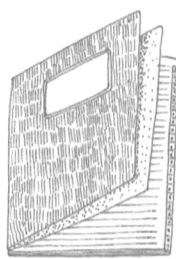

364. Index Book

Ending the year, as is my habit, by reading over it, I find where it starts, halfway through a hardback index book with a marbled cover and cloth binding. A Berlin flea-market book I'd kept unused, bought on a winter morning in 2008, with leaves from that day dried between its pages. Every time I pick it up the leaves fall out and I put them back in, a gesture which becomes as regular as taking up the pen and writing the day and date.

I clear off the desk and start to read, making two lists from the journal as I go. The first is what happened, the chronology. The other is a running list of moods and phrases, which form a softer link to the events surrounding them.

All still here – watching the golden sky and streetlights turning on – holding-pattern days – does it help to think of it as a story? Water like a kind of silky light – the longer way around, the harder road – legendary streets like Rainbow – it doesn't need to be jewel-like – everything changes, can't help but change – a helium balloon of a T-Rex escapes up into the sky – the pilot announces we're dodging storms – wanting to cling onto the feeling a little longer – racing thoughts, purple tulips – remember that everyone constructs a world from the one they see around them.

365. Perpetual Calendar

Move the blocks of the perpetual calendar and it could be any day that does or doesn't exist. It was Tuesday December 85th as I sat up at my father's desk, my legs dangling off the edge of the chair, not yet long enough to touch the ground. A blank sheet of paper was in front of me, as I play-acted my life on this impossible future date.

The calendar was made of wooden blocks inside a wooden stand, the blocks facing up on an angle as they nested inside, square ones for the date, and thin rectangular ones like sticks of gum for the month and day. The wood held its own time in its layers, smooth to the touch. Before I clambered down I turned the date back to the real one, to keep my fictional days a secret.

Now this calendar keeps count on my desk, containing any and all possible days in its configurations. I too carry all my days with me, the days that have been and might be, a perpetual shuffling into this or that or something else. The blocks are time, memory, imagination. I turn each of them over, in search of today.

Afterword: Blue Glass Cat

Two years later, in my father's apartment, everything was as if awaiting his return. Oranges in the fruit bowl, a cap and two folded reusable bags on the corner of the dining table, the EZ2C calendar above the desk with pension days shaded in red biro. The call had come, unexpected, a few days before, a doctor at the hospital telling me that he was not expected to survive the night. There was not enough time for me to travel there to see him. Now my strongest urge was not to move a thing, even though I was there to pack everything up, to decide what to keep and what to discard.

Starting in on the rooms I moved haphazardly between tasks, fighting the feeling that I was destroying the order that kept his life together. He had few, carefully chosen possessions, and anything he kept was for a reason, practical or sentimental. Inside the desk drawer, on top of pens and pencils arranged in a plastic tray, I found a glass cat figurine that I remember him always keeping around. The cat was a rich cobalt blue, with a missing ear and missing front paws, rough and shiny where the glass had been broken. I set it aside as a precious object, trying not to focus on the fact that my father was no longer here to tell me its significance.

Later that night, after a full, sad day of reckoning with objects, I had an urge to locate the blue glass cat again. Surely I had put it away safely but, true to my premonition, I couldn't find it. Not on the desk, not in my bag, not in the pencil case in which I was storing mementoes: a couple of poker chips from Wrest Point Casino, a lenticular ruler that flashed between imperial and metric measures, an engraved nametag from a 1970s trade show. These were all trivial things, unlike the precious glass cat which did not appear among them, no matter how many times I checked.

I could remember the feel of it, cool and heavy, with rough edges where it had been chipped. Of the few sentimental objects my dad had kept, this one was clearly destined for me to keep and treasure, this funny little cat with a smug expression and a broken ear. But somehow it was gone, even though I hadn't left the flat all day, and I could think of nowhere else to look. It was late, almost midnight, but I called S to talk through it. Maybe, I said, I have done something stupid with it. The only place I haven't looked is the bin, I added.

Earlier in the night I had wheeled the bin out to the kerb for collection the next morning. It was heavy, filled with bags of worn pillowslips, old cushions, stale cornflakes, plastic folders, all the things I was con-signing to landfill with a heavy heart. Surely you wouldn't have done that, S said. I'm not myself, I replied, I can't keep track of anything I'm doing.

An electricity was running in me, an immensity. My father's whole life, and mine within it, was wrapped up and squeezed tight and was here and also gone. I opened the sliding door slowly, as quietly as if I were sneaking out for the night and didn't want to be detected leaving. Out-side in the garden it was completely still, the sky clear and the moon a bright white disc. Nothing stirred. The lights in the houses were off, the streetlights shone weakly, there was only the faint ambience of faraway traffic. I tiptoed out to the street, where the bins were lined up all the way along, ready for the truck in the morning. I tried to make peace with the fact there was nothing to fear by slowing myself down to the pace of what was around me. I was the moon, I was the grass, I was the dark windows of the houses.

Back inside, in the kitchen, I sat with the bin bags I had dragged in with me, going through them, taking out all the things I had thrown away that had broken my heart a little to discard, the spare hats, the pairs of socks, the expired lotions from the bathroom cabinet, the worn-out tea towels, folders from medical technology trade shows in

Melbourne, Hawaii, Canada. I hadn't wanted to be throwing any of this away, didn't want it to be real that I was doing this at all, but I had told myself that I could bear it, that I only needed to do it once and then it was over.

Now I was back with it all, digging through the bags. The first bag, then the second, then the third, which had throughout it damp bunches of balled-up tissues from all my crying, and the sugar I had tipped out from the sugar bowl. The sugar stuck to my hands as I dug right down to the very bottom of the plastic bag. I couldn't quite believe that I actually saw it in there, the glass cat, gleaming blue among the sugar and tissues and dust.

Notes

13. *Exercises in Style* by Raymond Queneau, translated by Barbara Wright, published by John Calder, 1998.

18. *Swann's Way*, by Marcel Proust, first published 1913 as *Du côté de chez Swann*, translated by C. K. Scott Moncrieff, 1922.

24. *Premier Danseuse*, published by B. Shackman & Co., 1984.

36. 'Song of the Surf' by Edouard Mandon (1885–1977).

41. *Accident: a day's news* by Christa Wolf, translated by Heike Schwarzbauer and Rick Takvorian, Virago, 1989.

44. Chess column by Ian Rogers, *Sun Herald*, 13 February 2022.

49. *Modern Nature* by Derek Jarman, first published by Century in 1991.

61. *Portrait de Marcel Proust* by Jacques-Emile Blanche, 1892. 'But sometimes illumination...' from *Time Regained* by Marcel Proust, translated by Stephen Hudson, 1931.

68. *The Great Artists*, Marshall Cavendish Weekly Collection, 1985; 'The Sorrow of the King', Henri Matisse, 1952.

80. '"What I saw, I hope no one will ever see," says Greek diplomat returning from Mariupol', *Reuters*, 21 March 2022; 'Lismore flood victims call for climate action outside Scott Morrison's Kirribilli home', Carla Hildebrandt, *ABC news*, 21 March 2022.

84. https://www.tyreextinguishers.com/

85. *Looking in Junk Shops*, by John Bedford, published by Max Parish and Co Ltd in 1961, and *Still Looking for Junk*, by John Bedford, published by Macdonald & Co. in 1969.

87. *Jamie Livingston: some photos of that day*, https://photooftheday.hugh-crawford.com/03-28-92

88. *Nufashond Rick Rack Book of 1916*, The Narrow Fashion Co. Reading, PA. Antique Pattern Library.

90. 'Model of Pea pod (*Pisum sativum*)', Macleay Collections, Scientific Instruments And Apparatus, Chau Chak Wing Museum, Sydney.

93. Julia Child's *The French Chef*, 'Mousse au Chocolat', first broadcast 1971.

94. *The House in Paris* by Elizabeth Bowen, published by Penguin in 1946.

96. Drawn from newspaper articles from the *Leader* (Melbourne) 24 December 1869, *The Daily News* (Perth) 9 May 1903, *The Kalgoorlie Miner* 18 April 1903 and *Northwestern Courier* (Narrabri) 10 October 1929.

102. Nagakin Capsule Tower, 1970–2, designed by architect Kisho Kurokawa.

116. *From Caves to Canvas* by Donald Williams and Barbara Wilson, McGraw-Hill, Sydney, 1992; 'Le Thé', Berthe Morisot, oil on canvas, 1882.

117. '100-Year-Old Chalkboards, With Drawings Still Intact, Discovered in Oklahoma School', Maris Fessenden, *Smithsonian Magazine*, 9 June 2015.

122. *Mythologies* by Roland Barthes, translated by Annette Lavers, published by Paladin, 1973.

125. *The Tale of Tom Kitten* by Beatrix Potter, originally published 1907.

127. 'The Waterfall of Yoro, or the Fountain of Youth', transcribed in *Japanese Fairy World* by William Elliot Griffis, 1887.

129. 'How a priceless Roman bust ended up in a Texas thrift store', Chloe Kim, *BBC News*, 7 May 2022.

136. *The Art of Memory* by Frances Yates, first published 1966 by Routledge & Kegan Paul.

140. *The Pillow Book* by Sei Shōnagon, translated by Meredith McKinney, published by Penguin, 2006.

141. 'Thing Theory' by Bill Brown, in *Critical Inquiry*, vol. 28, no. 1, Autumn 2001.

152. 'Astrological Calendar and Moon Planting Guide' by Thomas Zimmer, 2022.

160. *Pink Steam* by David Haines and Joyce Hinterding, Biennale of Sydney, 2022.

162. *Le Savon* by Francis Ponge, published by Gallimard, 1992; *Mute Objects of Expression* by Francis Ponge, translated by Lee Fahnestock, published by Archipelago Books, 2006.

164. The Larrakia seasons calendar was devised by members of the Gulumoer-rgin (Larrakia) language group, in partnership with CSIRO: Lorraine Williams, Judith Williams, Maureen Ogden, Keith Risk, Anne Risk and Emma Woodward, 2012.

167. 'Sweet lemony wax' and 'coolwrapped soap' from the 'Lotus Eaters' chapter of *Ulysses* by James Joyce, first published 1922 by Shakespeare and Company.

173. *The Torquemada Puzzle Book: A miscellany* by Torquemada (Ernest Powys Mathers), published by Victor Gollancz Ltd, 1934.

178. 'National Geographic Smell Survey' in *National Geographic* magazine, September 1986; *La Chevelure* by Charles Baudelaire, from *Les Fleurs Du Mal*, first published 1857.

180. 'Hand mit Ringen', radiographic print, Wilhelm Conrad Röntgen, 1895.

193. *Woman in a Dressing Gown*, dir. J. Lee Thompson, 1957.

194. 'Fragment of an Analysis of a Case of Hysteria' by Sigmund Freud, translated by Alix and James Strachey, 1925.

196. *Time Loops: In conversation with Christa Wolf*, dir. Karlheinz Mund, 1992.

203. *Vertigo*, dir. Alfred Hitchcock, 1958.

207. Drawn from newspaper articles from *The Mail* (Adelaide) 9 December 1950, *Truth* (Sydney) 6 June 1954, *The Sun* (Sydney) 2 June 1954, and *Mirror* (Perth) 1 March 1952.

223. *Jules et Jim*, dir. François Truffaut, 1962.

224. *The Poems of Laura Riding*, 1986. Carcanet edition of the collection first published in 1938 by Random House.

225. 'The Magic Fish', Arthur Boyd, oil on canvas, c.1978.

232. *Madame Colette*, Robert Doisneau, 1950.

236. *Villette* by Charlotte Brontë, first published 1853.

237. *Namennayo Cats* by Satoru Tsuda, published by Shoichi Kusano, 1981.

241. *Dream Mapping* by Susan Hiller, 1973.

244. *Kitsch: The world of bad taste* by Gillo Dorfles, first published by Studio Vista Ltd in 1969.

246. *Snow Crystals* by Wilson Bentley and W. J. Humphreys, published by Dover Books, 2013.

252. *Life After God* by Douglas Coupland, first published by Pocket Books in 1994.

255. *Etty: A diary 1941–43* by Etty Hillesum, published by Triad/Panther Books, 1985.

256. *The Hidden Power of Everyday Things: A complete personology guide to your lifestyle for each day of the year* by Julie Gillentine, published by Atria, 2000.

258. 'The Cares of a Family Man' by Franz Kafka, first published in 1919.

272. *Langenscheidt's Lilliput Dictionary, German-English*, 1964.

274. 'Ruined, 60 Shop Windows', *The Sun*, 16 November 1931.

275. 'Venus on Earth' by Paul Lincke, published by Chappell & Co. Ltd, London, 1907.

277. *Letters to the Sphinx from Oscar Wilde: With reminiscences of the author by Ada Leverson*, published by Duckworth in 1930.

286. *L'Hôtel*, Sophie Calle, 1981.

291. *Fire of Love*, dir. Sara Dosa, 2022, with footage from volcanologists Katia and Maurice Krafft.

297. *My Winnipeg*, dir. Guy Maddin, 2007.

300. *Fishing in the Styx* by Ruth Park, Text Classics, 2019, first published by Viking in 1993.

303. 'The Writer's Technique in Thirteen Theses' by Walter Benjamin, first published in 1928. Translation by Edmund Jephcott, in *One Way Street*, published by Belknap, 2016.

304. *House of Dracula*, dir. Erle C. Kenton, 1945.

311. Widely reported, unverified, report from the Russo-Ukrainian war.

318. 'Tightrope Walker, Sydney', c.1936, photograph by Harold Cazneaux. National Library of Australia.

319. Drawn from newspaper articles from *The Sydney Morning Herald* 2 December 1933, *Evening News* (Sydney) 4 December 1922, *The Manning River Times* 23 December 1933, and *Cairns Post* 9 November 1927.

322. *Prometheus' Garden*, dir. Bruce Bickford, 1988.

341. *Jeanne Dielman, 23 quai du Commerce, 1080 Bruxelles*, dir. Chantal Akerman, 1975.

343. *A Literary History of Wallpaper* by E. A. Entwisle, published by B. T. Batsford Ltd, 1960.

346. 'Gratitude for the Machine' by Clarice Lispector, first published in *Jornal do Brasil*, 1968. Translated by Margaret Jull Costa and Robin Patterson in *Too Much of Life: The complete crônicas*, published by New Directions Publishing, 2022.

352. *Strawberry Hills Forever*, published by Local Consumption Press, 2007.

353. *The Universe: A three-dimensional study* by Heather Couper, published by Century, 1985.

362. 'He who has once begun to open the fan of memory never comes to the end of its segments...', Walter Benjamin, 'Berlin Chronicle', translated by Edmund Jephcott and Kingsley Shorter, in *One Way Street and Other Writings*, published by New Left Books, 1979.

Further Reading

Objects from April and May, Zena Agha, Hajar Press, 2022.

Proxies, Brian Blanchfield, Nightboat Books, 2016.

One Story a Day, Genevieve Callaghan, No More Poetry, 2022.

My Life with Things: the consumer diaries, Elizabeth Chin, Duke University Press, 2016.

A Catalog of Such Stuff as Dreams Are Made On, Kai-cheung Dung, Columbia University Press, 2022.

The Book of Delights, Ross Gay, Algonquin, 2019.

Calamities, Renee Gladman, Wave Books, 2016.

Significant Objects, eds Josh Glenn and Rob Walker, Fantagraphics Books, 2012.

Urban Tumbleweed, Harryette Mullen, Graywolf, 2013.

Important Artifacts and Personal Property from the Collection of Lenore Doolan and Harold Morris, including Books, Street Fashion and Jewellery, Leanne Shapton, Sarah Crichton Books, 2009.

An Anecdoted Topography of Chance, Daniel Spoerri, Atlas Press, 2015 (first published 1966).

Acknowledgements

This book was written on Aboriginal land. I acknowledge the ongoing sovereignty of the Aboriginal people on whose lands these stories take place and offer my deepest respects to the abiding and enduring wisdom within Aboriginal care for country. Much of *Calendar* was written on Gadigal land, and I offer my respects to Gadigal elders past and present.

Thank you to the guides, colleagues, friends, and readers who make my writing life possible: your support and encouragement sustains me. With special thanks to Kathryn Bird and Ross Gibson, Belinda Castles, Colin Chestnut, Christen Cornell and Pete O'Donoghue, Anwen Crawford, Emma Davidson, Morrin Delves, Michelle de Kretser, Paul and Tiffany Donnelly, Kuba Dorabialski and Katy Plummer, Briohny Doyle, Robin Edgerton, Johanna Ellersdorfer, Erin Fae, Kath Fries, Sarah Goffman, Keri Glastonbury, Katie Haegele and Joe Carlough, Tina Havelock-Stevens, Lara Hembrow, Peter Hobbins, Lesley-Anne Houghton, Simmone Howell, David Haines and Joyce Hinterding, Melissa Hardie and Kate Lilley, Lucas Ihlein and Lizzie and Albie Muller, Mireille Juchau, Daniel Juckes, Joy Lai, Anna MacDonald, Walter Mason, Julie McElhone, Chantelle Mitchell and Jaxon Waterhouse, Celia Morris, Daniel Mudie-Cunningham, Gemma Nisbet, Sarina Noordhuis-Fairfax, Cathy Perkins, Kirrilee Price, Tim Richards, Liz Rickman, Chiara Scott, Ryan Scott, Vanessa Smith, Anna Thwaites, Richard Vogt, Jessica Wilkinson, Beth Yahp, and my colleagues and students in English and Writing at the University of Sydney. Work on this book was supported by residencies at Bundanon and the Byron Writers' Festival.

Thank you to Upswell for bringing *Calendar* into being so beautifully. To Terri-ann for all of your support, to Becky for the wonderful design, and to Keith for all your care and skill in putting the book together: I appreciate it so.

With lifelong gratitude to Pat, John and Fiona, and with love to Simon, who is so much a part of this book and all my days.

About Upswell

Upswell Publishing was established in 2021 by Terri-ann White as a not-for-profit press. A perceived gap in the market for distinctive literary works in fiction, poetry and narrative non-fiction was the motivation. In her years as a bookseller, writer and then publisher, Terri-ann has maintained a watch on literary books and the way they insinuate themselves into a cultural space and are then located within our literary and cultural inheritance. She is interested in making books to last: books with the potential to still be noticed, and noted, after decades and thus be ripe to influence new literary histories.

About this typeface

Book designer Becky Chilcott chose Foundry Origin not only as a strong, carefully considered, and dependable typeface, but also to honour her late friend and mentor, type designer Freda Sack, who oversaw the project. Designed by Freda's long-standing colleague, Stuart de Rozario, much like Upswell Publishing, Foundry Origin was created out of the desire to say something new.